D0764341

Benjamin Lundy and the Struggle for Negro Freedom

BENJAMIN LUNDY

and the Struggle
for Negro Freedom

Merton L. Dillon

UNIVERSITY OF ILLINOIS PRESS, URBANA AND LONDON, 1966

PREFACE

This is an account of the leading figure in the American antislavery movement before 1830. The antislavery crusade of the 1830's and 1840's has always been counted an important episode in American history, and lately we have been reminded of the extent to which abolitionists helped to shape events during the Civil War and Reconstruction. But antislavery activity before 1830 has remained less well known.

It would be absurd, of course, to claim that such early antislavery reformers as Benjamin Lundy overshadowed their successors; yet their accomplishment was far from meager. The record of Lundy's life suggests that long before the abolitionists who were to win fame in the 1830's had entered the movement he and his associates had laid the foundation upon which they would build. It was not those later well-known men but their predecessors in the upper South and West who developed antislavery argument, rejected the racist claims of colonizationists, experimented with various techniques of antislavery propaganda and activity, organized antislavery political movements, and created centers of antislavery thought and influence. Perhaps most important of all in its implication is the fact that well before 1830 Lundy had tested and repeatedly found wanting the sincerity of claims made by and for slaveholders that they too wished to end slavery.

Lundy's preeminence during the pioneer period of antislavery reform has frequently been asserted, even if his accomplishment is less often specified. Not so well known is the fact that he also occupied a large place in the antislavery struggles of the 1830's. After a period when his influence among abolitionists had all but disappeared, the Texas Revolution brought him renewed prominence. Indeed, the abolitionist response to that event was in some sense Lundy's own creation. His role in shaping the crisis occasioned by the rebellion of American settlers in Mexico warrants his being recognized not only as a pioneer abolitionist but also as a major participant in the later phase of the antislavery movement.

Among the numerous obligations incurred while preparing this study, none is greater than the debt I owe Fred Landon, who, through protracted correspondence and during my visit to his home at London, Ontario, generously shared with me the results of his lifelong interest in Lundy. Others were similarly helpful. David M. Vigness allowed me to read his work on the Texas Revolution prior to its publication. Martin Duberman, Larry Gara, and William Pease brought to my attention important manuscript items relating to Lundy. Lowell Blaisdell read early drafts of certain chapters, and Betty Fladeland read and criticized the entire manuscript. Their aid was invaluable, but since I did not heed all my friends' suggestions, they must not be blamed for such flaws as still remain. The research for this volume was supported in major part by grants from the Organized Research Funds of Texas Technological College.

CONTENTS

CHAPTER I

To Break That Ponderous Chain

Benjamin Lundy was born on January 4, 1789, at Greens-
ville in Hardwick Township, Sussex County, New Jersey, the
only child of Joseph and Elizabeth Shotwell Lundy. We know
little about his boyhood except for the meager facts recorded
by his first biographer: He received only limited and interrupted schooling; he was reared by a kindly stepmother, Mary
Titus Lundy (his own mother had died when he was four
years old); he worked so hard on his father's farm that he overtaxed his strength, became ill, and developed a deafness that
was to become worse as he grew older.[1]

Not much more than that can be said about his early years,
except for the all-important fact that he was reared as a Quaker.
Through many generations the Lundy family had been devout
and important members of the Religious Society of Friends.[2]

---

[1] [Thomas Earle], *The Life, Travels and Opinions of Benjamin Lundy*
. . . (Philadelphia, 1847), pp. 13–14.
[2] *Ibid.*, p. 13; William Clinton Armstrong, *The Lundy Family and Their
Descendants of Whatsoever Surname with a Biographical Sketch of Benjamin Lundy* (New Brunswick, N.J., 1902), pp. 21–25.

For the Lundys, as for many other Quakers, this meant to be somewhat set apart from the world and to mistrust worldly values. It meant introspection and soul-searching, the constant exercise of vigilance to assure that the perishing things of time occupied only a subordinate place in their affections. For a select few ever since the sect was founded, it also had meant to have an all-compelling zeal to aid the wretched and oppressed. That is what it came to mean to Benjamin Lundy.

It is not necessary, even if it were possible, to locate some disturbing element in Lundy's infancy or childhood to account for the distinguishing features of his career. He was moved by no impelling neurosis to take up reform causes. Rather, he had wholeheartedly accepted the Quaker humanitarian ethic, and he applied it to slavery. This required not a warped personality but only a healthy mind, perceptive enough to reflect on the evils an impartial eye observed.

Precedents among Quakers for lives of such devotion were plentiful. No Quaker child, not even a little boy on a poor New Jersey farm, was likely to grow up without knowing in detail the careers of such saintly Friends as Benjamin Lay and John Woolman, who had spent their lives in humanitarian endeavor. From such examples constantly placed before them, Quaker children received early instruction about the equality of all men and their own philanthropic duties toward all God's creatures. Accordingly, they were likely to develop uncommon sensitivity to oppression and cruelty.[3] If their elders sought by strict supervision to shield their children from worldly allures, they had no desire to keep them from knowledge of the world's evils.

Benjamin Lundy must have learned these lessons at a tender age. His father scrupulously guarded him from worldliness,

---

[3] Sydney V. James, *A People Among Peoples; Quaker Benevolence in Eighteenth-Century America* (Cambridge, Mass., 1963), pp. 268–334.

although in a simple Quaker community that probably required no great effort.[4] The child's carefully taught humanitarian duties, too, must have seemed to him of only remote application among the farmers and mechanics of Sussex County, where extremes of wealth were few and signs of oppression seldom appeared. There was, to be sure, one glaring exception to that egalitarianism — slavery still flourished in New Jersey during Lundy's childhood. Only in 1804, when Lundy was fifteen, did the state provide for gradual emancipation. As late as 1810, of the nearly 750 Negroes living in Sussex County 478 were held as slaves.[5] Yet even by the time Lundy was born, the yoke of slavery, although persistent, had become rather light in New Jersey, as in other northern states. Lundy never credited the events or scenes of his early childhood with arousing his hostility to slavery and to the cruelties produced by caste. As a child he was offered by his environment no unusual opportunity for the practical exercise of Christian charity.

The child grew up small in stature, frail in health, and uncommitted to a career. In the summer of 1809 at the age of twenty he left his father's home,[6] not in rebellion — for the ties between Lundy and his family always remained close — but to travel, hoping in that way to recover his uncertain strength and also to establish his independence by finding a suitable occupation for his life's work.[7] He soon accomplished both aims.

---

[4] [Earle], *Life*, p. 14; Frank Sanborn, "Benjamin Lundy," *Friends' Intelligencer and Journal*, XLVI (May 18, 1889), 308.

[5] *Aggregate Amount of Persons Within the United States in the Year 1810. Third Census* (Washington, D.C., 1811), book I, p. 29.

[6] Armstrong, *Lundy Family*, p. 253; Wendell Phillips Garrison, "In Lundy's Land," *Pennsylvania Magazine of History and Biography*, no. 75 (October, 1895), p. 342.

[7] [Earle], *Life*, p. 14.

The change of scene proved a tonic to his health, and after a few months spent wandering among Quaker settlements in Pennsylvania and southeastern Ohio, he moved across the Ohio River into Virginia (the area now known as West Virginia) ready to look for work. There in the town of Wheeling he apprenticed himself to a saddler to start the arduous task of becoming expert in the making of leather goods.[8] He learned easily and became a good craftsman. The mechanical skills Lundy acquired in youth he continued to practice at intervals throughout the rest of his life. He could earn a living with his hands whenever he needed to or wanted to.

Lundy's new home was closely tied to the rising West. At Wheeling, where the great post roads that ran from Philadelphia, Baltimore, and western Virginia united, emigrants and merchants — travelers of all sorts — paused on the long journeys that would take them to Ohio, Kentucky, Tennessee, and even Louisiana. The freedom from restraints offered by the crowded town appealed to young Lundy. He enjoyed Wheeling's relaxed atmosphere as a contrast to the moral earnestness of his father's home.[9]

The young men he met in that enterprising place engaged in various frivolous activities. Since not even the most conscientious Quaker could be serious always, Lundy confessed attraction to their kind of life, even shared it for a time. Yet he saw that in most of those youths the Inner Light burned dim. His ways were not their ways, nor could they be. Lundy's carefully nurtured piety soon reasserted itself and after momentary temptation he became all seriousness. In an excess

[8] Nathan Macy Thomas, *Nathan M. Thomas, Birthright Member of the Society of Friends, Pioneer Physician, Early and Earnest Advocate of the Abolition of Slavery, Friend and Helper of the Fugitive Slave* . . . (Cassopolis, Mich., 1925), pp. 15–16.
[9] [Earle], *Life*, pp. 14–15.

of youthful enthusiasm he decided to put frivolity aside and concentrate on learning his trade; for the rest of his life he would wear the world as lightly as a garment. He resolved to remain true to the Friends' faith and custom; he would retain his plain dress and Quaker style of speech, indulge in no worldly amusements, read only instructive books.[10] Luckily for the success of his resolution, his roommate during some of those solemn months was Benjamin Stanton, a like-minded, sober Quaker boy, sent from his home at Mount Pleasant, Ohio, to study medicine in Wheeling.[11] The two earnest youths sustained each other, for they could find few other suitable associates in that impious, unchurched town. Lundy's isolation from youthful society, his early quarrel with the world, fostered his sympathy for the world's outcasts, because in his fashion he had become one of them himself.

In an alien society Lundy had kept his Quaker manners; he kept his Quaker conscience, too. With his religious and humanitarian sensitivities thus heightened, he was in a mood to respond to philanthropic calls whenever they should come. Accordingly, when in Wheeling he for the first time encountered coffles of chained and handcuffed slaves on their way to new plantations down the Ohio and Mississippi, his conscience rebelled.[12] Here were men homeless and alien, cut off from society somewhat like himself. They too were fellow sufferers far from home, out of communion with the world and victimized by it. Lundy imagined that he could understand their plight. His previous acquaintance with slavery had allowed him to know of its potential cruelties only in theory. He now saw slavery in its most unlovely aspect.

---

[10] *Ibid.*

[11] John Alexander Caldwell, *History of Belmont and Jefferson Counties, Ohio* . . . (Wheeling, W. Va., 1880), p. 545.

[12] [Earle], *Life*, p. 15.

There had always been some trade in slaves, of course, but such traffic before 1800 had been sluggish and infrequent, much of it confined to unruly Negroes sold by impatient masters. In earlier years the trade had been unorganized and easy to ignore. But with the birth of the cotton plantation and its westward expansion, the interstate slave trade became big business. An increasing number of slaveowners in the upper South now sold their excess human property to planters in the new Southwest.[13] "The selling of slaves," as a Maryland newspaper soon reported, had "become an almost universal resource to raise money." Within a few years a North Carolinian could write with little exaggeration that there were more droves of slaves on the public roads of his state than of cattle, horses, or hogs.[14]

Lundy had come to a good place to observe the new trade in slaves, for Wheeling served as a gathering point prior to their passage down the Ohio River. The young Quaker was shocked on his walks through town by the sight of "droves of a dozen or twenty ragged men, chained together and driven through the streets, *bare-headed* and *bare-footed, in mud and snow,* by the remorseless 'SOUL SELLERS,' with horsewhips and bludgeons in their hands!!" In Wheeling Lundy had at last been brought face to face with the institution that generations of Quakers had borne fervent witness against. He now understood as he had never understood before the implications of the Quaker belief in the equality of all men. At that moment in one of the most impressionable and devout periods of his life, he "made a solemn vow to Almighty God [that] he

---

[13] Frederic Bancroft, *Slave-Trading in the Old South* (Baltimore, 1931), pp. 19–44.

[14] *Federal Gazette* quoted in *Philanthropist* (Mount Pleasant, Ohio), I (March 13, 1819), 214–215; H. M. Wagstaff (ed.), *Minutes of the North Carolina Manumission Society, 1816–1834* (Chapel Hill, N.C., 1934), p. 51.

would break at least one link of that ponderous chain of oppression. . . ." [15]

The vow Lundy made at Wheeling determined the course of his life. It placed him directly within the Quaker antislavery tradition established in preceding centuries by John Woolman, George Fox, Benjamin Lay, and Anthony Benezet. His labors henceforth would be a continuation of theirs. His career would form the bridge connecting those early antislavery efforts with the expanded abolition movement of later times.

But before launching great philanthropic enterprises, Lundy needed to make arrangements for his own livelihood. Having learned the elements of saddlery at Wheeling, he now moved a few miles west to the little town of Mount Pleasant, Ohio, where he hired out as a journeyman saddlemaker to Jesse Thomas, brother-in-law of his Wheeling roommate.[16] No doubt he was drawn to Mount Pleasant at least in part by the prospect of living again among his own kind of people, for most of its residents were Quakers, some of them from New Jersey and acquainted with his relatives. The move would thus have the result of keeping him firmly within the community of Quakers, but equally important, it would also make a large contribution to his antislavery sentiment, for among these people lived many recent arrivals from the South, Friends whose distaste for slavery and the spreading plantation system had contributed to their decision to move to Ohio. One of those whom he would know the best was his employer, Thomas, an earnest opponent of slavery who had joined the Quaker exodus from North Carolina about ten years earlier.[17]

---

[15] [Earle], *Life*, p. 15; *The Genius of Universal Emancipation*, XIII (November, 1832), 8. This periodical is hereafter cited as *Genius*.

[16] Thomas, *Nathan M. Thomas*, pp. 15–16.

[17] *Ibid.*, p. 13.

Others of his new associates disliked slavery with similar fervor. On a farm at the west edge of town lived the large family of Thomas' mother-in-law, Abigail Macy Stanton, a Quaker woman of unyielding moral commitment who had moved from North Carolina after her husband's death in 1798, bringing the family's manumitted slaves with her and settling them on land nearby.[18] Many of Mrs. Stanton's children — Lundy's friends at Mount Pleasant — felt irresistibly drawn, as he did, to oppose slavery. Her son Benjamin, Lundy's roommate at Wheeling, would within a few years give his antislavery projects financial support.[19] Her daughter Lydia, who married William Lewis, Lundy's future brother-in-law, soon became one of the more intransigent abolitionists, first in Ohio and later in Illinois.[20] Mrs. Stanton's grandson Edwin would serve as Abraham Lincoln's Secretary of War. Another grandson, Nathan M. Thomas, would eventually move to Kalamazoo County, Michigan, to become one of Michigan's first abolitionists and a founder of the Liberty party.[21] Others Lundy knew at Mount Pleasant soon drifted northwestward into Lenawee County, Michigan, to swell the antislavery ranks of that important early abolitionist center.[22] Members of such families at Mount Pleasant could relate to Lundy their experiences in slaveholding communities and thus bolster his own antislavery determination. They supported his early antislavery

---

[18] *Ibid.*, pp. 6–12; [Nathan Macy Thomas], *Abigail Stanton* (Schoolcraft, Mich., 1881), p. 10.

[19] Richard Frederick O'Dell, "The Early Antislavery Movement in Ohio" (unpublished Ph.D. dissertation, University of Michigan, Ann Arbor, 1948), p. 218.

[20] Jesse Thomas, Jr., to Nathan M. Thomas, December 29, 1834, May 25, 1835, and Lydia M. Lewis to Nathan M. Thomas, December 6, 1855, Nathan M. Thomas Papers (Michigan Historical Collections, Ann Arbor).

[21] Nathan M. Thomas, "History," *ibid.*

[22] Elizabeth M. Chandler to Jane Howell, September 2, November 11, 1833, Elizabeth M. Chandler Papers (Michigan Historical Collections).

efforts, and together they helped seed the states of the old Northwest with abolitionism.

But for the present Lundy plodded on at his apprenticeship. After working two years for Thomas and proving his skill at leatherwork, Lundy decided the time had come for him to set up his own saddle shop. For a few months during the winter of 1813–14 he worked again in Wheeling, and during the spring at his father's urging he visited New Jersey to consider eastern job prospects.[23] But he finally decided to settle permanently in the West. There, he believed, he would find business opportunities more promising than any the East offered, and there he could work the most effectively against slavery. These were not the only reasons, however, that led him to leave New Jersey to return to Ohio. At Mount Pleasant he had become acquainted with Esther Lewis, a pious Quaker girl of his own age. Now that he had reached a station in life when marriage seemed desirable and possible, his thoughts increasingly turned across the mountains toward the girl he had left behind.

In February 1815 he returned to Mount Pleasant to marry Esther Lewis.[24] Shortly afterward the young couple moved ten miles farther west to St. Clairsville, the rapidly growing seat of Belmont County, where Lundy established his own saddle and harness shop.[25] These important events only temporarily interrupted his determination to take positive action against slavery. "I have long had [this cause] in contemplation," he wrote, "and have resolved, and fully determined, never to lay it down while I breathe, or until the end be attained." [26]

---

[23] Lundy to Joseph Lundy, May 20, 1814, Benjamin Lundy and Paxson Vickers Collection (Library of Congress); [Earle], *Life*, p. 15.

[24] Armstrong, *Lundy Family*, p. 353; Thomas, *Nathan M. Thomas*, p. 17.

[25] [Earle], *Life*, pp. 15–16.

[26] "Circular, to the Advocates of African Emancipation, Who Are Sensible

He soon built up a thriving leather business. He did good work, and customers sought him out from miles around. His business prospered, and he was happy with his new wife. But such satisfactions never blotted from his mind the sights of slave coffles in Wheeling. While sitting at his clamp stitching at saddle skirts, wagon harness, and bridle reins, he brooded over the injustice and cruelty of slavery.

The antislavery movement, Lundy concluded, had lost much of its earlier momentum and needed fresh leadership. Clearly the cause languished, especially in those older parts of the South that had once formed the very center of antislavery thought. The Negro uprisings in Haiti in 1792–93 and the plot of the slave Gabriel Prosser to seize Richmond in 1800 had discouraged antislavery action everywhere in the slave states. "This is, indeed, a melancholy crisis to us," the Virginia Abolition Society had reported soon after the disclosure of the Gabriel conspiracy. The Virginia society had fallen into decline, its secretary explained, because many "who were once hearty in the cause of emancipation, taking a retrospect view of the recent plot . . . have now thought proper to abandon it as dangerous to the well-being of society."[27] After such events southerners could easily imagine that they lived atop a human volcano. Greater repression, not freedom, seemed to be called for.

But economic considerations, in the long run, probably proved a more important force than concern for the public safety in discouraging southern antislavery activity. As slaveholdings in the upper South rose in value, especially after the

of the Wrongs of Those Unhappy Beings," St. Clairsville, Ohio, January 4, 1816. Broadside (Chicago Historical Society).

[27] *Minutes of the Proceedings of the Seventh Convention of Delegates from the Abolition Societies Established in Different Parts of the United States . . .* (Philadelphia, 1801), p. 22.

end of the foreign slave trade in 1808, fewer criticisms of slavery and still fewer proposals to end it were voiced by slave-owners in that region. Shrewd observers early recognized the financial motives for perpetuating slavery. "Gain was the original cause of slavery. — Gain has been the cause of the blacks being kept in slavery, and gain will be the cause of perpetuating their slavery," commented Daniel Raymond, a Maryland abolitionist. "If the people were only willing to deny themselves of the gain of oppression, the trumpet of jubilee would soon be sounded," observed another.[28]

Thus if Lundy were to venture publicly to raise his voice in favor of abolition, he would defy not only a racially inspired fear but a powerful, entrenched economic interest as well. This meant that he could expect to find few sympathizers among the former philanthropists of the upper South. Men in Virginia and Maryland who had once spoken out strongly against slavery took second thought as they watched the price of slaves advance. This was true even of some of America's greatest exponents of liberty. Thomas Jefferson, while retaining theoretical opposition to human bondage, still kept his slaves — and not alone because he feared the social consequence of freeing them. Like many another Virginian he had become aware of the profit to be made by raising men for market. Concerned in 1819 by the heavy mortality among infants on his plantation, he admonished his overseer to provide adequate leisure for pregnant slave women and nursing mothers. "I consider the labor of a breeding woman as no object," he wrote, "and that a child raised every 2. years is of more profit than the crop of the best laboring man." And with that

---

[28] Daniel Raymond, *The Missouri Question* (Baltimore, 1819), p. 36; *The Emancipator (Complete), Published by Elihu Embree, Jonesborough, Tennessee, 1820* (Nashville, 1932), April 30, 1820, p. 4. All further citations to the *Emancipator* are to this reprint of the original.

serenity for which he was famous, he added, "in this, as in all other cases, providence has made our interest & our duties coincide perfectly."[29]

As long as a market for slaves existed, it would be hard to curb the avarice of those profiting from the system. "Neither the moral force of precepts and examples, nor the enactment of penal laws, will have their proper effect while the 'breeding' of slaves is considered lucrative . . ." Lundy commented.[30]

If the philanthropy of such great emancipated spirits as Jefferson had been compromised by the love of gain, what support could Lundy expect from younger men born too late to share in the liberalizing traditions of the Enlightenment? Now envisioning rich futures for themselves based on the perpetuation of human bondage, they inclined even less than their elders to oppose slavery and thereby imperil their own anticipated wealth. Most exceptional was the aristocratic young Virginian Edward Coles, who in 1819 freed his numerous slaves and moved with them to Illinois.[31] Even most of those antislavery leaders who remained true to their earlier convictions had resigned themselves to the conclusion that with the abolition of slavery in the northern states and the ending of the foreign slave trade all readily attainable antislavery goals had been reached. Further victories, it appeared, could not be won in their lifetime.

Thus at the time Lundy moved to Ohio, a momentary lull had appeared in the antislavery movement. But it did not last long. As Lundy put it, "Altho' the spirit of reform has slumbered a while, it only rested a little season to obtain new vig-

---

[29] Edwin M. Betts (ed.) *Thomas Jefferson's Farm Book with Commentary and Relevant Extracts from Other Writings* (Princeton, N.J., 1953), p. 43.
[30] *Genius*, I (November, 1821), 65.
[31] Clarence W. Alvord (ed.), *Governor Edward Coles* (Springfield, Ill., 1920), pp. 23, 28, 43, 261–263.

or." [32] Even while Lundy observed the decline, the new strength of slavery was generating renewed opposition. Lundy's own vow to fight slavery constituted evidence of that development.

In the new phase of the antislavery movement some old centers of opposition — most notably Philadelphia — remained active, although the Quaker philanthropists now restricted themselves for the most part to giving quiet antislavery testimony and aiding free Negroes. They united their efforts in a rather ineffectual organization called the American Convention for Promoting the Abolition of Slavery and Improving the Condition of the African Race, which generally met every two years to discuss problems and plan antislavery strategy. New Englanders in those years joined men in the Middle States to allude occasionally to slavery as an evil, but they lived too far removed from its direct influence for many to be aware of the magnitude of the problem. Although men in that section had once held slaves themselves, much as did their southern brethren, for most of them awareness of their own complicity in the slave system had all but vanished. If pressed, they might admit that slavery had indeed once flourished in their own neighborhoods, but for most of the present generation it was as though it had all happened in another country, and they now felt small concern for deeds done far from their own borders.

Nearly unique in New England at that time was the work of John Kenrick, an elderly philanthropist of Newton, Massachusetts, who had waged a lonely campaign against slavery during long years of general apathy. When Lundy's antislavery activities began, Kenrick would be one of the first men in New England to support his efforts. In 1817 he published at his own expense 3,000 copies of an antislavery pamphlet, *Hor-*

---

[32] *Genius*, III (July 18, 1823), 9.

rors of Slavery, and circulated it as far west as Tennessee.[33] Although less lurid than its title suggested, the book still contained a harsh arraignment of slavery, an institution Kenrick called "impolitic, antirepublican, unchristian, and *highly criminal.*" The remedy, Kenrick said, was immediate emancipation. "If slavery is 'a violation of the divine laws,' is it not absurd to talk about a gradual emancipation? We might as well talk of gradually leaving off piracy — murder — adultery, or drunkenness." [34] On April 4, 1818, the year after Kenrick's book appeared, Representative Arthur Livermore of New Hampshire introduced into Congress a constitutional amendment to abolish slavery everywhere in the nation.[35] But despite such noteworthy exceptions as these, New England lagged for many years in antislavery thought and action. Lundy could expect little immediate support from that quarter.

Stronger and more persistent antislavery effort could be found after 1815 in parts of the nonslaveholding upland South and the newly settled West, the theater of Lundy's early operations. Men there — many of them recently arrived from small farms in plantation areas — early recognized slavery's new dynamism and, having no economic stake in slavery and few powerful slaveholding neighbors to bid them be silent, found themselves free in their new locations to speak boldly against it. Although for various reasons Lundy was to become

---

[33] Lydia Maria Child, *An Appeal in Favor of That Class of Americans Called Africans* (Boston, 1833), p. 230; Elihu Embree to Joseph M. Paul, August 6, 1820, Papers of Elihu Embree (Historical Society of Pennsylvania, Philadelphia); *The Liberator* (Boston), April 6, 20, June 8, 1833.

[34] John Kenrick, *Horrors of Slavery* . . . (Cambridge, Mass., 1817), pp. 38, 48.

[35] Herman V. Ames, *The Proposed Amendments to the Constitution of the United States During the First Century of Its Existence* (Washington, D.C., 1897), p. 334.

the most important of slavery's new critics, he at no time stood alone. His was not the first voice in the upland South and West to speak out against slavery, nor was his condemnation the strongest and most comprehensive heard in those early years.

Much the most outspoken of slavery's new opponents appeared in Virginia itself. At Short Creek in the Shenandoah Valley the Reverend George Bourne, an English-born Presbyterian, preached for seven years, all the while investigating the rapidly spreading slave system and brooding over its effect on both whites and blacks. From his meditations came a powerful and angry tract, *The Book and Slavery Irreconcilable*, published at Philadelphia in 1816. Bourne expressly repudiated gradual emancipation, demanding instead "immediate and total abolition." In addition he castigated churches and clergymen for their failure to act against slavery.[36] Such sentiments, so out of harmony with the society within which they were expressed, led a Presbyterian council to condemn him for heretical views, and public opinion to drive him from Virginia.[37] Whatever the immediate effect of Bourne's work, it ultimately served as a major source book for abolitionists. By 1830 William Lloyd Garrison had absorbed both its argument and rhetoric. Garrison credited Lundy with bringing him into the antislavery movement, but he credited Bourne's book next to the Bible itself with shaping his views of slavery.[38]

---

[36] George Bourne, *The Book and Slavery Irreconcilable, with Animadversions upon Dr. Smith's Philosophy* (Philadelphia, 1816), pp. 3–4, 7–8, 16.

[37] Louis Filler, *The Crusade Against Slavery, 1830–1860* (New York, 1960), p. 17.

[38] *Liberator*, March 17, 1832; Wendell Phillips Garrison and Francis Jackson Garrison, *William Lloyd Garrison, 1805–1879* (Boston, 1885–89), I, 306, and "postscript" following p. xiv. John L. Thomas, *The Liberator*,

Kentucky and Tennessee had produced critics of slavery
even before Bourne wrote, and long before Lundy had moved
to the West. As early as 1797 the Presbyterian David Rice had
formed a short-lived antislavery society in Kentucky, and in
1807 the Kentucky Friends of Humanity, a group of obscure
Baptists, adopted a catechism denying church membership to
those "friendly to perpetual slavery." Their example was gradually copied by a few of their fellow churchmen until by the
early 1820's little Baptist organizations calling themselves
Friends of Humanity could be found scattered across southern
Illinois and Missouri as well as Kentucky. In 1808 Baptists
and others formed the Kentucky Abolition Society, one of the
first antislavery societies in the West. One of its founders,
David Barrow, in 1807 published a thorough indictment of
slavery as a violation of natural and religious law in his closely reasoned pamphlet, *Involuntary, Unmerited, Perpetual,
Absolute, Hereditary Slavery Examined; on the Principles of
Nature, Reason, Justice, Policy, and Scripture.*[39]

Lundy may not have read Barrow's pamphlet or even heard
of the Friends of Humanity when he launched his own antislavery career. But activities among the Quakers of east Tennessee almost certainly did influence him directly. While
Lundy, working in his saddle shop at St. Clairsville, pondered
ways to move against slavery, Jefferson County in Tennessee,
an area settled by Quakers from Pennsylvania and North
Carolina, had already become the site of one of the first organized antislavery movements in the West. Foremost among
its leaders was Charles Osborn, a North Carolina Quaker who
had joined the trek to Tennessee, where about 1806 he became

William Lloyd Garrison, a Biography (Boston, 1963), p. 105, asserts that
"Garrison never admitted a debt to Bourne's pamphlet. . . ."
[39] Dwight Lowell Dumond, *Antislavery: The Crusade for Freedom in
America* (Ann Arbor, Mich., 1961), pp. 133–134.

a Quaker minister. He had then set himself to wandering
from one Quaker meeting to another, there to preach and bear
witness, a practice typical of Quaker ministers before and
since. His travels through the Carolinas and Virginia seem to
have awakened his sympathy for the slaves and led to his determination to work for emancipation.[40] On February 25, 1815,
he and seven other men met at the Lost Creek meetinghouse
in Jefferson County to organize the Tennessee Society for Promoting the Manumission of Slaves. Later in the year delegates from Osborn's society and other local antislavery groups
that had sprung up among Presbyterians and Quakers met at
the Lick Creek meetinghouse in Greene County, expanded
the earlier organization, and renamed it the Manumission Society of Tennessee. Their goal was gradual emancipation, and
members agreed to withhold their vote from state officials who
did not sympathize with their cause. The next year Quakers in
North Carolina, apparently stimulated by Osborn's example,
also formed antislavery societies.[41]

In June 1815 Osborn left the prospering Tennessee movement to tour Kentucky, Indiana, Ohio, and Pennsylvania,
where he communicated to sympathetic Friends his views on
the necessity for action against slavery. One of his stops that
summer was Mount Pleasant, Ohio, the village just north of
the town where Lundy had settled. Lundy may well have met
Osborn at that time; certainly he learned of his work. Although direct proof is lacking, circumstances strongly suggest
that Lundy's decision to form an antislavery organization in

[40] Charles Osborn, *Journal of That Faithful Servant of Christ, Charles Osborn* . . . (Cincinnati, 1854), pp. 88, 91, 98.
[41] Asa Earl Martin, "The Anti-Slavery Societies of Tennessee," *Tennessee Historical Magazine*, I (December, 1915), 261–281; *Emancipator*, April 30, 1820, p. 10; *History of Tennessee* (Nashville, 1887), V, 881.

Ohio owed its immediate inspiration to Osborn and his example.[42]

In any event, not many months after Osborn's visit, Lundy decided to act. Following a long period of brooding over slavery and his responsibility toward it, he invited several of his friends to his home in St. Clairsville to form an antislavery association. Plans for organizing went forward during the winter. In a circular dated January 4, 1816, his twenty-seventh birthday, Lundy explained the goals of his ambitious project.[43] He intended to form a national society to embrace all existing antislavery organizations and thereby create a grand concert of antislavery sentiment and activity. Nothing but an effort on a monumental scale, he had concluded, could halt the new momentum of the slave system. Only a man moved by uncommon zeal and willing to disregard the realities of his situation could have formulated such a program. Limited as he was by deficiencies in training, experience, location, financial resources, and access to centers of power, his aim seemed unrealistic as well as unattainable. The society's immediate goals, however, were less grandiose.

According to the constitution, drafted by Charles Hammond and adopted at Mount Pleasant on April 20, 1816, the Union Humane Society derived its principles from the Golden Rule and the Declaration of Independence. It would try to end racial prejudice and, by seeking to repeal legal disqualifications and to remove other impediments to civil rights, help Negroes already freed to become useful members of society. All legal means would be used to secure the freedom of Negroes illegally held in bondage and to protect the rights of free Negroes entering Ohio. Following the precedent set by the

---

[42] O'Dell, "Early Antislavery Movement in Ohio," pp. 194, 206.
[43] Thomas Hedges Genin, *Selections from the Writings of the Late Thomas Hedges Genin . . .* (New York, 1869), p. 13.

Manumission Society of Tennessee, members of Lundy's society pledged themselves to vote only for politicians who opposed slavery. The constitution also stated that the society hoped ultimately to achieve gradual emancipation, but it was vague as to how the members expected to accomplish that end.[44] Lundy as yet had developed no plan for reaching into the South to destroy slavery. Clearly, though the society hoped to see slavery ended, its chief activity would be to aid free Negroes and to eliminate racial prejudice and legal discriminations. As its name implied, the Union Humane Society aimed primarily to extend humanitarian assistance to Negroes in Ohio. In this respect it closely resembled the ineffectual Quaker antislavery societies that had operated for decades in Pennsylvania to aid free Negroes and fugitive slaves. The Union Humane Society was a beginning, but scarcely more than that, in Lundy's evolution as a major antislavery reformer.

---

[44] Dumond, *Antislavery*, p. 136.

CHAPTER II

Perplexities

The Union Humane Society grew rapidly. Within a few months its membership had increased to nearly 500 and its locals to at least eight, each of which sent delegates to semiannual meetings held at Mount Pleasant.[1] Lundy's antislavery zeal had easily found support among his neighbors, for Belmont and Jefferson counties in southeastern Ohio already contained a population sensitive to injustice and hostile to slavery. No tension developed between the antislavery society and the community; indeed, Lundy's organization secured the backing of some of the area's most prominent men, among them Charles Hammond, later to become an influential Cincinnati editor and lawyer; James Wilson, Steubenville editor and grandfather of Woodrow Wilson; and Joseph Howells, grandfather of William Dean Howells.[2]

[1] [Earle], *Life*, p. 16.
[2] O'Dell, "Early Antislavery Movement in Ohio," p. 202; Dumond, *Antislavery*, p. 136; William Cooper Howells, *Recollections of Life in Ohio from 1813 to 1840* (Cincinnati, 1895), p. 33; Genin, *Selections*, p. 13.

Yet, after its first prosperity enthusiasm for the society rapidly declined, partly no doubt because the efforts it proved capable of seemed inadequate to accomplish very much. The growing colony of free Negroes west of Mount Pleasant had served constantly to remind humanitarians of the fate of southern slaves and of the hardships Negroes must labor under even in the North. But when Jefferson County's philanthropy had freed local Negroes from the most flagrant abuses, what more could be done? How could Ohio reformers, with the best will in the world, lessen the grip of slavery on the South? The Union Humane Society supplied no answer. Even Lundy soon lost enthusiasm for the organization he had created. Within a year of its founding he was writing to important men in other parts of the country, appealing for their suggestions for ways to achieve more effective antislavery action.[3]

Charles Osborn helped him find a better method. The Tennessee reformer had been convinced by his visit to Mount Pleasant in 1815 that hardly a more strategic spot existed anywhere from which to influence Quaker opinion. Situated in the path of thousands of Quaker families moving West and containing a great two-story brick meetinghouse that periodically drew Quakers from miles around, Mount Pleasant seemed destined to become the center of western Friends' religious and intellectual life. Osborn moved to that important place in October 1816 in the hope that there he could take steps to mold Quaker thought and direct Quaker action toward new philanthropic accomplishment. He was joined the next spring by another outstanding antislavery Quaker, Elisha Bates from Yorktown, Virginia, a sometime schoolmaster

---

[3] Joseph Doddridge to Lundy, December 8, 1816, in *Philanthropist*, I (October 10, 1817), 38.

and dedicated humanitarian who had already tried to found antislavery societies in his home state.[4]

This constellation of philanthropists — Osborn, Bates, and Lundy — stood in a position, Osborn believed, to direct Quaker opinion throughout the Northwest toward sympathy for reform causes of many kinds. Their instrument would be the press.

On August 29, 1817, Osborn published at Mount Pleasant the first issue of a weekly journal called the *Philanthropist*, to contain — as he said — "such religious, moral, agricultural and manufacturing information, as may tend to the great aim of giving 'ardour to virtue and confidence to truth.' "[5] Osborn scattered among its immediately practical articles essays on Quaker religious belief, admonitory letters from London Yearly Meeting to Friends in western America, addresses from the newly formed manumission societies in North Carolina and Tennessee, and antislavery articles.

Lundy became the *Philanthropist*'s agent at St. Clairsville, and from the first shared in producing the newspaper. In hours saved from saddlemaking, he poured over exchanges from other editors. From those newspapers he helped select articles for republication in the *Philanthropist*, sending them to Osborn along with contributions of his own; the first antislavery essay from his own pen appeared in the issue of October 10, 1817.[6] With the discovery that he could write effectively himself, new possibilities opened to his inventive mind.

---

[4] Ellen Starr Brinton, "The Yearly Meetinghouse of Mount Pleasant, Ohio," *Bulletin of Friends Historical Association*, XXXI (autumn, 1952), 93; Robert J. Leach, "Elisha Bates and the Mount Pleasant Printing Press, 1817–1827," *ibid.*, XXIX (spring, 1940), 17; Osborn, *Journal*, p. 144.

[5] *Philanthropist*, I (August 29, 1817), 3.

[6] *Ibid.* (September 19, 1817), p. 12; (October 10, 1817), pp. 37–38. Lundy used the pseudonym "Philo justitia." See [Earle], *Life*, p. 18.

He began to weigh the utility of journalism as the means he had been seeking to advance the antislavery movement. The *Philanthropist*, for all its humanitarian appeal, ranked slavery as only one of many evils to be eradicated from American society. Osborn's reformist concern ranged far and wide; Lundy's focused on slavery alone. A journal dedicated solely to abolition rather than to general reform, Lundy decided, might do much to mobilize opinion in favor of the antislavery cause and to stimulate discussion of the strategy its proponents should adopt. If such a journal could be directed not exclusively to Quakers but to all persons of humanitarian bent, it might prove to be the effective antislavery instrument Lundy had sought. But however reasonable all this seemed, it nonetheless wore the attributes of a dream of the sort an ambitious craftsman might conjure in the silence of his workshop, for at that point Lundy had only the scantiest financial resources to implement such a scheme, and, in any event, another aspect of antislavery reform soon distracted his interest.

As discussion of slavery increased, Lundy discovered that any program designed to abolish slavery presented greater complexities than his limited experience had thus far allowed him to imagine. These became apparent with the controversy aroused by the founding of the American Colonization Society at Washington during the winter of 1816–17. On the surface, at least, the society's plan to send free Negroes to Africa appeared to be a humanitarian project, for hardly any group in the country needed aid more desperately than those oppressed people. In that respect its aim did not differ greatly from that of Lundy's own Union Humane Society. The new society's advocates appealed to philanthropists for support on the ground that colonization would accomplish several desirable aims. It would aid free Negroes by giving them a fresh start in the land of their origin, and thereby it would also help Christianize heathen Africa. Even more important, some colonizationists claimed, the plan would lead gradually to the ending of slavery by encouraging masters to free their slaves with the understanding that they must leave the country.[7]

An organization that promised reformers so much naturally aroused interest in southeastern Ohio as elsewhere, with Lundy among its local proponents. Late in 1817 a colonization society was organized at the courthouse in St. Clairsville, presumably with Lundy's aid, certainly with his approval. There is no evidence, however, that Lundy ever held formal membership in the American Colonization Society. Indeed, late in life he denied that he had even attended one of its meetings.[8]

But join the society or not, any man who had set himself to the task of ending slavery could hardly avoid coming to terms with the issues the colonizationists had raised, and this was not an easy thing to do. Those issues plagued Lundy during the rest of his career. Of immediate concern was the effect the colonization society's program would have on emancipation. Would its operations really hasten the ending of slavery, as its advocates claimed, or would they, by removing the free Negroes, simply make slavery a stronger institution? A humanitarian had to ask himself too whether the deportation of American Negroes to Africa would in itself be a wise and humane act. Would the freedmen themselves substantially benefit by moving to a strange and perhaps inhospitable land? Certainly many Negroes did not think so. There were other practical considerations as well, not of immediate concern to antislavery men but important nonetheless and not easy to

---

[7] P. J. Staudenraus, *The African Colonization Movement, 1816–1865* (New York, 1961), pp. 19–22.

[8] *Philanthropist*, I (October 10, 1817), 38; *National Enquirer* (Philadelphia), March 18, 1837.

ignore. What, for instance, would be the effect upon the nation's economy of the removal of so many productive laborers? Did America not really need the Negro?

Important as all those considerations undoubtedly were, the fundamental question posed by the American Colonization Society was this: What shall be the ultimate racial composition of the United States? This question tested the American conscience and caused many reformers extreme mental anguish as they struggled to arrive at an answer.

Even though in actuality whites had never been alone on the continent, colonizationists assumed with many others of their time that America was intended to be and ultimately must become a white man's country. Although the American Colonization Society contained some members who looked upon its operations as a means of strengthening and perpetuating slavery, others just as sincerely wished to end it. But the philanthropy toward the Negro of even the most benevolent of them was severely limited by their views of his inherent nature. Like Jefferson before them, they found it hard to believe that Negroes ever would be qualified to share full citizenship in the United States. Accordingly, they planned to banish them to Africa.[9]

In spite of the racism nearly all colonizationists shared, an important segment within the society readily admitted that slavery was a wicked institution. Therefore, they said, slavery should be gradually ended, and then all evidence of the evil it represented should be expunged by sending the freedmen to Africa. It was as though they sought to restore the nation's lost innocence. America, they assumed, was to have been a

[9] Staudenraus, *African Colonization*, pp. 1–3, 29; Dwight Lowell Dumond, *Antislavery Origins of the Civil War in the United States* (Ann Arbor, Mich., 1939), pp. 16–18; see the remarks by South Carolina's William L. Smith in *Annals of Congress*, 1 Cong., 2 Sess., p. 1455.

new Eden. Obviously this had not happened, for avarice and pride had accompanied Adam from the Old World to the New. Evidence of that fact in the form of Negro slaves was present for all to see. Even the ending of slavery would not by itself remedy the situation, for after emancipation the Negro still would remain, the badge of America's lost innocence. Colonizationists longed for a white America, its innocence restored, the nation purged of the evidence of its centuries of guilt. So long as the Negro remained — even if free —white men would be tempted to repeat against him their well-rehearsed crimes of tyranny and exploitation, vanity and lust.

Some Americans, on the other hand, could accept both the presence of the Negro and the fact of the nation's indelible guilt. They saw no way to avoid the burden imposed on the present generation by history. Slavery had flourished in America for nearly two centuries, and abolitionists were willing to accept that long-standing sin as irremediable. They had no delusion that innocence once lost could ever be recovered. They asked, rather, that guilt be recognized and accepted and justice be done to those whom the nation's sins had caused to suffer. Even *retribution* was in their vocabulary. From the strength granted by such wisdom, abolitionists envisioned a biracial America built on the recognition and acceptance of the equality of all men.

Since the colonization program thus involved matters of great magnitude and social effect, differences of opinion as to its merits inevitably appeared. The abolitionist George Bourne dismissed the idea of colonization even before the American Colonization Society had been formed — "totally impracticable," he called it.[10] In southeastern Ohio Osborn, a gradual emancipationist ("We see [slavery] in all its dif-

---

[10] Bourne, *The Book*, p. 134n.

ficult and delicate aspects," he had written), also saw through
the scheme at once. He charged that by removing free Negroes and the natural Negro leaders to Africa, the American
Colonization Society would only rivet closer the chains of
the slaves. Furthermore, he expressed "great doubts of the
justice" of colonization. The free Negroes of Philadelphia, he
pointed out, had already met to protest plans to deport them
to Africa. He suggested either hypocrisy or misinformation on
the part of those religious advocates who proposed to evan-
gelize Africa by sending it America's manumitted slaves: He
who has observed "the ignorance and vice with which Slavery
has enveloped the Children of Africa can hardly be persuaded
that they are *now* fit instruments for propagating the gos-
pel."[11]

Lundy could not agree with Osborn's criticism. His own understanding — not yet very extensive — of southern whites and
slaves led him to believe that thousands of slaves would be
freed if only their owners could be assured that they would
be removed from the United States. He believed too that most
slaves would gladly accept such conditional manumission. In
short, Lundy thought no price too great for a slave to pay in
order to win release from bondage.[12] He never changed his
views on that matter. Furthermore, he had seen enough of the
treatment popularly accorded free Negroes in the North to
make him doubt that they were likely soon to be granted equal
rights with white men. Racial prejudice, he predicted, would
have a long American history. He supposed on that account
that many Negroes would prefer to live in Africa rather than
endure seemingly hopeless degradation in America. But quite
apart from all this, Lundy in those years considered the Amer-

[11] *Philanthropist,* I (October 17, 1817), 44; (February 7, 1818), p. 172;
II (September 3, 1818), 189–190.
[12] *Ibid.,* I (October 17, 1817), 45.

ican Colonization Society to be a genuine antislavery instrument, even if a most imperfect one. As he pointed out, colonization agents in their efforts to persuade masters to free their slaves often thought it expedient to emphasize the cruelties of slavery. Some masters would yield to those arguments, Lundy believed, and the total burden of slavery would be lessened by that much. Still more important, he said, was the educative work the society could be expected to accomplish among nonslaveholders. "The arguments used in support of the plan of colonization," he explained, "generally tend to sap the foundation of the system of slavery itself." Not only would some individual slaves immediately be freed as a result of the society's operations, but the slave system itself would be undermined as the society helped the public to grow increasingly aware of slavery's iniquity.[13]

Lundy altered but never fundamentally changed his views on these matters. He soon became thoroughly disenchanted with the American Colonization Society as all abolitionists did, but his views on the efficacy of colonization — or emigration — as an antislavery instrument remained the same. Not until the end of his career did he finally condemn the American Colonization Society in its entirety as a foe of immediate abolition.[14]

Lundy was thoroughly committed to the ending of slavery, and he never made compromises with racial prejudice to the point of denying the right of Negroes to remain in the United States as citizens. He never justified the slave system; he never defended it in any way or excused those guilty of its practice and perpetuation. He never suggested that slavery could be ameliorated; he never attempted to palliate its evils. He never implied that slavery was less than a monstrous crime for

---

[13] *Ibid.*
[14] *National Enquirer*, March 18, 1837.

which God someday would exact awful vengeance unless men speedily reformed. But he refused ever to be doctrinaire about how slavery should be ended. Any method that would weaken the system and at the same time free individual slaves won approval from him. To him the goal seemed all important, the method less so.

Lundy was a genuine abolitionist and as such never believed that the United States could or should banish the Negro from its bounds. He had no vain ambition to make of it a white man's country. He supported colonization not because he himself distrusted or despised Negroes but because he thought the removal of some of them would speed the ending of slavery. "I have no idea that *ever* they will *all* be colonized, or that it will be necessary that they should be," he explained. "I am not anxious to support this measure any further than it will subserve the cause of emancipation." He considered colonization a necessary prerequisite "to pave the way for the completion of that grand and benevolent work, the Abolition of slavery." [15]

Lundy's persistence in advocating emigration arose from his belief as to how slavery finally would be ended. Already the notion that the federal government might by legislation destroy slavery in the states had been tested and denied.[16] Therefore, it remained for the state legislatures to pass the laws that would end it. But obviously no state legislature would act until public opinion within the state forced it to do so. The majority of southern people — most of whom themselves reaped no profit from slavery — presently refused to consider emancipation, Lundy believed, because of their racial prejudice and especially because they feared insurrections by Negroes freed from slavery's restrictions. They al-

---

[15] *Philanthropist*, I (December 12, 1817), 110–111.
[16] *Annals of Congress*, 1 Cong., 2 Sess., pp. 1473–74.

ready dreaded the prospect of further increasing the number of free Negroes, hence their exertions "to perpetuate the galling chain of servitude, and their aversion to the enlightening of their minds, or diminishing the burdens of those who remain in a state of bondage." Such anxieties could be allayed, Lundy supposed, if the white population were assured that some of the freedmen would be removed. The opposition of the whites to emancipation would diminish in ratio with the number of Negroes colonized. For economic reasons slaveholders would never agree to legislative action to end slavery, but the nonslaveholding southerners, who constituted the majority, might be persuaded to force the state legislatures to pass such laws if they could be assured that emancipation would not be socially disastrous.[17] Such was also the prediction of persons better acquainted than Lundy with the realities of the southern situation. Emancipation, they reasoned, was unlikely to come unless many Negroes could be removed from the southern states.[18]

However realistic Lundy's views may have been, they met powerful opposition in southeastern Ohio, not only from Osborn and Elisha Bates but also from another outspoken abolitionist, Thomas Hedges Genin, a rising young lawyer who had arrived in St. Clairsville from New York City in 1817. On May 18, 1818, Genin, then aged twenty-two, addressed the semiannual meeting of the Union Humane Society at Mount Pleasant to urge emancipation and to condemn the American Colonization Society, which, he said, would only "perpetuate and extend" slavery. Colonization was a dream, he insisted, for the Negroes "will ever remain among us." Since this was a certainty, all thought of deporting them should be abandoned,

---

[17] *Philanthropist*, II (March 14, 1818), 5–6.
[18] Address by Aaron Coffin, September, 1824, in Wagstaff (ed.), *Minutes*, p. 84.

and they "should be enlightened and formed for good citizens." Humanitarians should work to aid the free Negroes rather than waste their energies on vain plans to get rid of them. Genin went further than most men of his day toward envisioning a biracial America, and he was more optimistic than most about the Negro's capacity. The Negro, he declared, "is not inferior in nature to the rest of mankind. . . ."[19] He combed ancient and medieval history for evidence to prove his assertion. Through long and praiseful passages he sought to demonstrate that Africans had been "the first learned people, and that letters [were] chiefly indebted to the swarthy race!"[20]

In 1819 Genin's views were carried from Mount Pleasant to Philadelphia, where his speech was presented as a message from the eight branches of the Union Humane Society to the American Convention, the loose association of the nation's antislavery societies. There the assembled delegates were informed of Genin's objections to colonization: "It is doubtful whether the expense of colonizing the blacks at any place, might not be appropriated more advantageously for humanity: those that are now free, are in as good a country as any to which they could be transported; if it be expected that the slave-holders will manumit their slaves that are useful, to be colonized, the expectation must be founded upon the supposition that man will act as he ought to and not as he has done. . . ."[21]

While Lundy in the midst of many dissenters continued to believe the best of the American Colonization Society, Osborn printed a lengthy article calling attention to the society's official denial that it aimed to end slavery. The writer ap-

---

[19] Genin, *Selections*, pp. 109–111.
[20] *Ibid.*, p. 102. Punctuation as in the original.
[21] *Ibid.*, p. 19.

praised colonization as damaging to the antislavery cause, a mere diversionary tactic which "might amuse our minds with the mistaken idea of doing something valuable. . . ." Not the free Negroes but the slaves demanded first attention, he insisted. Measures to aid free Negroes or to promote civilization in Africa, however desirable in themselves, still should not be the philanthropist's first concern. "The great object still is, to devise some system, by which slavery may ultimately be terminated." African colonization, whatever its other merits, was not directed to that object or capable of effecting it. The rational mind, he concluded, must agree "that the colonization of Africa, can never remove from our country the evils of slavery; nor atone for the injuries we have done, and are doing." [22]

Osborn recognized that in spite of his differences with Lundy over colonization their conflict was not really fundamental. Both agreed that slavery must be ended and justice done to the freedmen. Lundy's developing literary ability and his dedication led Osborn, now tiring of his editorial role, to consider making him a full partner in his printing establishment. Lundy, having become increasingly enthusiastic about writing and editing, decided to arrange his business affairs in order to accept the proposal.[23] He would need money, and in order to get it, he made plans to liquidate his prospering saddle business by taking his stock of leather goods to Missouri Territory, where he believed they could be sold to advantage. The trip down the Ohio River and back took nearly six months. As the weeks dragged on, Osborn grew impatient for Lundy's return and in the absence of any firm commitment decided not to wait longer for him. Early in October 1818 he announced that he had sold his newspaper

22 *Philanthropist*, II (August 27, 1818), 181–182.
23 Genin, *Selections*, p. 14; [Earle], *Life*, p. 18.

to Elisha Bates and would himself soon leave Mount Pleasant and move to a Friends' settlement in Indiana.[24]

Lundy returned to Ohio a few weeks later to find his hopes for sharing in the publication of the *Philanthropist* dashed. The new editor, unlike Osborn, sought no partner. Lundy, with little money of his own, could hardly hope to publish an independent newspaper. Furthermore, another western antislavery journal no longer seemed necessary, for in January 1819 Elihu Embree in Jonesboro, Tennessee, founded the *Manumission Intelligencer* as the official organ of the Tennessee Manumission Society. Lundy apparently had no immediate function to serve in antislavery journalism. The decade was ending, and Lundy had passed his thirtieth birthday with little but resolution and deepening antislavery conviction to show for his years of antislavery concern.

---

[24] [Earle], *Life*, p. 18; *Philanthropist*, II (October 8, 1818), 204. All later writers have copied Earle's error in dating the sale of the *Philanthropist* in 1819 during Lundy's second trip to Missouri.

CHAPTER III

The Genius of Universal Emancipation

During his stay in Missouri Territory in 1818 Lundy had become more intimately acquainted with slaveholders than he had ever before found possible, and he also met slaves lately brought by their owners to that frontier region. It was an educative experience, for in both slave and slaveholder he saw revealed once more the vitality of the slave system and the comparative weakness of its opponents. Here he encountered men who — unlike many planters in older sections of the country — made no effort to apologize for slavery. Instead, they publicly avowed their plans to perpetuate it and extend it into new states; here he found exposed for the first time the ambitions of some slaveholders to spread slavery across the country. He must have listened to their predictions of the great wealth Missouri's admission as a slave state would bring and heard the specious claim that expanding slavery into new territories would make it a more humane institution by diffusing the nation's slave population.[1] All these ex-

---

[1] Glover Moore, *The Missouri Controversy, 1819–1821* (Lexington, Ky., 1953), pp. 46–47, 51, 292–293.

periences could only have reinforced his conviction that the times required far greater antislavery effort than any yet exerted.

In February 1819, soon after Lundy's return to Ohio, Representative James Tallmadge, Jr., of New York introduced into the congressional debates over the admission of Missouri his amendment to bar the future introduction of slaves to that state. Antislavery groups everywhere rejoiced. This was the sort of action in high places which they believed necessary if the rapid growth of slavery were to be halted. For the first time since the outlawing of the African slave trade, an issue directly concerned with slavery was presented to the nation in easily understood political terms and in a form inviting commitment and action. Rousing itself from months of lethargy, the Union Humane Society at its spring session in Mount Pleasant commended Tallmadge and others in Congress for their antislavery efforts, and appointed Lundy to a business committee with Elisha Bates, Thomas Hedges Genin, and Joseph Steer to handle the society's affairs during that time of increasing sectional tension.[2]

Although Lundy welcomed such gestures and agreed on the importance of letting all the world know where good men stood on this issue, he knew very well that commendatory resolutions from the citizens of Ohio would have little influence on the course of events. Words possessed power, as he had learned from experience; yet he considered them in this instance inadequate to halt the drive for slavery's expansion. He felt personally obliged not merely to frame antislavery declarations but to take some action that might contribute to

[2] *The Philanthropist, a Weekly Journal* (Mount Pleasant, Ohio), I (May 1, 1819), 47. Bates ignored the numbering of Osborn's two published volumes of the *Philanthropist* and started his own editorship with volume I.

the efforts such men as Tallmadge had made to block the admission of another slave state. Furthermore, he must act at the very center of events rather than on their periphery. Concluding that next to the halls of Congress the spot where the most effectual steps could be taken to prevent the extension of slavery was Missouri itself, he decided that he must return to Missouri and stay there until the issue had been settled. He would make his living by establishing himself as a saddler, and then do whatever might be done to help Missouri become a free state.[3]

Late in the fall of 1819 after borrowing 300 dollars to help finance his plans,[4] Lundy once again said good-bye to his wife and his two small daughters, Susan and Elizabeth, and with three indentured apprentices left for Missouri to set up his saddle and harness shop at Herculaneum, a new but rapidly growing village on the Mississippi River midway between St. Louis and Ste. Genevieve. As a business enterprise the move could hardly have been a greater failure. The depression following the Panic of 1819 cut the demand for saddles and lowered prices; one of his apprentices ran away; and Lundy soon found himself so preoccupied with politics that he neglected his shop. But these misfortunes troubled him hardly at all, for antislavery work, not saddlemaking, had brought him to Missouri.[5]

On March 6, 1820, a few months after Lundy had arrived in Herculaneum, Congress authorized the people of Missouri to form a constitution without the Tallmadge amendment. That is, Congress placed no restriction on the status Missouri

---

[3] [Earle], *Life,* p. 19.
[4] District Court of Philadelphia, Execution Docket, September term, 1835, no. 263 (Department of Records, City Hall, Philadelphia).
[5] St. Louis *Gazette and Public Advertiser,* April 19, 1820; [Earle], *Life,* p. 19.

might accord to slavery. Since Congress did not *require* Missouri to have slavery, there remained at least the chance that its constitutional convention might be prevailed upon to draft an antislavery document. It was this remote possibility that had drawn Lundy back to Missouri, and by the spring of 1820 enough other men also had recognized that possibility to produce a movement within the territory designed to elect antislavery delegates to the convention.[6]

Since Missouri's population was overwhelmingly of southern origin, the cause seemed lost from the start; yet the opponents of slavery felt an obligation to principle not to concede without giving battle. The Baptist Friends of Humanity, scattered along the Mississippi, held meetings to oppose the constitutional establishment of slavery, and John Mason Peck, a Connecticut-born Baptist missionary, traveled through the territory delivering sermons of such character as to cause the proponents of slavery to accuse him of turning his evangelical camp meetings into antislavery forums.[7] Lundy, by his efforts, revived old sectional antipathies among southern emigrants, who charged him with being an emissary of New England antislavery Federalism, and used against him such pejorative epithets as "Tory," "Hartford Convention Man," and "Blue Light" — words associated with alleged Federalist treachery during the War of 1812.[8]

Lundy, now somewhat practiced in the arts of antislavery journalism, wrote numerous letters to the newspapers in Missouri and Illinois in an effort to sway voters, but he never

---

[6] Moore, *Missouri Controversy*, pp. 263–266.

[7] *Missouri Intelligencer* (Franklin), June 17, 1820; St. Louis *Enquirer*, April 15, 1820; Merton L. Dillon, "John Mason Peck, a Study of Historical Rationalization," *Journal of the Illinois State Historical Society*, L (winter, 1957), 385–390.

[8] St. Louis *Enquirer*, April 29, 1820; *Genius*, II (November, 1822), 68.

imagined then or later that propaganda alone could destroy slavery.[9] Just as he had earlier organized the Union Humane Society in Ohio in the hope of furthering emancipation, he now helped organize groups in Missouri for political anti-slavery action.

On April 22, 1820, a few men met at John Geiger's home in Herculaneum to launch a political campaign to elect anti-slavery delegates to the constitutional convention. David Bryant was elected chairman; Lundy, who never enjoyed making speeches, served as secretary. The meeting resolved that the slaveowners then in Missouri be allowed to retain their slaves but that no more slaves be admitted and that all residents — not freeholders alone — be allowed to vote. The latter measure was designed, of course, to permit such relatively poor newcomers and temporary residents as Lundy to cast votes in the ensuing critical elections. They resolved to support Abner Vansart as delegate to the convention from Jefferson County. The group then appointed Lundy chairman of a committee to draft an address to the voters explaining the antislavery position.[10]

Lundy's essay attempted to refute the claims proslavery advocates had made to justify their stand. He denied the frequently heard argument that the admission of slavery would increase land values and lead to a rapid influx of white population. Land prices in slave states, he pointed out, generally lagged behind those in the North. Neither would Missouri's attractiveness to settlers be enhanced by making it a slave state — more persons were leaving the South to escape from

---

[9] Although these cannot be positively identified, probably those signed "Anthony Benezet" and "Howard" were from his pen. See St. Louis *Gazette and Public Advertiser*, April 12, 19, 1820, and St. Louis *Enquirer*, quoted in *Emancipator*, July 31, 1820, p. 60.
[10] St. Louis *Missouri Gazette*, April 26, 1820.

slavery, he thought, than were being drawn there because of its presence. He denied the frequently heard argument that slavery would become a more humane institution if it were diffused through new regions. Slavery, he insisted, was slavery wherever it existed. Spreading it into the West would solve no problem, would serve only to expand the evil implicit in the system. "The wise and virtuous in all parts of the union," had long opposed it, he wrote, "*and* the only question with them is how to get rid of it?" How ironic, then, that the people of a new territory at the moment when they held within their hands the power to exclude slavery forever should consider introducing this "dangerous system of cruelty and injustice," this "hydra of iniquity." [11]

Lundy's appeals proved useless, for he had centered his arguments on the effects of slavery on society. Such arguments were discarded easily by frontiersmen. What difference did it make to those highly individualistic men if slavery harmed society in general? They could not think in such terms, for society in their eyes scarcely existed. Furthermore, the ambitious Missouri settlers knew very well that the slave system *was* profitable, at least for the lucky few, among whom they confidently expected to be numbered. And, as practical, unreflecting men they were little influenced by arguments centering about the "cruelty and injustice" implicit in slavery.

The election for delegates to the constitutional convention turned out to be a disaster for the restrictionists, who found themselves outnumbered by at least seven to one. Not a single antislavery delegate was elected anywhere in the territory. Even though the proslavery vote in Jefferson County, where Lundy lived, was split between two candidates — Samuel Hammond, who had been a business associate of Moses Aus-

---

[11] *Ibid.* "A very violent piece . . . exactly in the Northern style," said the St. Louis *Enquirer*, April 29, 1820.

tin, the father of the founder of Texas, and John W. Haney
— Vansart, the antislavery candidate, still ran a poor third.[12]
The simple truth was that in spite of all efforts antislavery
ideas had not penetrated very far among the voters of Missouri or among the people of the slave states from which they
came. The prospect of economic gain and personal advantage
had counteracted all moral arguments. Accordingly, the Missouri constitutional convention could be counted on to admit slavery without restriction.

Although the outcome could hardly be doubted, Lundy
nonetheless felt obliged to remain in Missouri to await the
issue's final settlement.[13] The convention framed a proslavery
constitution as expected. Upon hearing the news, Lundy no
doubt concurred with Elihu Embree's remark when word of
the event reached that Tennessee abolitionist: "Hell is about
to enlarge her borders; and tyranny her domain. . . ."[14] With
that defeat behind him Lundy set out for home in December
1820, having only thirteen and a half dollars in his pocket
and walking most of the way. "My bed, at night, was the floor,
or the ground," he remembered, "— my knapsack was a substitute for a pillow."[15]

Yet in spite of this failure Lundy returned from Missouri
optimistic rather than depressed by recent events. The nationwide controversy precipitated by Missouri's admission had
in itself aided the antislavery cause, he decided, for it had

---

[12] Moore, *Missouri Controversy*, p. 266; John L. Thomas, "Old Land-
marks of Jefferson County. . . . Vansart Mill, Abner Vansart and the
Slavery Question," *Missouri Historical Review*, VII (1912–13), 136.

[13] Lundy to Isaac Barton, January 21, 1829, Pennsylvania Abolition
Society Manuscript Collection, vol. X (Historical Society of Pennsylvania).

[14] *Emancipator*, September 30, 1820, p. 89.

[15] Lundy to Isaac Barton, January 21, 1829, Pennsylvania Abolition
Society Manuscript Collection, vol. X.

once again brought slavery under review. The widespread discussion over the issue suggested the existence of much latent antislavery sentiment that might be further developed and organized. Even during the controversy many new antislavery societies had been established, especially among southern Quakers. More important, however, was the fact that the complacency of those who had supposed slavery would in due time wither and die had itself been destroyed. Some men now realized that they could not depend upon the benevolence of history to eradicate such evils from American society. They themselves would have to act. The antislavery message that Lundy resolved to convey to his countrymen would thus reach minds made receptive by recent events.[16]

At the same time that the Missouri controversy stimulated antislavery people to new exertions, it also made slaveholders more sensitive to the peril of their situation and less willing to tolerate criticism of their institutions. Other events contributed to the new southern concern. Some of the recently freed Spanish colonies in South America had abolished slavery, and a persistent agitation in England and the United States against the African slave trade had produced expressions of humanitarian ideas that could easily be turned against slavery itself.[17] Southerners began to feel themselves besieged, the defenders of an anachronism. They would meet increased antislavery activity with redoubled defenses against both external foes and those within the South who might question the virtue of local institutions.

The Missouri controversy had been of similar importance

[16] *Genius*, I (January, 1822), 104; (November, 1821), pp. 65, 67–68; William Goodell, *Slavery and Anti-Slavery; a History of the Great Struggle in Both Hemispheres; with a View of the Slavery Question in the United States* (New York, 1852), p. 383.

[17] Goodell, *Slavery*, pp. 385–390.

in the development of Lundy's own ideas. His participation in the contest, slight and ineffective though it was, had awakened him to the political aspects of slavery and to the uses of political power in the antislavery cause.[18] Slavery could have been kept out of Missouri if enough votes had been mustered in Congress against it or if enough votes had been cast in the territory to elect an antislavery constitutional convention. It was as simple as that. Lundy would never forget the implication of those facts. If an antislavery majority could somehow be achieved, slavery was doomed, for it could then be destroyed at the ballot box. Having learned that lesson, he would become one of the earliest and most persistent advocates of antislavery political action.

Most opponents of slavery before 1830 took for granted its political aspects and assumed that it could be ended by political means. Some later abolitionists would so emphasize their program of moral suasion that for a few years the use of politics as an antislavery weapon would be minimized. The appearance of the Liberty party in the late 1830's would thus seem to many to be a new departure, a turning away from established and orthodox methods, whereas, in fact, confidence in the efficacy and moral value of politics had never been lost by such western abolitionists as Lundy.

But before successful political antislavery action could be taken, public antislavery sentiment must be created. Lundy looked to journalism as the instrument for molding public opinion in the desired form. In his efforts to achieve that goal, he was persistent and determined beyond the ordinary. Lundy was by no means the only antislavery spokesman in the country during the 1820's, nor was he necessarily the most able, but he was one of the few who would speak boldly and

---

18 *Genius*, I (January, 1822), 104.

consistently against slavery and virtually the only person in the entire land willing to make antislavery agitation his career.

He could not avoid comparing his own zeal with the moderate enthusiasm of others, even of those professedly dedicated to the abolition of slavery. In particular he decided that the antislavery newspapers currently published ill served the cause. During Lundy's absence from Ohio Osborn's successor, Elisha Bates, had proved to be a not altogether satisfactory antislavery editor. Under his charge the *Philanthropist* had evolved from a general reform publication emphasizing slavery into an interesting journal of the times. Although it still opposed slavery and colonization with no compromise whatever, it now included so much material on unrelated subjects that its antislavery character had become obscured. Furthermore, Bates, like Osborn before him, directed his journal principally toward Quakers, thereby minimizing its influence with other groups. But Quakers, as Lundy well knew, could never destroy slavery by themselves. They might possess great zeal and much moral integrity, but their numbers were few and their power limited. When Lundy later claimed that Bates's antislavery journalism did not come up to his own standards,[19] he could have meant only that Bates's editorial efforts were sectarian in their appeal and not devoted solely to the antislavery cause as Lundy believed they ought to be.

The only other antislavery newspaper in the country seemed similarly inadequate. If Lundy happened to see copies of Elihu Embree's *Manumission Intelligencer*, published for the Tennessee Manumission Society at Jonesboro, Tennessee, he could not have been pleased with the extent of that journal's emphasis on slavery. By Embree's own admission his newspaper was "too barren on that important subject in gen-

---

[19] [Earle], *Life*, p. 19.

eral. . . ." [20] He did not exaggerate. In one issue, for example, Embree provided his readers with agricultural advice and numerous pieces of foreign news but printed no antislavery items at all.[21] His excuses for such neglect were plentiful and frank. He considered himself "illy calculated to write for the press," and claimed he was unable to find persons in east Tennessee to contribute to his columns "for want of more leisure among those who can write at all, which are but few that dare appear in public. . . ." Furthermore, he complained, the burdens imposed on him by his ironworks and mercantile business left little time to give the paper due attention.[22] Readers of the *Manumission Intelligencer* could hardly have been surprised when Embree gave up the newspaper as a failure before the year had ended.

But in April 1820, apparently moved by the new antislavery zeal fostered by the Missouri controversy, Embree decided to neglect his business and devote his time to publishing a new journal.[23] The result fell little short of Lundy's own view of what an antislavery newspaper should be. Embree's monthly *Emancipator*, sponsored like its predecessor by the Tennessee Manumission Society, concentrated all its attention on slavery. The paper had been founded ostensibly for only local needs — to provide a means of communication among the branches of the Tennessee society in order "to facilitate the abolition of slavery, and alleviate the condition of slaves" in Tennessee.[24] Yet Embree's vision was not parochial. He ventured to circulate his newspaper throughout the entire country and found interested readers everywhere. The appearance

[20] Elihu Embree to Joseph M. Paul, December 19, 1819, Embree Papers.
[21] *Manumission Intelligencer* (Jonesboro, Tenn.), April 27, 1819.
[22] Elihu Embree to Joseph M. Paul, December 19, 1819, Embree Papers.
[23] *Emancipator*, April 30, 1820, p. 2.
[24] Prospectus in *East Tennessee Patriot* (Jonesboro), February 1, 1820.

of the *Emancipator* in the wake of the Missouri controversy, he reported, "opened such an extensive correspondence all over the United States that it seems likely to engross the most of my time." Now he experienced no trouble in finding writers and securing antislavery materials. "People from different parts [of the country], & many without giving their names," he said, "are kind enough to forward to me pieces on slavery." [25]

The favorable public response to the new publication demonstrated the accuracy with which Lundy had gauged the temper of the times. Much latent antislavery sentiment did exist, wanting for its expression only the stimulus and direction that a vigorously edited newspaper could supply.

As long as Embree continued the *Emancipator*, there would be little need for other western editors to enter the field. But, as it turned out, the *Emancipator* proved short-lived. While Lundy made his slow and poverty-stricken way from Missouri back to Ohio, he learned that Embree, fallen suddenly ill, had died on December 6, 1820, at the age of thirty-eight, leaving no one in Tennessee to carry on his work. [26]

That event constituted a turning point in Lundy's career. It arranged the situation that gave him his place in history, for Embree's death left Lundy free — indeed, from his point of view, obliged — to start an antislavery newspaper himself. He now made his plans accordingly. Almost as soon as he returned to Ohio, he moved his wife and small daughters from St. Clairsville to Mount Pleasant in order to be at the center of Ohio's reform movements. There in June 1821 Bates published the prospectus for Lundy's *Genius of Universal*

---

[25] Elihu Embree to Joseph M. Paul, August 6, 1820, Embree Papers.
[26] Mark Reeve to Joseph M. Paul, December 8, 1820, and Elijah Embree to Paul, June 28, 1821, *ibid.*; [Earle], *Life*, p. 19; *Philanthropist*, V (February 24, 1821), 267.

Emancipation, a newspaper to be devoted "almost exclusive-ly" to slavery.[27]

Lundy selected the lofty name for the *Genius* from a phrase the Irish orator John Philpot Curran had used in 1794 in his eloquent defense of Archibald Hamilton Rowan against the charge of sedition.[28] In that way Lundy self-consciously placed himself in an Anglo-American tradition of resistance to in-justice, tyranny, and despotism. The time had come, he wrote, when the advocates of emancipation must speak boldly "to arouse and awaken the American people to a sense of the in-consistency, the hypocrisy, and the iniquity of which many of them are chargeable" because they tolerated slavery. He promised to work to make his paper "an active instrument in the attempt to abolish that cruel and disgraceful system in the American Republic." [29]

All this sounded grand and brave, but an impartial observer would have been compelled to admit that there was little sub-stance to support such ambitious attitudes and statements. Lundy started his newspaper with few assets beyond convic-tions of the righteousness of his cause and the urgency of the need for immediate action. He had almost no money, no more than six subscribers, no press, and no knowledge of printing. A more unpromising beginning could hardly be imagined.[30]

Of necessity his first printing arrangements were remark-ably haphazard. Elisha Bates printed the first number of the *Genius* at Mount Pleasant, and James Wilson the next six on his press at Steubenville. The eighth was printed at Zanes-

---

[27] [Earle], *Life*, pp. 19–20; *Philanthropist*, VI (June 2, 1821), 72–73.

[28] *Speeches of Right Hon. John Philpot Curran* (Philadelphia, 1854), p. 111.

[29] *Philanthropist*, VI (June 2, 1821), 72–73.

[30] *Genius*, I (November, 1821), 65; (January, 1822), p. 102; Lundy to Isaac Barton, January 21, 1829, Pennsylvania Abolition Society Manu-script Collection, vol. X.

ville as Lundy made his way toward Tennessee. While the arrangement with Wilson remained in effect, Lundy sometimes made the complete trip between Mount Pleasant and Steubenville on foot, carrying his printed papers home on his back. In Steubenville he usually lodged at the home of Benjamin Stanton, his roommate at Wheeling who now practiced medicine and served as one of the *Genius'* subscription agents. Sometimes while waiting for type to be set, Lundy worked at his old trade of saddler to pay the expenses of publication; sometimes Stanton lent him money. Many years later Lincoln's Secretary of War, Edwin M. Stanton, remembered that as a small boy he often had sat on Lundy's lap during Lundy's visits at his Uncle Benjamin's home in Steubenville.[31]

While Lundy made this shoestring beginning, he received an invitation from Thomas Embree, Elihu Embree's father, to move to Jonesboro, Tennessee, and resume publication of the suspended *Emancipator*. Lundy could use the same printing press that the Tennessee Manumission Society had furnished his son, the elder Embree promised. Lundy decided not to accept the invitation under those conditions, for he was vain enough to wish to continue on the independent course he had begun.[32] Although he did make arrangements with the Tennessee society to use its printing equipment (the society faced the loss of the press to creditors if it were not employed),[33] he insisted that the society exercise no control over his editorial policy. Except for the fact that the *Genius* would be printed on the same press as the *Emancipator*, it would

---

[31] O'Dell, "Early Antislavery Movement in Ohio," pp. 216–218; Henry Wilson, "Edwin M. Stanton," *Atlantic Monthly*, XXV (1870), 243; Henry Wilson to William Lloyd Garrison, February 11, 1864, in Garrison and Garrison, *William Lloyd Garrison*, IV, 116.

[32] Thomas Embree to Joseph M. Paul, June 16, 1823, Embree Papers.

[33] *American Economist and East Tennessee Statesman* (Greeneville, Tenn.), July 29, 1824.

have no connection with Embree's newspaper. Neither would it be officially sponsored by the Tennessee Manumission Society.

Early in 1822 Lundy settled at Greeneville in east Tennessee, established an office, and took the first steps toward learning to be a printer under the guidance of Isaiah Osborn, Charles Osborn's twenty-year-old son, who had accompanied him to serve temporarily as his printer and printing instructor. Lundy's wife decided to remain in Ohio until spring, for she had given birth in December to their third child and first son, whom they named Charles Tallmadge in honor of Representative James Tallmadge of Missouri Compromise fame.[34]

Lundy moved to Tennessee for much the same reason that he had traveled to Missouri in 1819 — in order to live near the people whom he hoped to persuade to act against slavery. The move into the South might be expected to increase the influence of the *Genius* among those who had it within their power to abolish slavery, for almost certainly it would now reach more southerners than if it had continued to be published in Ohio. Furthermore, Lundy would now be close to the Quaker antislavery groups that flourished in North Carolina and elsewhere in the upper South. Above all, he could expect to receive the patronage of the members of the Tennessee Manumission Society, one of the largest and most active antislavery societies in the country. Already its influence was being felt in state politics. There seemed at least the chance, if antislavery sentiment continued to grow, that the Tennessee legislature might eventually be induced to end slavery. But even if nothing so desirable soon occurred, Lundy still saw his newspaper as serving in Tennessee the same symbolic purpose as an antislavery society in a slave state. In a region

---

[34] [Earle], *Life*, p. 21; Ruth Anna (Ketring) Nuermberger, *Charles Osborn in the Anti-Slavery Movement* (Columbus, Ohio, 1937), p. 38.

where slavery flourished as an accepted institution, "the bare existence of a Manumission society, is an important thing," he remarked; "it raises a kind of ensign with something like this inscription, 'slavery is wrong, it is an unreasonable violation of justice, and opposed to our own best interest —.' " [35]

Of course the move might also arouse considerable antipathy. Lundy would now be in the country of the enemy; he would be attacking an institution cherished by the men who held power within the state. Slaveholders had already demonstrated their displeasure at critics of their labor system. Since the day in the preceding decade when abolitionist George Bourne had been driven from Virginia, planters had become ever more intolerant toward any action or the expression of any sentiment that might weaken slavery. The trend could be noted even in Tennessee. Two years before Lundy arrived, the Presbyterians and Methodists in Sumner County had combined to organize a Sunday School for Negroes, but others, who feared the results of such philanthropy, "rose in mobs, and dispersed the scholars, and broke up the school." [36] Although antislavery sentiment obviously still existed in the South, the fact that it was the sentiment of a minority became every day more evident.

Elihu Embree, Lundy's predecessor, had aroused widespread hostility even during his brief antislavery career. His *Emancipator*, founded in the immediate aftermath of the Missouri controversy, had "met with some opposition where it was little expected," Embree had reported. "Some say I strike too hard. . . ." [37] Embree believed that his enemies pillaged copies of the *Emancipator* from the mails. Some-

[35] *Genius*, I (June, 1822), 183; II (September, 1822), 24.
[36] *Emancipator*, September 30, 1820, p. 82.
[37] *Ibid.*, May 31, 1820, p. 17; Elihu Embree to Joseph M. Paul, May 10, 1820, Embree Papers.

times the packets were opened, he charged, and parts removed; on some copies addresses were altered; a few postmasters even refused to deliver the papers.[38] How much of these troubles resulted from the unavoidably primitive character of the western mails and how much from intent can hardly be determined, but that Embree's activities aroused vast opposition that might have given Lundy pause cannot be doubted.

Governor George Poindexter of Mississippi, to whom Embree sent an early copy of his newspaper, accused him of representing *"an association of individuals, in another section of the United States, who bear the expense of the work you have undertaken,* and reward your labours; and . . . your position in the western country, has been selected with a view to economy. I regard it as an effort, mischievous in its tendency, designed to *sever the bond of social harmony,* which ought to be cherished, and strengthened in every part of the union. . . ." Embree's paper, the governor warned, was calculated "to excite passions and prejudices, the most unfavorable to domestic tranquility, and national prosperity." [39] If Lundy, among others, had begun to suspect the existence of an organized "slave power," southerners now imagined an antislavery conspiracy directed against their interests. The task of an abolitionist editor in the South would not be easy.

The Reverend John Finley Crowe of Shelbyville, Kentucky, who printed his short-lived *Abolition Intelligencer and Missionary Journal* for the Kentucky Anti-Slavery Society at about the time Lundy moved to Tennessee, reported that his editorial efforts also "excited the alarm and provoked the abuse

---

[38] *Emancipator,* July 30, 1820, p. 64.
[39] George Poindexter to Elihu Embree, July 31, 1820, in *ibid.,* September 30, 1820, p. 91.

of certain characters." [40] He had aroused opposition in spite of advocating what would appear to be the least offensive of programs. In an editorial address which promised "candour and forbearance" in dealing with slavery, Crowe had outlined carefully limited aims: "to *prepare* the public mind for taking the necessary *preparatory* measures for the *future* introduction of a system of laws, for the *gradual* abolition of slavery. . . ." [41] A more cautiously phrased statement of purpose could hardly be imagined, yet even that expression of what might be called "gradual gradualism" aroused hostility.

Predictably, Lundy's *Genius* did not escape criticism. His first number printed in Ohio had encountered opposition in the North as well as the South — an editor in New Brunswick, New Jersey, had accused him of "too much severity." [42] After moving to Tennessee, Lundy reported that he "was often threatened in various ways" and subject to "pretty severe criticism." Opponents menaced him with threats of "corporeal chastisement," he said, and subjected him to "the language of premeditated assassination." [43] Thomas Foley, editor of the *Correspondent and Ste. Genevieve Record,* warned that the *Genius* might be expected to stir the slaves to commit "acts of fire and blood, in a fruitless struggle for liberty." But slavery need not be ended by "Mr. Lundy's firebrand sweeping system," the Missouri editor assured his readers, for Lundy could be driven from the South. Let the people of Tennessee "remove the fuse before the shell explodes among them," Foley counseled. [44] Southern Quakers in their

[40] *Abolition Intelligencer and Missionary Journal* (Shelbyville, Ky.), June, 1822.

[41] Quoted in *Genius,* I (June, 1822), 191–192. Italics added.

[42] *Genius,* I (August, 1821), 18–19.

[43] *Ibid.,* II (October, 1822), 49; (April 30, 1823), p. 146; [Earle], *Life,* pp. 20–21.

[44] Quoted in *Genius,* II (November, 1822), 65–66.

own communities could be allowed to give their quiet antislavery testimony among themselves, for they possessed little
power or influence outside their fellowship. But antislavery
newspapers, in contrast, might fall into any hands at all and
ought therefore to be destroyed.

Proslavery opposition mingled with remnants of Anglo-
phobia to bring wildly imaginative charges against Lundy.
A correspondent signing himself "Citizen of Illinois" claimed
that Great Britain fostered emancipation as a scheme to re-
gain control of America. The British cabinet, he charged,
sponsored Bible societies in the United States, subsidized such
editors as Lundy, and controlled the Bank of the United
States in order to direct American elections.[45] "We very much
suspect that friend Lundy is only the puppet of the show,"
wrote a Missouri editor.[46] Such suspicions persisted. Robert
J. Turnbull of South Carolina hinted toward the end of the
decade that the operations of the *Genius* (which he thought
was edited in New York) suggested the existence of an Anglo-
American combination to end slavery.[47] Southerners easily
imagined that malevolent foreign influences were directed
against them, for it was hard to conceive of one's own countrymen as having originated proposals for the destruction of
the southern social order.[48]

Hostile southern reaction to the *Philanthropist* and the
Genius was understandable, for Lundy and Embree had lev-
ied harsh and fundamental criticism against slavery. They

---

[45] *Genius*, II (January, 1823), 103.

[46] *Correspondent and Ste. Genevieve Record*, quoted *ibid*. (November,
1822), p. 65.

[47] "Brutus" [Robert J. Turnbull], *The Crisis, or Essays on the Usurpa-
tions of the Federal Government* (Charleston, S.C., 1827), pp. 127–129.

[48] "A Warm Friend" to R. R. Gurley, December 16, 1828, American
Colonization Society Papers (Library of Congress).

made no effort to conciliate slaveholders or spare their feelings. The antislavery advocates of the 1820's were far less restrained in their attacks and less gentle in their discourse than has sometimes been assumed. If most of them were "gradualists" rather than "immediatists," this does not mean that forbearance characterized their discussion of the system they hoped gradually to abolish. On the contrary they presented an untempered condemnation of slavery scarcely exceeded in severity by that of their successors of the 1830's.

Even in their rhetoric the early antislavery advocates were far from laggard. They let their hatred of slavery slide easily into hatred of slaveholders, whom they charged with horrid crimes and attributes. Embree had pictured slaveowners as "monsters in human shape" and marveled at the mercy of a God who had refrained from destroying them "with fire unquenchable! ! !" Slaveholders, Lundy asserted, were "too depraved to blush, and too wicked to repent" of their crimes. They were "actuated by a domineering spirit, puffed up with pride, and inflated with self-consequence." "Blood suckers," a Tennessee writer called them in the *Genius*. Others referred to them as "Miserable sons of avarice," and "Infant Nero's . . . these Caligulas of the North American Republic." [49]

A passage more insulting in its implications can scarcely be found anywhere in abolitionist literature than one Lundy penned in 1823: "Many of [the slaveholders] are ipso facto the most disgraceful whoremongers upon earth; they make a *business* of raising bastards and selling them for money; — they keep poor miserable degraded females for this identical purpose; they compel them to submit to their abominable

---

[49] *Emancipator*, April 30, 1820, p. 8; *Genius*, I (January, 1822), 102–103; II (July, 1822), 12; (October, 1822), p. 49; (May, 1823), p. 163.

avaricious, and brutal lusts; they oppose the work of emancipation *on this ground. . . .*" [50]

To those who may have objected to these harsh charges hurled at slaveowners, Lundy offered an explanation. " I have no idea of a reformation being effected by oily words . . . flowing in honied accents," he said; ". . . shielded with the breastplate of power, and elated with the idea of self-sufficiency, they laugh to scorn every thing like mildness and persuasion, and must be addressed in such language as will reach their adamantine hearts. . . ." [51]

Slaveowners endured Lundy's rhetoric with relative calm, when compared with their response to similar charges made in the next decade; yet the great southern opposition aroused by the abolitionist crusaders of the 1830's resulted less from the increased severity of those later critiques than from the fact that slaveholders had by that time become thoroughly aware of the danger they faced. By the 1830's antislavery criticisms could no longer be regarded as the vagaries of eccentrics. The effects of abolitionist activity proved to be cumulative. However limited the influence slaveholders in the 1820's may have thought Lundy's newspaper to have possessed, by the next decade they could not possibly evade the fact that increasing numbers of their countrymen regarded slavery as an evil which must be destroyed. Lundy's journalistic enterprise was then to achieve its aim.

---

[50] *Ibid.* (June, 1823), p. 171.
[51] *Ibid.,* I (June, 1822), 101–102.

CHAPTER IV

Plans and Rationale

Shortly after Lundy founded the *Genius*, several ill-informed skeptics asked him whether he really expected to find enough antislavery material to fill its columns through future issues. Lundy could only scorn their ignorance of what he regarded as the nation's most compelling problem. "If these people had thought *one fourth* of as much as I have upon the subject of slavery," he replied, "they would never *think* of asking such a question as that." [1] No shortage of material developed as month after month the *Genius* carried across the country the news, ideas, and programs of the early antislavery movement.

Lundy devoted less space than might have been expected to condemnations of slavery, although he occasionally printed a "Black List" of its horrors so shocking both in substance and language as to give little warrant for calling him a gentle Quaker.[2] There was never a dearth of sensational items in the *Genius* and no lack of strong language, yet in spite of a certain

---

[1] *Genius*, I (October, 1821), 49.

[2] *Ibid.* (September, 1821), pp. 10–11; (March, 1822), p. 146.

asperity that occasionally colored his writing, Lundy clearly was more interested in discovering a way to abolish slavery than he was in merely condemning it or arousing hatred of slaveholders. "There is no kind of use in canvassing the subject by the fireside . . ." he wrote; "the huge fabric of oppression *must go down*, and I am not so anxious to listen to the question *whether it shall be razed?* as I am to learn *how* it shall be done." [3] From its first issue the *Genius* provided a sober chronicle of the efforts of humanitarians to discover an acceptable solution to that problem.

Early in his editorial career Lundy published a plan for emancipation based on proposals he had presented six years earlier to the Union Humane Society. Even though he had labored many months in its drafting, he maintained a detached, impersonal view toward it. It did not become for him a permanent, unalterable program which he insisted upon on all occasions, but neither did he ever renounce any part of it. He was never doctrinaire about this proposal or any other, and declared himself willing to accept any emancipation plan "consistent with justice . . . that might be agreed upon by the people at large. . . ." [4] Lundy's plan comprised a set of interconnected proposals; the acceptance of each was necessary to the success of the whole. It was a carefully articulated program, moderate and cautious in its demands. If it had been implemented, slavery would have been ended gradually, without rancor or bloodshed. But the plan was impossible. Its weakness lay not in its substance but in its impracticality, for its success would have required a degree of unified action in all parts of the nation and at all levels of government that could hardly have been achieved. Nowhere could a majority have been marshaled to support any one of the measures, let

---

[3] *Ibid.* (January, 1822), p. 107.
[4] *Ibid.* (September, 1821), p. 33.

alone all of them. The means did not exist to create the degree of unified sentiment necessary to effect such a program.

Lundy proposed that the national government abolish slavery in all the territories and districts under its immediate control and prohibit the admission of new slave states; it should also prohibit the interstate slave trade. These measures were the responsibility of the government at Washington, but the states — both North and South — had responsibilities too. Each state should appoint delegates to attend a national convention for the purpose of gathering information about antislavery operations and then report their findings to the state legislatures. The slave states should arrange for "gradual though *certain*" emancipation and repeal laws that discriminated against free Negroes. At the same time the free states should agree to admit Negroes as citizens on the same basis as whites. Free Negroes willing to leave the country should be aided to do so by the national and state governments and by private philanthropy. Finally, the three-fifths compromise, which gave southern white voters more power in the national government than their actual numbers would have allowed, should be abolished by constitutional amendment.[5]

Although this plan foresaw a large role for the national government in restricting slavery, Lundy expected slavery finally to be abolished by the southern state legislatures themselves, just as northern legislatures had provided for gradual emancipation in earlier years. On this account his plan placed much reliance on political action; in fact, as far as he could see, there was no other feasible way to end slavery.[6] Most of his antislavery contemporaries agreed with him. Some, like the members of the usually cautious Manumission Society of Tennessee, could imagine no other means of ending slavery

---

[5] *Ibid.,* pp. 33–34.
[6] *Ibid.,* pp. 35, 37.

than "by the consent of a majority of the members of our civil government, in whom rests the sovereign power of reform, in the civil law code. . . ." [7] Lundy himself believed that the national importance of slavery — connected as it was with "the internal policy, the welfare, and even the *existence* of our *republic*" — demanded action at all governmental levels. Over and over again he repeated his view of the necessity for antislavery political action in contrast with sole reliance upon single-minded antislavery propaganda. "I do not expect to *'persuade' the advocates of slavery* to do justice," he explained. "Such persons cannot be honest; and I am not for making a covenant with dishonesty. WE MUST VOTE THEM DOWN." [8]

The obstacles to the success of such a political program appeared enormous, of course, and the difficulties nearly insuperable of overturning an institution as well entrenched as slavery. Indeed, so gloomy was the prospect that unlike many later abolitionists, Lundy and his contemporaries seldom allowed themselves to imagine that their goal would soon be attained. "The chief actors in the great work of African emancipation," are now "merely 'boys,' " Lundy wrote in 1822. "So unconquerable are the prejudices of a great portion of those more advanced in years, it seems they will never wear off but with their lives." [9] Those whose acquaintance with the South was even more intimate than Lundy's shared his view. "Bear in mind," warned the antislavery reformer James Jones, after a lifetime spent among Tennessee slaveholders, that "under the existing interest and prejudices of the community in general, the abolition of slavery is not the work of a day, or a

---

[7] "Address of the Seventh Convention of the Manumission Society of Tennessee," *ibid.* (April, 1822), p. 152.
[8] *Ibid.*, III (November, 1823), 70; see also *ibid.* (March, 1824), p. 131.
[9] *Ibid.*, I (January, 1822), 107.

year — no, nor perhaps of a life time." [10] Such men as Jones and Lundy did not find the prospect of immediate abolition undesirable; rather, they considered it wildly visionary.

Despite the general pessimism about the chances for early abolition, Lundy had no doubt that so great an anomaly within the American system must someday end. He placed his faith in Providence; God sided with the abolitionists, he declared, not with slaveholders.[11] Lundy saw abolition as a great rational movement that would progress through stages preparatory to the recognition of the full freedom and equality of the Negro. Although God's mysterious ways could not be predicted, Lundy speculated that Divine intervention would take the form of the gradual spread of reason and the consequent elimination of racial prejudice, which taken together would serve to end slavery. He thought he could read signs of slavery's ultimate doom in the recent appearance of antislavery movements throughout the hemisphere. "The field of Slavery in North America is surrounded," he wrote in 1822. "The free states of this Union are on the east, the north, and the west, Hayti and Colombia on the South. The mighty force of *Public Opinion*, in the former, powerfully aided in its march, shall bear resistless down the majestic Mississippi" destroying slavery as it advances.[12]

It was certainty of this sort that allowed Lundy to assert that "neither the powers of earth or hell can move me from my purpose, until the lamp of life shall be extinguished."[13] His conviction of his responsibility to help fulfill the plans of Providence led him to persist in his antislavery campaigns against obstacles of poverty, overt hostility, and repeated dis-

---

[10] *Ibid.*, II (December, 1822), 92.
[11] *Ibid.*, I (November, 1821), 67.
[12] *Ibid.*, II (July, 1822), 4.
[13] *Ibid.* (April 30, 1823), p. 146.

appointment. Continued publication of the *Genius* through many kinds of adversity was his means of fulfilling his early pledge.

Lundy's newspaper primarily reflected his own views, but in its reports of antislavery societies and correspondence from all over the country it also consistently mirrored the ideas upon which the early antislavery movement was based. Much of the argument clearly derived from the Bible, not only from such admonitions as the Golden Rule but also from Old Testament prophecies that God's wrath would be directed against those who broke His law.[14] Fear of Divine retribution for national as well as personal sins spurred abolitionists to new efforts. The Illinois Friends of Humanity, a union of Baptist antislavery groups, interpreted recent tornadoes, epidemics, and earthquakes as but precursors of the "main storm" to come. Conscientious Bible readers thought they saw parallels between their own situations and the tribulations of the Ancients. "Have we not every reason to suppose that the God of Justice, that God who spared not the slaveholders of Egypt . . . will visit our nation with a scourge for its iniquity?" asked one of Lundy's correspondents.[15] Recognizing and perhaps sharing such fears, Lundy intended by his own activities to awaken Americans "to a sense of their situation, and [thus to cause them to] be willing to exert themselves to do away with the evil ere the vengeance of Retributive Justice is let loose upon us." For some persons antislavery activity thus constituted an end in itself. It became the means of release from the imputed guilt of the nation's most conspicuous sin and, presumably, personal escape from the pains of retribution. "How can we see the oppression of our fellow men, and

[14] Raymond, *Missouri Question*, pp. 25–26; *Genius*, II (July, 1822), 10.
[15] Edwardsville (Ill.) *Spectator*, November 9, 1822; *Genius*, I (April, 1822), 151.

not reprove the oppressor, and yet be clear of their blood?" asked an early reformer.[16]

On a more secular level slavery appeared to violate the natural rights philosophy expressed in the Declaration of Independence. It conflicted with republican government, abolitionists said, and constituted a serious flaw in the otherwise admirable American system. "Many things [were] left undone, by our great political reformers, which it is our duty to attend to," explained Lundy; "a countless number of evils yet remain in the body politic, for us to root out and destroy." The founders of the nation were undoubtedly great men, abolitionists conceded, but they had not been perfect — their toleration of slavery proved the assertion. Lundy and other early abolitionists thought of themselves as completing the unfinished work of the Revolutionary generation and moving the nation toward the goals set by its founders.[17]

"Humanitas," one of Lundy's correspondents, neatly summed up both the secular and religious aspects of the argument in an appeal to the clergy for stronger antislavery action: "If 'life liberty and the pursuit of Happiness' are undeniable rights of man, if 'all the nations of men who dwell upon the earth are created of one blood;' if all are sons of one common father, and equally objects of a Redeemer's love; let the professors of Christianity arise from their thoughtless lethargy." [18]

Although nearly all early abolitionists might properly be described as "religious," Lundy and his contemporaries were not motivated to antislavery action principally by the demands of revivalistic religion. Their rationale belonged not to romanticism but to the nearly outworn persuasion of an

---

[16] Ibid. (March, 1822), p. 136; (February, 1822), p. 123.
[17] Ibid. (March, 1822), p. 134; Wagstaff (ed.), Minutes, p. 115.
[18] Genius, I (November, 1821), 69.

earlier age. The abolitionists of the 1820's still lived close
enough to the eighteenth century to be able to conceive with
the philosophers of that age of a perfectly articulated world
in which each person and institution occupied a place in the
great chain of being and bore a necessary relation to the
whole. They conceived of an orderly universe operating in
accord with natural law. Therein lay much of their horror of
slavery, for as an offense against natural law, slavery in their
eyes destroyed the moral order of the universe. The Greene
County branch of the Manumission Society of Tennessee endorsed the statement that "slavery is contradictory to that relation which man bears to man, in the scale of being, that
was fixed by the Almighty Creator; and can never be rendered
justifiable by any law, usage or custom of man, either in a religious, moral, or political point of view." [19] Lundy's friend
James Jones of Tennessee explained his opposition to slavery
in more colorful terms: "We feel impelled . . . to view slavery as a daring attempt to arrest the sceptre from the moral
governor of the world, and bury all laws human and divine,
in the devouring vortex of ambitious power." [20] John Swaim
of North Carolina similarly pictured the anarchistic tendency
of slavery: "[It] appears to represent the universe peopled
with beings left to the caprice of each others will, with the
privilege of doing to each other just as their pleasure, interest,
or ambition may direct." [21] By its disregard of the natural
obligation that rational beings owed to each other, slavery
created moral chaos.

Given the republican quality of early America, the abolitionists' commitment to order easily issued into crusading

[19] *Emancipator*, May 31, 1820, p. 20.
[20] *American Economist and Weekly Political Recorder* (Greeneville,
Tenn.), September 28, 1822.
[21] *Genius*, I (May, 1822), 172.

egalitarianism. As a matter of national policy slavery should be ended, Lundy believed, because the aristocracy it created and the arrogance it fostered tended to undermine the wholesome republic of simplicity and virtue projected by the founding fathers. Class lines were sharpened in a slave society, Lundy charged, for rich slaveholders monopolized the posts of honor and profit within their states, denying opportunities to their poorer neighbors.[22] "The Farmer," one of Lundy's contributors, blamed slavery for creating a class of "rich money holders" who extended their haughty behavior even to their white neighbors. At the same time, slavery degraded all kinds of labor and lowered wages so that white workers tended to sink to the level of slaves — or so thought emigrants who on that account had left the South. Free white men in the South, abolitionists charged, generally became "abject and obsequious" in the face of slaveholders; even the children of slaveholding parents learned at a tender age to behave like small tyrants.[23]

"It is not a republic — this," concluded Morris Birkbeck, an English emigrant who had visited Virginia on his way to settle in Illinois; "it is a confederacy of tyrants, pure aristocratical despotism!"[24] Abolitionists of Lundy's time commonly pictured the slaveowner as a wealthy despot, living in luxury and vice, exploiting his slaves, and dominating his white neighbors. "He is the chief of a petty principality, but little dependent on his neighbors," wrote Birkbeck. "The lash goads from his slaves all that he deems necessary to his per-

---

[22] Wagstaff (ed.), *Minutes*, p. 115; *Genius*, I (January, 1822), 102–103; (March, 1822), p. 134.

[23] *Genius*, II (July, 1822), 11–13; I (July, 1821), 1–2, 13; Edwardsville *Spectator*, September 6, 1823.

[24] Morris Birkbeck, *An Appeal to the People of Illinois on the Question of a Convention* (Shawneetown, Ill., 1823), p. 10.

verted appetites; and he cares for no more. To improve the
condition of his poor neighbors, is a thought that but rarely
enters his head." [25] Slavery is the "hot bed of tyranny," said
Lundy, "and those districts in which it is tolerated are the
nurseries of aristocracy and despotism." The vaunted republicanism of slaveholders, he charged, was confined to members
of their own class. Far from accepting the equality of all men,
they would reduce even the whites to slavery "if they had the
power, and conceived it to be their interest to do so." [26] The
abolitionists saw slaveholding planters as congenital enemies
of republicanism.

Despite all these religious and philosophical imperatives
for emancipation, neither Lundy nor many other abolitionists
before 1824 demanded the immediate freeing of all the slaves.
Their policy of gradualism no doubt derived in part from
their knowledge of the practical difficulties inherent in the
southern situation. A majority of these men were themselves
southerners who shared the common opinion that most slaves
had been prevented from acquiring the habits and attitudes
necessary to live successfully as free men. Furthermore, they
recognized the obstacle created by the violently proslavery
convictions of their neighbors. They were more willing than
some who came after them to accept social conditions as given
and insusceptible to revolutionary change. More readily than
their successors they adjusted their program to meet existing
circumstances.

Just as their opposition to slavery was rooted in eighteenth-
century thought, so their caution derived from their concept
of an orderly universe run by natural law in which each part
was necessarily related to the whole. They shrank from

25 [Thomas Lippincott and others], *To the People of Illinois* (Edwardsville, Ill., 1824), p. 8.
26 *Genius,* I (July, 1821), 1–2.

revolutionary change. They were aware, not only as southerners but also as remote heirs of the Enlightenment, of the
subtle connections binding together all men and institutions.
They understood that sudden emancipation must destroy delicate adjustments in southern society with resultant chaos.
Thus they could not easily demand an immediate change in
the status of slaves because they knew that this must rend the
social order and in itself create grave new problems.

Patience was a virtue many of them deliberately cultivated,
for they confidently expected time to remedy many evils. Man
could gradually progress in social relations and thereby move
step by step toward a better society in which all would enjoy
life, liberty, and happiness. Man could reach that happy goal
by solving his problems through rational persuasion and moderate adjustment without resort to violence or upheaval.
Early abolitionists as much as Jefferson himself took for
granted the benign influence of reason. They assumed that
great evils could be removed by goodwill and moderate efforts
and through mutual consent. They had confidence in the efficacy of piecemeal reform. The reforms they earnestly sought
to bring about should be accomplished with the least possible
disturbance to the social order. Revolutionary change was not
for them. That is one reason why they considered so carefully the problem of what should be done with the slave after
he was freed. That is one reason why colonization programs
held so great an attraction for them. That is also why they
accepted the necessity of obtaining the consent of a southern
majority for the ending of slavery.[27]

Lundy belonged to that company of early reformers who
believed that slavery, like the rest of the world's dark evils,

---

[27] David Brion Davis, "The Emergence of Immediatism in British and
American Antislavery Thought," *Mississippi Valley Historical Review*,
XLIX (September, 1962), 213–214.

might be expected gradually to disappear before the ever-advancing light of reason. In the 1820's he was a gradualist whose Quaker views allowed him fully to share the common faith in a benevolent universe. Yet in some respects he diverged from the gradualists and adopted points of view held by all important later radical abolitionists. He accepted, for example, the necessity for compulsion; he did not believe that many slaveholders would voluntarily free their slaves. And to the frequently asked question, "If the slaves are freed, what shall be done with the freedmen?" he gave the same answer many of his most extreme successors would have given: "*Let justice be done*, and the God of nature will do the rest. . . ." [28]

A few early abolitionists, governed by more specifically religious ideas than Lundy was, remained unmoved by the demands of caution and often skirted near the frank calls for immediate emancipation. Thus the Presbyterian George Bourne, with no apparent concern for consequences, had called for the immediate ending of slavery. Somewhat later the Baptist John Mason Peck, then living in Illinois, observed that by "the eternal principles of natural justice, no master in the United States has a right to hold his slave in bondage for a single hour. . . ." Yet practical considerations held him back from endorsing immediate emancipation. [29]

So rare were such extreme views that Lundy felt justified in asserting that *nobody* urged an " 'immediate' liberation of the slaves. The friends of emancipation recommend the *gradual* abolition of the system." [30] Even among southern antislavery Quakers, however, this was not strictly true. According to the North Carolina Manumission Society in 1825, one-

[28] *Genius*, III (July 4, 1823), 3.
[29] Bourne, *The Book*, pp. 7–8, 16–19, 136, 139–140; Edwardsville *Spectator*, August 16, 1823.
[30] *Genius*, II (September, 1822), 50.

thirtieth of the people in that state already favored immediate emancipation.[31] Forbearance was even more commonly ignored in northern states where here and there in the 1820's a few outspoken and impatient individuals boldly rejected gradualism. An agent of the American Colonization Society to his dismay found among Philadelphia Quakers in 1829 several advocates of "an immediate and general emancipation . . ." and another encountered "a perfect bear of an opponent" to gradualism and colonization in the person of Judge Benjamin Tappan of Steubenville, Ohio (a brother of the later abolitionists Lewis and Arthur Tappan), who told him "with an oath" that he hoped the slaves would rise up and cut the throats of their masters.[32] But such extremists were rare, as Lundy knew. Most abolitionists in those early days still followed counsel similar to that given in 1826 by Moses Swain, president of the North Carolina Manumission Society, to "avoid all unnecessary Irritation of those deep-rooted prejudices which have grown up with our Countrymen, and cannot be suddenly eradicated without sensible pain. . . ."[33]

Lundy recognized the temptation to seek short cuts to abolition. To some persons, he knew, the problem of slavery would "appear of easy solution: Immediate, universal emancipation." But this, he said (repeating a statement endorsed in 1821 by the American Convention), would "cut rather than untie the Gordian knot." At that time he accepted a method far more rational but also far slower: The slaves should be prepared for freedom as partial payment of the debt white Americans owed them for their years of servitude; they should be given an interest in the land they cultivated and paid

---

[31] Wagstaff (ed.), *Minutes*, p. 103.
[32] Mathew Carey to R. R. Gurley, December 2, 1829, and Benjamin O. Peers to Gurley, October 13, 1826, American Colonization Society Papers.
[33] Wagstaff (ed.), *Minutes*, p. 126.

wages; their children should be educated to prepare them for life as free citizens.[34]

The abolitionists' continued adherence to such moderate and gradualist views would depend finally upon the appearance of visible signs of progress toward the desired goals. They had developed a comprehensive indictment of slavery. They found slavery so at variance with American values that it was quite unthinkable that they would ever be reconciled to its perpetuation. If the abolitionists were not villains, neither were they saints. They were, after all, human and therefore unwilling to allow their lives to pass without seeing evidence of tangible accomplishment for years of exertion and sacrifice in the cause of extending human freedom. Further, their entire program depended upon winning sympathy and support from the southern majority. If progress were not made, if the abolitionist argument aroused hostility and opposition rather than support in the South, would they then feel compelled to retain their program of gradualism? Could they reconcile themselves to perpetual failure? If slaveowners gave no indication that they ever intended to begin the gradual process of freeing their slaves, abolitionists might well be expected to seek alternative methods and to put forward new, even revolutionary proposals.

During the next few years Lundy would place himself among the leaders of the campaign to present gradualism to the South as a means for ending slavery. He would thoroughly test the efficacy of the program and the strength of its appeal. If that plan did not work, it might be expected that he and his fellow abolitionists eventually would abandon it and adopt some other.

---

[34] *Genius*, III (December, 1823), 88–89.

CHAPTER V

An Established Influence

With Lundy's move to Tennessee his influence slowly expanded as he sent the *Genius* far and wide and arranged with sympathizers, many of them Quakers, to act as his subscription agents in twenty-one states and territories.[1] In this way he managed each month to circulate antislavery ideas into most parts of the country, uniting individuals and scattered antislavery groups into at least the semblance of a coordinated effort. But the *Genius* accomplished a purpose beyond the diffusion of a body of antislavery thought, essential though that was. By its constant reminders to humanitarians that slavery remained a national problem of major proportions, Lundy's newspaper served to dispel the apathy that always threatened the early antislavery movement. The *Genius* helped to keep the movement alive at a time when no similar journal existed.

The importance of the *Genius* bore little relation to the meager financial returns it brought its editor. Paid subscriptions were almost always too few to support Lundy and his

---

[1] *Genius*, II (July, 1822), 16.

growing family. In the first struggling months in Tennessee
the lack of money was remedied by loans from James Jones,
leader of Tennessee's abolitionist forces, and Valentine Sevier,
a sympathetic merchant at nearby Jonesboro.[2] Fortunately,
Lundy developed a more financially profitable enterprise
than the monthly *Genius* in the *American Economist and
Weekly Political Recorder,* a weekly which he also published
after the middle of June 1822, as a means of keeping the
manumission society's press efficiently employed. A newspaper
filled with political and market news, poetry, and anecdotes,
it was obviously of wider local appeal than the single-minded
Genius. Lundy valued the *American Economist* chiefly for the
profits it brought, but it had another use as well. The occa-
sional antislavery items he scattered in its columns among the
price quotations for corn and wheat reached a group of readers who would not have dreamed of allowing the *Genius* to
enter their homes.[3] The moderate success of the weekly newspaper and the generosity of his friends soon helped Lundy
rise a little above the state of poverty. By the summer of 1823
his affairs had progressed well enough to enable him to move
his family into a new frame house at the "northwest corner
of Water Street and Church Alley" in Greeneville.[4] But he
was never out of debt at any stage in his career, and he maintained the *Genius* only by rigid economies and the most severe
exertions on his part supplemented at critical times by slender contributions from antislavery supporters.

As soon as Lundy arrived in Greeneville, he joined the

---

[2] Deed Records, Greene County, Tennessee, book 14, pp. 89–93 (Greene
County Courthouse, Greeneville, Tenn.).

[3] *American Economist and Political Recorder,* September 28, 1822, May
10, 1823. With the issue of July 26, 1823, the name of this newspaper was
changed to *American Economist and East Tennessee Statesman.*

[4] *Ibid.,* May 10, 1823.

local Humane Protecting Society, a philanthropic organization similar in purpose to the Union Humane Society he had earlier founded in Ohio, and his prominence as an editor soon took him to a position of leadership in it.[5] His activities in Greeneville were not confined to the slavery question and aid to free Negroes, however, but extended to other matters which he thought should concern ordinary citizens. Thus in an address to the Greene County Agricultural Society in April 1824 he put forward his views on the problems faced by the Tennessee yeomen. Small farmers, not slaveholding planters, he assured his rural audience — again revealing his republicanism — formed "the bone and sinew, the strength and support of the nation." Yet, steady economic decline threatened the yeomen's position and thereby also undermined the foundation of the republic. Slavery contributed to their difficulties, he suggested, but that was not the only source of their troubles nor even the chief menace confronting them. Lundy warned his audience, most of whom cultivated rolling farms in east Tennessee, of the danger of soil depletion. Small farmers in the upland South faced impoverishment as their topsoil washed away with every shower. Agriculture, Lundy told them, should be made a subject for scientific investigation. He advocated the use of manure, compost, and lime to increase soil fertility, and crop rotation and deep plowing to reduce erosion.[6] Lundy's remedy for the Tennessee farm problem was like his remedy for slavery — pragmatic, rational, and based on an appeal to the self-interest of the men chiefly concerned.

Lundy's main interest, of course, remained the abolition of slavery, and his chief instrument in accomplishing it, the publication of the *Genius*. Its paid circulation slowly increased,

---

[5] *Ibid.*, September 16, 1823.
[6] *Ibid.*, May 1, 1824.

and he sent complete files wherever he thought they might be of influence. Thus George Easton, president of the Philomathian Society of Ohio University, received such a gift upon his promise to spread antislavery ideas among the students at Athens.[7]

Although the *Genius* had no official connection with any antislavery society, it now served as an organ for societies throughout the upper South, especially those in Tennessee, Kentucky, and North Carolina, and Lundy faithfully published their reports and notices. By that means these widely separated groups were kept informed of each other's sentiments, activities, and difficulties. Lundy did not intend his journal to be local or regional, however, and he was careful not to allow local concerns and interests to dominate its pages. He published communications from all parts of the country and reprinted antislavery items from newspapers everywhere. The abolition of slavery, he believed, should not be considered the responsibility of any particular sect or class or region. Slavery was a national evil to be eradicated by national efforts. Consequently, the *Genius* as Lundy edited it could have as much value for an interested reader in Massachusetts as for one in Tennessee.

He used his newspaper both as a means of disseminating antislavery news and as an instrument to intervene directly in situations touching upon the antislavery interest. Of major concern to him in 1823 and 1824 — and to antislavery groups wherever located — was the effort then made to call a state constitutional convention in Illinois, presumably with the intent of establishing slavery.[8] Once again as in 1820 foes of

---

[7] George Easton to Lundy, June 7, 1823, in *Genius*, III (July 4, 1823), 3–4.

[8] Theodore C. Pease, *The Frontier State, 1818–1848* (Chicago, 1922), pp. 70–91.

slavery were obliged to exert themselves to prevent the spread of slavery outside its customary bounds. With recent events in Missouri still fresh in his mind, Lundy interpreted the effort in Illinois as another scheme of southern slaveholders to extend slavery, this time by subverting free institutions. The Illinois affair proved of major importance in developing Lundy's interpretation of the nature of the slaveholders' threat. They had formed a conspiracy, he charged, to spread slavery into the states of the old Northwest from which it had presumably been excluded forever by the Northwest Ordinance of 1787. According to his interpretation their purposes were to create new markets for slaves and to expand still further their political power within the national government.[9] Lundy would retain his view of the slave-power conspiracy for the rest of his life and succeed in transmitting it to most other abolitionists.

Even though much of the wealth and power in Illinois was arrayed in favor of holding a constitutional convention, neither Lundy, Illinois antislavery groups, nor abolitionists located far from the crisis area accepted defeat as foreordained. Even the Philadelphia Quakers, led by Roberts Vaux and Nicholas Biddle, supplied Illinois opponents of the convention with ideas and information to use in the struggle.[10] From his outpost in Tennessee Lundy too encouraged the foes of the convention movement. In particular he kept in touch with Hooper Warren, Vermont-born editor of the Ed-

---

9 *Genius*, III (February, 1824), 115.
10 Nicholas Biddle to Edward Coles, May 20, 26, 1823, and Roberts Vaux to Coles, May 27, 1823, in Alvord (ed.), *Governor Edward Coles*, pp. 123–124, 126; [Roberts Vaux], *An Impartial Appeal to the Reason, Interest and Patriotism of the People of Illinois on the Injurious Effects of Slave Labour* (Philadelphia, 1824).

wardsville (Illinois) *Spectator*, who helped organize the local antislavery forces. Warren, a patron of Embree's *Emancipator*, reprinted antislavery articles from Lundy's *Genius*, thereby multiplying their circulation in Illinois. Edward Coles, Illinois' antislavery governor, also read the *Genius* and recommended it to opponents of the convention as a valuable source of antislavery facts and arguments.[11] James Lemen, Jr., leading member of the Illinois Friends of Humanity, wrote Lundy of his gratitude for the inspiration he had gained from the *Genius*.[12] Lundy's newspaper thus proved to be an important source of antislavery ideas for the voters in Illinois as they organized to defeat the convention proposal.

When the vote on the proposed convention was taken in August 1824, Lundy again was presented with proof of the utility of political antislavery action, for the measure failed by a vote of 6,640 to 4,972.[13] The outcome also demonstrated the utility of antislavery journalism, for through his conduct of the *Genius* Lundy could properly claim an important share in the most spectacular of the decade's few antislavery victories.

While the convention debate convulsed Illinois, the slavery issue assumed new importance in national politics as sectional legislative programs developed and popular interest in political campaigns grew. With the approach of the national presidential election of 1824 Lundy again expressed his concern for the uses of politics, urging his readers to vote for no

---

[11] Edwardsville *Spectator*, September 5, 1820, August 21, 1821; Edward Coles to Morris Birkbeck, April 12, 1823, in Alvord (ed.), *Governor Edward Coles*, p. 146.

[12] James Lemen, Jr., to Lundy, January 1, 1824, in Edwardsville *Spectator*, February 17, 1824.

[13] Theodore C. Pease (ed.), *Illinois Election Returns, 1818–1848* (Springfield, Ill., 1923), pp. 27–29.

candidate who held slaves or defended slavery. He thought the Kentucky slaveholder Henry Clay a particularly bad choice.[14]

In preparation for the election Lundy urged the nation's churches to take an antislavery stand. The antislavery Baptists in Illinois who had withdrawn from their congregations to form the Friends of Humanity provided a worthy example for others, Lundy thought. " 'Come out from among them, come out from among them,' " he urged.[15] That radical call for the dissolution of the churches, though not typical of Lundy and little noticed at the time, revealed a strand of antislavery thought pregnant with danger. The temptation was always present for abolitionists to separate from institutions that failed to heed their call for reform and to break with a society that did not attain their high standard of purity. Moreover, withdrawing from evil associations and thereby cleansing oneself of imputed guilt was a characteristic Quaker — indeed, Christian — solution to the problem of sin. But however tempting and time honored, it was still a dangerous course and one Lundy seldom advocated, although some of his successors, most notably Garrison, would commonly preach such doctrine. Lundy, aware (as Garrison was not) of the network of society and institutions that enmeshed all men, hesitated to advocate policy that would destroy it. Instead, he characteristically urged abolition through political action, an instrument of institutionalized power. Perhaps at the time of his early flirtation with radicalism Lundy had not yet recognized that implicit in his call for separation was a demand

---

[14] *Genius*, II (February, 1823), 113. At this time he also queried Andrew Jackson to learn his views on slavery. Lundy to Andrew Jackson, September 4, 1823, in John Spencer Bassett (ed.), *Correspondence of Andrew Jackson* (Washington, D.C., 1928), III, 206–207.
[15] *Genius*, II (February, 1823), 114.

for the destruction of institutions and even for the dissolution of the Union. Certainly he never repeated his recommendation.

In the summer of 1823 he began to consider another, more moderate aspect of antislavery argument, quite in harmony with the rationalism of his time. He had concluded that whether slavery was right or wrong it was in any event not profitable and might well be abandoned on that ground alone. Advocates of the extension of slavery almost always urged its profitability as a point in its favor. Lundy thought them mistaken. Free labor, he insisted, always outproduced slave labor; slavery was profitable only when the goods it produced enjoyed freedom from competition with the products of free labor.

Lundy referred, of course, to the profitability of slavery for southern society in general. He would doubtless have agreed that slavery often constituted a source of wealth for individual planters and slave traders, but for society at large, he insisted, it stifled economic progress. Lundy believed that arguments in this vein helped to halt the convention movement in Illinois, and he imagined that they might also be used in the South to persuade voters to do away with the institution. Accordingly, he printed a letter in the *Genius* comparing the prosperity of New York and Pennsylvania with that of Virginia. Virginia's economic growth lagged behind the free states, and slavery, he said, was responsible. Fascinated by this idea, Lundy now began in earnest to collect materials on the comparative value of slave and free labor.[16]

---

[16] *Ibid.* (June 19, 1823), pp. 190–192; III (July 18, 1823), 16. Note that Lundy's economic argument anticipated that of Hinton Rowan Helper in *The Impending Crisis of the South: How to Meet It* (New York, 1857), *passim.*

This proved to be one of the most fateful intellectual decisions he ever made, for so absorbed did he eventually become with his effort to demonstrate the superiority for society of free labor that he allowed it to determine much of his activity for the next ten years of his life. It was largely wasted effort because in its appeal to social responsibility it ran counter to a dominant fact of the time. To a highly individualistic age arguments about the social good, however well documented, were not very compelling. Older ideas of society and community were disappearing in the disintegrative frontier process. Few potential slaveowners saw any reason to weigh the effect on society of their buying slaves. Like most other Americans they concerned themselves not with the welfare of the community but with promoting their own individual wealth, and as they knew from observation, individual slaveholders often found slavery extremely profitable and convenient. Those few critical southerners who did venture to calculate its social value were as likely as their more individualistic neighbors to conclude that slavery must be perpetuated, for even if they did not think in terms of dollars and cents, they nonetheless considered slavery a necessary means of maintaining white supremacy.

If Lundy's economic argument met with trifling success among slaveholders, it also in the long run cost him support within the organized antislavery movement, for later abolitionists — as individualistically oriented as slaveholders — would find arguments about profit and loss to society demeaning. They largely ignored economic calculation. To them the moral effect of slavery on individual masters and slaves seemed all important, and they emphasized the necessity for individual decision rather than social action to do away with it. They were no more concerned about society and no more capable of dealing with social concepts than their southern antagonists.[17]

The morality of slavery mattered to Lundy, of course, and it impelled all his actions, but he also believed that through the use of statistics demonstrating the economic cost of slavery to society he could prevail upon rational men — whose moral sense might otherwise be blunted — to put away an unprofitable institution. Very few heeded his argument, and Lundy was to be proved mistaken in his optimism, though hardly more so than his fellow abolitionists who imagined they could sway slaveholders by appeals to their moral sensibilities. Neither Lundy nor his successors ever found ways to cope with the irrationalities and the calculations of self-interest that helped to account for the defense and perpetuation of slavery.

While Lundy wrestled with the problem of developing effective antislavery argument, he also began to consider more effective means of furthering the organized antislavery movement and of increasing the authority of the *Genius*. Despite the cohesive influence of Lundy's newspaper the antislavery movement remained fragmented and largely unorganized. Societies had been founded in many places, but except for those in Pennsylvania, Tennessee, and North Carolina their membership was small and their activities poorly developed and uncoordinated. Only the *Genius* provided communication lines among them. Although it reached a fairly wide audience and its contents were probably endorsed by a majority of its readers, the *Genius* spoke in actuality only for Lundy. Its editorial views carried only such authority as their inherent wisdom gave them; Lundy's preeminence in the antislavery movement had never received sanction from any organized

---

[17] Stanley M. Elkins, *Slavery, a Problem in American Institutional and Intellectual Life* (Chicago, 1959), pp. 147–157, 164–178.

antislavery group. He had never joined even the Manumission Society of Tennessee, whose press he used. His intention had been, by maintaining complete independence of thought and action, to establish himself as a national, not merely a local, antislavery leader. In this goal he had been somewhat successful, but he also saw the practical value to himself, to his newspaper, and to the movement against slavery of a more thorough organization than presently existed.

In the fall of 1823 the biannual meeting of the American Convention for the Abolition of Slavery was scheduled to be held in Philadelphia. Weak and loosely organized as the American Convention was, it still constituted a semblance of a national antislavery society, the only one in existence. It had been founded in 1794 to unite the efforts of various local antislavery groups, most of them Quaker dominated, which sent delegates to its biannual meetings. Its efforts had always been limited and of slight effect, yet Lundy thought he could see in the convention the means for obtaining support and authority for the *Genius*, thereby strengthening the entire antislavery enterprise.

As a preliminary step to the accomplishment of this goal, he now reversed his policy of remaining aloof from antislavery groups in Tennessee. On September 8, 1823, he held a meeting at his home to form the Greeneville Branch of the Manumission Society of Tennessee. Seven charter members attended, including Lundy and his helper, Isaiah Osborn. Lundy was elected president.[18] It now became possible for Lundy to proceed to Philadelphia and join the meeting of the American Convention as a properly qualified delegate from the Manumission Society of Tennessee.

While young Osborn remained in Greeneville to conduct the *Genius*, Lundy traveled on horseback to Philadelphia to

---

[18] *Genius*, III (September, 1823), 33–34.

meet with delegates from antislavery societies in the East.
Never before had a representative attended from so far west
as Tennessee; Lundy, for his part, had never met with so
cosmopolitan a body of philanthropists. Most of them were
Quakers from New York, Pennsylvania, and Rhode Island,
and though their record against slavery was long and honor-
able, most exercised great caution in the actions they were
willing to recommend. Although each in his fashion was a
dedicated humanitarian, few seem to have experienced in
themselves anything like Lundy's commitment to devote his
life to accomplishing the destruction of slavery. Indeed, a certain air of complacency and self-satisfaction could be detected
in the convention's proceedings.

Among the first business of the convention was the presentation of reports from the state societies. The New York Manumission Society sent a thoroughly optimistic account of antislavery progress, which it derived from undisclosed sources.
The condition of the slaves constantly improved, the New
York report declared. They enjoyed better food and in every
way were treated more kindly than in earlier days. The domestic slave trade had declined, and few slave families any
longer were being separated because of the demands of com-
merce. In attempting to account for improved conditions, the
report concluded on an altogether happy note: "As the light
of Reason and Religion have [sic] advanced, Slavery has re-
ceded." [19]

If all this were true, Lundy and the convention could
congratulate themselves on work well done and prepare
to conclude their operations in anticipation of the day of universal emancipation. But the Pennsylvania society, better in-

---

[19] *Minutes of the Eighteenth Session of the American Convention for
Promoting the Abolition of Slavery, and Improving the Condition of
the African Race . . .* (Philadelphia, 1824), pp. 5–6, 8.

formed about southern conditions, presented an assessment
of the vigor of slavery which contradicted its northern neighbors at every point. It was a picture of slavery that Lundy
could accept as in accord with the facts: ". . . instead of
witnessing the gradual advancement of emancipation to reduce the number of slaves in the United States, we have
had with sorrow to observe their numbers progressively increase: — raised like cattle for the market, they are driven
from one State to another, and sold to the highest bidder." [20]
The Pennsylvania delegates also reminded the convention
that northerners themselves shared the racial antipathies that
lay at the root of slavery. They called attention to the plight
of the free Negro in the North, shut out by prejudice from
sharing in the profits of a growing economy: "Turnpikes,
canals, coal-mines, brick-making, street-paving and cleaning,
which engage so many thousands, give no employment to
them. . . ." [21] This report, following hard on the one submitted from New York, demonstrated that though slavery had
become sectional, prejudice flourished nationally. Northerners, it appeared, were as much in need of education about
slavery and racial bias as the slaveholders themselves. Lundy's
work had scarcely commenced.
The convention recognized Lundy's leadership in the antislavery movement by appointing him to its important committee on arrangements, the group that prepared the convention's agenda. After short deliberation the committee
brought in proposals for action which, if carried out, might
have made the convention a more vital force than it had
yet been. It recommended drafting a memorial to Congress
and the state legislatures asking for the abolition of slavery in
the District of Columbia; it requested the convention to dis-

[20] *Ibid.*, p. 11.
[21] *Ibid.*, pp. 12–13.

cuss concrete plans for general emancipation; it asked for consideration of Haiti as a site for the emigration of free Negroes; it recommended a memorial to Congress against the interstate slave trade and for recognition of the competency of slaves to testify in court; and it recommended efforts to obtain aid from churches for the antislavery cause.[22]

All this, if agreed upon, would have converted the American Convention into a pressure group seeking to influence the centers of American political and moral power, and it would have brought slavery once more into the focus of public attention. The report received a cool reception, however, almost as though the only purpose of the convention were to say *no*. The convention accepted the proposal to investigate the possibility of Negro emigration to Haiti, but either tabled or rejected all others as "inexpedient." [23] Nothing more was needed to demonstrate the ineffectual character of the American Convention and to support the view that Benjamin Lundy himself represented one of the few sources of dynamism in an otherwise moribund antislavery movement.

After that defeat Lundy introduced the matter that had brought him to Philadelphia, although in view of the convention's expressed conservatism acceptance of the proposal must now have seemed to him less vital than before. He asked the convention to consider sponsoring an antislavery newspaper with the hope, of course, that it would adopt the *Genius* as its own. He was appointed to a committee with Arnold Buffum, John Keating, Jr., John Wales, Robert F. Mott, and Lea Pusey to consider the proposal. After much deliberation and in spite of Lundy's attempts at persuasion, the committee issued an unfavorable report on the ground that the con-

22 *Ibid.*, p. 24.
23 *Ibid.*, pp. 28–32.

vention lacked financial resources to support such an enterprise and that the long intervals between its sessions would
prevent "due supervision of the press." [24]

The reasons given for rejecting Lundy's proposal may be
taken as the real ones, for though Lundy's course was indeed
more extreme and aggressive than many eastern Quakers
would have favored, the convention nonetheless willingly indicated its support for him in other tangible ways. In partial
compensation for the rebuff it had handed him, it recommended the *Genius* to the patronage of its member societies
and agreed itself to subscribe to ten copies, thereby granting
him a small, much-needed subsidy. The convention's approba-
tion of Lundy was shown further by his appointment to the
important "acting committee," which had responsibility for
handling the convention's affairs between sessions, and to a
special committee to investigate slavery in the District of
Columbia. [25]

Lundy had been sorely disappointed in not obtaining the
convention's endorsement for the *Genius*, and the conservative temper of many of its members must also have discouraged him; yet, on balance the trip to Philadelphia had not
been without value. Besides assuring him a limited amount of
financial aid, it had had the result of acquainting him with
the leaders of antislavery thought in Philadelphia and other
eastern centers, whose experience in antislavery work was
much longer than his own and whose prestige was great. It
had also introduced him to British antislavery pamphlets, a

---

[24] *Ibid.*, pp. 33, 37; *Genius*, III (May, 1824), 165, 171–172.
[25] *Minutes of the Eighteenth Session of the American Convention*, p. 42;
Edward Needles, *An Historical Memoir of the Pennsylvania Society for
Promoting the Abolition of Slavery* (Philadelphia, 1848), p. 84; Isaac
Barton to Lundy, July 26, 1825, Pennsylvania Abolition Society Manu-
script Collection, vol. X.

rich source of information about the rapidly growing British reform movement. For many months Lundy had followed newspaper accounts of the developing British opposition to slavery. As early as June 1823 he had reprinted William Wilberforce's remarks to Parliament on abolishing slavery in the West Indies,[26] but British antislavery publications, which reached eastern reformers in abundance, had seldom penetrated as far west as Tennessee. Now upon his return home friends he had made in Philadelphia sent him British materials, including such important sources of information and argument as Thomas Clarkson's *Improving the Condition of the Slaves in the British Colonies, with a View to Their Ultimate Emancipation* and James Cropper's *Relief for West Indian Distress*.[27]

Soon he was reprinting in the *Genius* numerous extracts from these and similar publications sent to America by British antislavery workers and relayed to him from Philadelphia. Within a few months they were sending them directly to him at Greeneville. By the end of 1827 James Cropper of Liverpool had arranged with Thomas Pringle, secretary of the London Anti-Slavery Society, to mail Lundy a complete set of its publications.[28] This development was of the greatest importance. American humanitarians who read accounts of the efforts made to eradicate slavery from the British Empire were likely to resolve not to allow the United States, which they chose to regard as the land of liberty, to lag behind England in antislavery reform. The expanded circulation of British antislavery writings through their republication in the *Genius*

---

[26] *Minutes of the Eighteenth Session of the American Convention*, p. 33; *Genius*, II (June, 1823), 174–175, 177.

[27] *Ibid.*, III (January, 1824), 99.

[28] *Ibid.*, pp. 108–110; IV (November, 1824), 25; Thomas Pringle to Lundy, September 9, 1827, in *ibid.*, VII (December 29, 1827), 203.

provided a strong stimulus to increased American antislavery effort.[29]

Of more immediate significance to Lundy, however, was the fact that the trip to Philadelphia led him to make the decision to move his newspaper from the isolation and poverty of east Tennessee to the Atlantic coast, nearer to centers of information, wealth, and political power. Tennessee had offered him the absolutely essential advantages of a press and local support at a time when he possessed nothing, but he recognized that an eastern location would now provide him with opportunities for more effective operation. He felt that he had discharged any responsibility he may have had to aid the Manumission Society of Tennessee, for its press could now be steadily employed without his help. Furthermore, like Embree before him, he found the western mails unreliable, and he used this annoyance to justify to his western supporters his decision to move from Tennessee.[30]

Leaving his wife and children behind in Greeneville until he could prepare a new home for them, Lundy shouldered his knapsack and set out on foot for Baltimore in the spring of 1824. He made a leisurely and roundabout trip, visiting on the way with friends and relatives in North Carolina and Virginia. In each of the Quaker settlements where he stopped, he found strong antislavery sentiment. He held meetings wherever he could — even at house raisings and militia musters — and helped to organize new antislavery societies.[31] These local successes might have encouraged him to believe the tide of antislavery sentiment was rising had he not also known of the

[29] Gilbert Hobbs Barnes, The Antislavery Impulse, 1830–1844 (New York, 1933), pp. 29–37, dates the British influence from 1830.
[30] Genius, III (June, 1824), 191; American Economist and East Tennessee Statesman, July 29, 1824.
[31] [Earle], Life, pp. 21–23.

recent close call in Illinois, the rapid increase in the domestic slave trade, and the growing political and economic power of the slaveholding planters. Despite his successes among his Quaker brethren, he arrived in Baltimore with his vision unclouded by illusions of early or cheap triumph. The day of victory for abolitionists and deliverance for slaves remained far off, as Lundy knew, and many costly battles yet waited to be fought.

CHAPTER VI

Emigration Experiments

When Lundy reached Baltimore in the summer of 1824, enthusiasm was running high among practically all antislavery groups for a new project to send Negroes outside the United States. Opponents of slavery had long been caught in a predicament. Fervently hoping to end slavery, they yet saw severe problems growing out of its destruction. On the one hand they were confronted with doubts about the Negro's capacity to live in America as a free man, on the other by surmises that white Americans would never accept him as an equal. As a way out of this dilemma, they had hit upon colonization, which they hoped would solve the twin problems of race and slavery. But after a half-dozen years of costly efforts to transport Negroes to Africa, the American Colonization Society still could show little success. Out of disappointment some of its backers had withdrawn support from the African program altogether, and many others had begun to doubt the morality of the program even if it were feasible.[1]

---

[1] *Poulson's Daily American Advertiser* (Philadelphia), March 21, 1827;

Confidence in the necessity for some Negro emigration remained all but universal, however, and those abolitionists —
Lundy among them — who still believed that some Negroes
would have to be sent from the United States as a prelude to
the ending of slavery now turned to Haiti as a spot more
suitable than Africa for emigration. At the American Convention late in 1823 when the subject had come up, Lundy had
voted with the majority to authorize the convention's vice-
president to visit the island to investigate its possibilities.
Haiti's President, Jean Pierre Boyer, encouraged their rising
interest in the hope of luring much-needed population to his
island republic. Even a few of the free Negroes, who had been
notoriously unenthusiastic about accepting transportation to
Africa, let it be known that they considered Haiti the promised land.[2]

Like most other philanthropists Lundy had watched the
political progress of Haiti with the greatest interest because
it demonstrated that Negroes could govern themselves, that
they were not hopelessly inferior and fit only for slavery as
many took for granted. It seemed to him providential that
an opportunity had now presented itself to make use of the
infant Negro republic to further the success of American
antislavery efforts. Haiti, he believed, possessed obvious advantages over Africa as a site for emigration. For one thing
transportation costs — a nearly insuperable barrier to the success of African projects — would be much reduced; furthermore, as Lundy observed, its climate was apparently more

Elliott Cresson to R. R. Gurley, August 23, 1828, and J. F. Polk to
Gurley, December 17, 1829, American Colonization Society Papers.
2 Staudenraus, *African Colonization*, p. 83; *Minutes of the Eighteenth
Session of the American Convention*, pp. 28–31; Lundy to Isaac Barton,
January 30, 1826, Pennsylvania Abolition Society Manuscript Collection,
vol. IX.

congenial than Africa's, and its nearness to the United States
would probably make it more attractive to American Negroes.
Lundy soon let it be known that he would offer complete editorial support to Haitian emigration projects.[3]

He was associated in Baltimore, however, with men who
had no faith whatever in colonization as a means of ending
slavery. Most notable among these was the lawyer Daniel
Raymond, who had early declared the impossibility of ever
returning the Negroes to Africa. Three of Lundy's Negro
friends in Baltimore — William Watkins, Jacob Greener, and
Hezekiah Grice — also remained adamant in opposing the removal of their race from the United States.[4] But despite their
opposition Lundy shared the widespread enthusiasm for
Haitian emigration.

John Kenrick, the Massachusetts reformer who had early
established his own lines of contact with Haiti, put officials
of the republic in communication with Lundy. They ordered
a file of the *Genius,* and soon Lundy and members of the
Haitian government were exchanging letters in which they
developed elaborate plans for transporting freed slaves to the
island.[5] Lundy found that the Haitian cabinet had already
agreed upon a policy of aiding Negroes to move from the
United States and now stood ready to receive emigrants on
liberal terms, including offers of land and the promise of full
civil rights. "Make known, sir, to the unfortunate descendants of Africa, in the United States," ran a dispatch from the
Haitian Secretary of State, "that when they may be at liberty

[3] *Genius,* II (September, 1822), 46; III (supplement, 1824), 193.
[4] Raymond, *Missouri Question,* pp. 5–6; Herbert Aptheker, *A Documentary History of the Negro People in the United States* (New York,
1951), p. 100; Garrison and Garrison, *William Lloyd Garrison,* I, 145n.
[5] *Genius,* III (June, 1824), 177.

to come hither, they will find in us brothers, ever ready to receive them. Haiti will become to them a tender Mother." [6]

The President of Haiti extended generous offers of assistance directly to American Negroes through the Reverend
Loring D. Dewey of New York, a disenchanted agent of the
American Colonization Society. In reply to Dewey's inquiries
for more information about Haitian policy, Boyer reported
that he had arranged to provide land grants for prospective
settlers and in a circular of December 24, 1823, had instructed
district officials to prepare for their arrival. He would also
supply them with tools and other essentials, and most important of all, so far as the unaffluent American philanthropists
were concerned, he promised to bear part of the cost of transporting the emigrants. [7]

In publicizing the Haitian project, Lundy took special
pains to make clear that his goal was to free slaves, not to rid
the country of its Negro population. When he learned that a
new society had been formed in Maryland whose aim did not
extend beyond sending free Negroes out of the country, he
hastened to reject its claims. "I am sick of the continual clack
about the removal of the *free people* of color," he wrote with
unconcealed irritation. "It will never, of itself, do a pin's
worth of good. I could not give the toss of a copper for a
system of philanthropy that extends no further than this." [8]

He left no ground for cynics to suspect that in supporting
emigration he had joined those whose racial bias made it impossible for them to accept the prospect of free Negroes living
permanently as citizens in the United States. Negroes had a

---

[6] B. Inginac to J. Kenrick, January 20, 1824, *ibid.*, p. 178.

[7] Jean Pierre Boyer to Loring Dewey, April 30, 1824, *ibid.* (supplement,
1824), pp. 194–195.

[8] *Genius of Universal Emancipation and Baltimore Courier*, I (January
7, 1826), 149. This periodical is hereafter cited as *Genius and Courier*.

perfect right to remain in this country, he repeated, but, he added, one must also accept the world as it is and recognize the disagreeable fact that "prejudice too often presents itself to us as an insurmountable barrier to the attainment of happiness. . . ." Lundy entertained few illusions about the rationality and generosity of his countrymen. Although he hoped Americans were improving in those qualities, he expected no early millennium, nor did he anticipate in any near future a frictionless adjustment between the races. Realistic men must agree, he wrote, that the degraded condition of the free colored people of the United States and the discriminations that plagued them would be much ameliorated by their removal to Haiti, where they could enjoy social and legal equality. "This they cannot expect here, for many generations to come," he warned, "for the causes that produced the prejudices now existing, on the part of the white inhabitants, will have a tendency to prolong them, and to give them force and effect." [9]

Lundy was plagued by a more frightful prospect that added urgency to his support of the emigration plan. He could see no reason to expect the end of slavery for at least another century. Before that time had passed, there would be (according to his calculation) some 3,000,000 Negroes in the United States. Would so many human beings held in hopeless subjugation long refrain from rebellion? Could the United States avoid becoming in its turn a Santo Domingo? Visions of the horrors of racial warfare had long contributed to the zeal with which Lundy worked against slavery. Now that same specter stimulated his efforts for emigration, which he regarded as an auxiliary necessity to abolition. [10]

---

[9] *Genius*, IV (October, 1824), 2–4.
[10] *Ibid.* (November, 1824), p. 17.

Since slavery appeared destined to continue for many years, prudence required that the nation's slave population somehow be reduced. This could best be accomplished by encouraging as many manumissions as possible and transporting the Negroes thus freed to Haiti. The Haitian plan, he thought, would make possible the sending out of 50,000 Negroes a year at a cost of only 720,000 dollars, thereby eliminating at small expense the annual increase in slave population plus 15,000 of the old stock. While the nation waited for complete emancipation to be accomplished at some distant time through a remote confluence of events that philanthropists could now only hope for, Haiti would serve as a safety valve for the slaves' explosive discontent. But besides all those prudential considerations to Lundy the plan seemed equally important as a means of helping to free at least some Negroes from otherwise hopeless bondage. President Boyer, he said, would rank as history's "second Moses." [11]

The project went forward with some success, aided by "Citizen" Jonathan Granville, a special agent sent to the United States by the Haitian government. Early in September 1824 Granville arrived in Baltimore and met at once with a group of Negro leaders to discuss the plan. Although they received him with evident skepticism, he answered their objections so satisfactorily that when he had finished speaking the group resolved "to use all honourable means to procure a speedy and effectual emigration of the free people of colour" to Haiti. With support from some leading Negroes thus secured, Granville arranged for more than 600 emigrants to leave from Baltimore, Philadelphia, and New York during a four-month period in 1824.[12]

As Lundy hoped, some slaveholders gave the new project

---

[11] *Ibid.* (March, 1825), p. 81.
[12] *Ibid.* (November, 1824), pp. 27–28.

their blessing. David Patterson of Orange County, North Carolina, freed eleven of his slaves and sent them from Baltimore to Haiti. Antislavery groups, too, began formally to endorse the project. The Society of Friends in North Carolina voted to transport the 700 Negroes that had been placed under its care, and in September 1824 the North Carolina Manumission Society agreed to support Haitian emigration. During the summer of 1824 Lundy described the plan to the officers of the Manumission Society of Tennessee, and within a few months the society passed a resolution of confidence in the "humane overtures" of the Haitian government.[13]

Lundy also received encouragement from other philanthropists who, like himself, saw little hope for fair treatment for the Negro so long as he remained in the United States. As early as 1822 George Flower, an English settler in Edwards County, Illinois, had given publicity to the advantages Haiti offered American Negroes. Flower had employed some of them on his Illinois farm and by 1819 had developed plans to establish a communitarian society with the object of freeing slaves and giving employment to free Negroes. But some of his neighbors, obsessed by racial prejudice, abused both him and the Negroes, menaced his property, and even threatened his life. Frustrated by what appeared a hopeless situation, he had helped twenty of the Negroes to move to Haiti in the spring of 1823. Flower informed Lundy that the letters they had written to him since their arrival were full of encouraging reports about the country and their prospects in it.[14]

---

13 *Ibid.* (February, 1825), pp. 65, 67; (December, 1824), p. 33; Lundy to Isaac Barton, March 8, 1825, Pennsylvania Abolition Society Manuscript Collection, vol. IX.

14 Arthur Eugene Bestor, Jr., *Backwoods Utopias: The Sectarian and Owenite Phases of Communitarian Socialism in America, 1663–1829* (Philadelphia, 1950), p. 49; Edwardsville *Spectator*, December 7, 1822; Flower to Lundy, July 23, 1824, in *Genius*, IV (October, 1824), 9–10.

Other sources confirmed the promise Flower saw in Haiti. In February 1825 Loring Dewey reported to Lundy's friend Daniel Raymond that more than 700 Negroes had already arrived at Cape Haitian, where most of them worked on land of their own near the city. Few had died. He assured Raymond that the government had fulfilled all its promises to the settlers. This report together with all the other encouraging recent events led Lundy to extend his support for the project beyond the writing of editorials. In March he announced that in cooperation with the board of managers of the newly organized Haitian Emigration Society he had opened an office for transacting business concerned with the project. He would take the names of Negroes wishing to leave the United States, and he would supply them and other interested persons with information about the island. An emigrant ship would depart from Baltimore on April 15, he announced.[15]

No sooner was the Haitian plan well launched than opposition began to appear, most vocally from the American Colonization Society itself, which justifiably looked upon the program as a rival to its own efforts to develop Liberia. Rumors spread too that the settlers in Haiti encountered conditions nearly as bad as those that had killed so many emigrants to Africa. Lundy refused to recognize any validity to those objections, claiming that they originated with persons whose zeal to preserve slavery led them to try to discredit the Haitian plan. He printed favorable letters from Haitian settlers in the hope of dispelling rumors of intolerable conditions on the island.[16]

Then came a far more serious, nearly fatal blow to the project. With no warning the Secretary General of Haiti an-

[15] *Ibid.* (March, 1825), p. 81; Loring Dewey to Daniel Raymond, February 3, 1825, in *ibid.*, pp. 88–90.

[16] *Ibid.* (January, 1825), pp. 49–52, 72.

nounced that after June 15, 1825, all payments to aid the transport of emigrants would be ended. The new settlers quickly became discontented, he explained, and refused to stay; many had demanded permits to leave the island nearly as soon as they arrived. Dewey denied the truth of the report, stating that only 200 out of the 6,000 whose passage had been paid by the Haitian government had returned to the United States. Lundy himself thought the charge could apply to only a few emigrants, but even his optimism about the efficacy of the program as an antislavery measure had to be tempered with knowledge of the relatively small numbers of slaves who had been freed and sent to Haiti and the slight financial support the project had received from American sources.[17]

The government's withdrawal of financial support did not diminish his enthusiasm for the plan, however, and he continued to give it publicity and aid. He announced that he continued to receive many inquiries from planters interested in manumitting their slaves on condition they go to Haiti. The inquiries led to a few spectacular results. A young man in Camden, South Carolina, applied to him for advice and aid in freeing his seventy slaves. David Minge of Charles City County, Virginia, freed his eighty-eight slaves and with Lundy's help sent them to Haiti at his own expense.[18]

If only more money were available, Lundy said, he could free hundreds of slaves in this way.[19] Ever optimistic, Lundy for a moment supposed that such men as Minge personified a new spirit that had struck slaveholders, whereas in fact they were to prove most unusual. Although here and there a few exceptional masters did free their slaves, and others contin-

---

[17] Ibid. (April, 1825), pp. 114, 125; (August, 1825), p. 174.
[18] Ibid. (June, 1825), p. 129; (July, 1825), pp. 143–144; (September, 1825), p. 178.
[19] Genius and Courier, I (October 16, 1825), 57.

ued to express the desire to do so, they were much outnumbered by those many southerners who aspired, rather, to qualify for entrance into the slaveholding gentry or, if they already
belonged there, to add to their present holdings. It was therefore hardly remarkable that even though Lundy's emigration
project had removed in theory the long-expressed basis for
southern opposition to emancipation, little money came from
slaveholders to aid in its execution.

In October 1825 while he still remained deeply committed
to Haitian emigration, Lundy presented as an adjunct to it a
plan for "gradual abolition of slavery in the United States
without danger or loss to the South." [20] It represented an
amalgam of the ideas on the subject that he had developed
through years of thought: the necessity for gradual emancipation, the superiority of free over slave labor, the need for at
least some Negro emigration, and, especially, his conviction
of the efficacy of economic appeals addressed to slaveholders.
Any antislavery plan, he explained, must consult the pecuniary interests and the prejudices of planters if it were to
succeed. His new proposal appeared to satisfy that require-
ment. It also demonstrated the vogue then enjoyed by the
communitarian ideas of Robert Owen and George Rapp.

Adapting for his own purposes their plans to create model
societies, Lundy proposed to buy land in Alabama or Mississippi and place on it as many as one hundred slaves purchased from their owners. These he would put to work raising
cotton on a cooperative system modeled after the Rappite
communities at Harmony, Indiana, and Economy, Pennsylvania. He would establish on the plantation a "school of industry," using the popular Lancastrian plan of education to

[20] Benjamin Lundy, *A Plan for the Gradual Abolition of Slavery in the United States Without Danger to the Citizens of the South* (Baltimore, 1825).

prepare the workers and their children for freedom. According to Lundy's calculation, the slaves would have returned their purchase price and expenses by the end of five years. Having fulfilled their obligation, they would then be free to settle wherever they wished, although Lundy would encourage them to move to Haiti or to Texas. The experiment would then be repeated with other groups of slaves until gradually the South would be drained of its slave population, which would be replaced by free white workers. Planters, observing the superior efforts and productivity of the Negroes released from slavery, would gladly substitute free for slave labor.[21]

Only the details of Lundy's plan were original. A similar scheme had earlier been given publicity through the activities of one of Robert Owen's disciples, Frances Wright, whose society of Nashoba in Shelby County, Tennessee, also intended to purchase slaves and allow them to work to discharge their debt to the community and then become free. Lundy consulted Miss Wright about his plan, but she could give him little encouragement. Nashoba had fewer backers than he supposed, she informed him, and her project was but poorly supported.[22]

Lundy's proposal aroused no enthusiasm whatever in the South, and for the best possible reason. No more than other men would slaveholders accept any program, however prudently arranged, which would remove the basis of their position, wealth, comfort, power, and self-esteem. However openly they might upon occasion admit to fear of the Negro and to convictions of his innate inferiority, the fact remained that they needed him for both material and psychic reasons, and they believed he would best serve their purposes if he were

---

[21] *Ibid., passim.*
[22] Frances Wright to Lundy, January 10, 1826, in *Genius*, V (January, 1826), 1.

kept in the servile position he then occupied. The removal of Negroes from the South and their replacement by white labor, even if this could have been accomplished without financial sacrifice, would have worked a revolution that few planters could have accepted. John Calhoun's later remark that a "mysterious Providence had brought the black and white people together from different parts of the globe, and no human power could now separate them," doubtless betrayed vast quantities of self-satisfaction, but it also gave authoritative recognition to the fact that the southern need for the Negro was at least as great as the southern need for slavery.[23] The remark also, of course, constituted an authoritative and unanswerable objection to all emigration projects and a final, devastating rebuttal to those who still dreamed of creating a white America.

Lundy nonetheless still cherished the quite unrealistic belief that somehow, through the use of economic incentives, he could develop a plan that would end slavery peacefully and with the consent of slaveholders. While he still adhered to a remnant of hope that something would come from his proposal to establish a communitarian emancipating society in the South, he decided that the prospects appeared better for founding one elsewhere. Accordingly, he announced that he would seek support to plant a Negro community in Haiti for the purpose of securing *"the release of slaves from bondage,* and *the total abolition of slavery in this country."* The society would itself free some slaves, but even more important, he thought, it would encourage additional manumissions by demonstrating that free Negroes worked more efficiently than slaves. In advancing his proposal, Lundy explained that he also had "something of a *commercial* nature" in view.

[23] *Congressional Register,* 24 Cong., 2 Sess., XIII, 566.

That is, the products from the free-labor colony would be sold in a free-produce store which he and Michael Lamb, an experienced merchant, planned to establish in Baltimore to cater to persons whose scruples prohibited their consumption of goods produced by slaves.[24]

He conferred with some Negro residents of Baltimore about his new plan and received promises of their support. John Peirce, treasurer of the Maryland Anti-Slavery Society, agreed to receive donations to finance the venture. Any money Peirce could raise would be welcomed, of course, but Lundy expected little help from Maryland. In a bid for northern support Lundy arranged to have Loring Dewey undertake a tour of New York, New Jersey, Pennsylvania, and Delaware to seek contributions for the Haitian undertaking while he also took subscriptions for the *Genius*.[25] Lundy already recognized that significant backing for antislavery programs must now be looked for outside the South. This change in view was of the very greatest importance, for it signaled an ultimate shift in the geographic base of the antislavery movement from South to North, with a consequent increase in sectional antipathy.

But even if additional aid were secured somewhere in the United States for Lundy's project, the Haitian government's precipitate withdrawal of financial support for emigration stood as a major obstacle to putting it into effect. Accordingly, Lundy made plans to visit Haiti himself to try to persuade officials to reverse their decision. He arranged with Daniel Raymond to take charge of both the monthly *Genius*

---

[24] Lundy to Isaac Barton, January 23, 1826, Pennsylvania Abolition Society Manuscript Collection, vol. IX; *Genius and Courier*, I (August 5, 1826), 388. His partnership with Lamb was dissolved September 11, 1826. *Ibid.*, II (September 11, 1826), 8.

[25] Lundy to Isaac Barton, January 30, 1826, Pennsylvania Abolition Society Manuscript Collection, vol. IX; *Genius and Courier*, I (December 24, 1825), 139; (December 31, 1825), p. 141.

and the weekly edition that he had published since July 4, 1825. A matter not so easily dealt with was the problem posed by his wife Esther, who was again pregnant and suffering besides from a rheumatic ailment that had left her an invalid much of the time. But Lundy, with her acquiescence, decided that his obligations to the antislavery cause were more compelling than his family responsibilities. With a promise to return to Baltimore within eight weeks — just before his wife's confinement — he embarked for Haiti accompanied by Negroes sent in his care by the North Carolina Quakers.[26]

He found Haitian officials still implacable. The Secretary of State explained that of the 6,000 American Negroes aided by the Haitian treasury one-third had become dissatisfied and only "returned evil for good. . . ." Some of them, the secretary charged, had turned out to be "a set of idle vagabonds." Lundy's own investigations revealed a quite different situation, at least as far as those emigrants who had remained on the island were concerned. Most of the settlers, he observed, worked diligently and lived contentedly in their new homes. To potential emigrants from the United States he sent back encouraging advice. They still might move to Haiti, and in spite of the disillusionment of government officials a display of industry and good conduct on the part of new settlers would still secure them friendship, hospitality, and wealth in Haiti, and, most important of all, "that respectable distinction in society which is denied them in the United States."[27]

Although the Haitian government remained unyielding in its decision to provide no more money for emigration, Lundy succeeded in persuading the members of the Haitian Philanthropic Society to make one more effort on behalf of their

[26] Lundy to Isaac Barton, January 23, 1826, Pennsylvania Abolition Society Manuscript Collection, vol. IX; [Earle], *Life*, pp. 23–24.
[27] *Genius and Courier*, I (June 3, 1826), 315; II (June 23, 1827), 261–262.

American brethren. Members agreed to advance up to 150 dollars for the transport of each settler from the United States. This was in no sense to be a gift. Indeed, the conditions exacted for repayment were so onerous as to raise doubts about the philanthropic character of the society. The emigrants would be bound to work for the society for three years, turning over to the sponsors one-half of their produce. In addition they must repay the cost of their transportation within three years. After some eight weeks of negotiation, Lundy concluded that these harsh terms were the best he could obtain, and he prepared to return to the United States to make the best of them that he could.[28]

These arrangements would not suffice to end slavery, he admitted, but they would help, and he announced upon his return to Baltimore that he intended to put them into effect by dispatching an emigrant ship to Haiti in February 1828. The plan worked out with the Haitian Philanthropic Society did not prove attractive, however, and Negroes who accepted transportation under its terms generally found them overly burdensome. As the prospects for the success of Haitian emigration dwindled, Lundy salvaged such consolation as he could from the disappointment. Despite its failure, he said, the project could be credited with stimulating a "general spirit of inquiry," thus bringing "thousands" into the cause as active workers. He thought that the fifty antislavery societies recently founded in the South owed much to its influence. "Men in general will not take the trouble to think upon any subject whatever," he explained, "unless, it presents itself to them in a shape that appears interesting, either favorably or unfavorably."[29] Haiti had interested them. But his optimism proved misplaced. Haiti soon ceased to appear as a

---

[28] *Ibid.*, I (June 3, 1826), 315.
[29] *Ibid.*, p. 313.

suitable refuge for American Negroes, and within a year or two Lundy himself had abandoned interest in it as a useful project.

The negotiations with the Haitian Philanthropic Society had kept Lundy out of the country several weeks longer than he had planned. The consequences of the delay were tragic. Just as he made ready to sail for home, a vessel arrived from Baltimore bringing news that on April 4 his wife had died in childbirth. Lundy reached Baltimore late in May to find his house empty and his five children, including newborn infant twins, Esther and Benjamin, scattered among his friends. To add to his distress, many of his associates and fellow Quakers harshly criticized him for leaving his wife at so inopportune a time.[30]

Lundy made such arrangements for his children as he could, placing them with Quaker friends and relatives to whom he surrendered nearly all the responsibility for their care. The three older children were reared by his father and stepmother; he hired nurses for the infants until they were three years old, when his sister-in-law in Ohio took them into her home.[31] Never again would he be in a position to establish a home for his motherless children, nor would he — until the very last months of his life — ever again have a home himself.

The death of his wife intensified Lundy's attachment to the antislavery cause. His life, long dedicated to the crusade for freedom, now became indistinguishable from it. Few distractions remained to impede his single-minded pursuit of that cause. Released, however tragically, from the responsibilities

---

[30] E. A. Snodgrass, "Benjamin Lundy, a Sketch of His Life and of His Relations with His Disciple and Associate, William Lloyd Garrison," *Northern Monthly*, II (March, 1868), 509; [Earle], *Life*, p. 24; *Genius and Courier*, I (June 3, 1826), 317.
[31] [Earle], *Life*, p. 309.

that had tended to bind him to place and to family, he now found himself even freer than before to devote himself to the very limit of endurance wherever the need seemed greatest and wherever his presence might accomplish the most for the antislavery cause. No domestic obligations absorbed his energies or impeded his efforts in the next few years as he journeyed thousands of miles within the country and outside it seeking ways to end slavery. But despite such exertions the obstacles to the success of such an undertaking seemed to become greater with every passing year.

CHAPTER VII

Defeats and Trials

While southern planters were demonstrating their devotion to slavery by adding to their slave holdings and refusing to support emigration schemes such as those Lundy had developed, they also increased their resentment toward all who ventured to criticize their institutions. Unfortunately for them criticism irresistibly grew. On January 17, 1824, the Ohio legislature passed resolutions asking Congress to appropriate funds to aid gradual emancipation and the emigration of free Negroes. It also used the opportunity to justify its request by branding slavery a national evil of such dimensions as to demand action from the national government. The resolutions were sent to other state legislatures for endorsement. Vermont, Massachusetts, Connecticut, Pennsylvania, New Jersey, Delaware, Indiana, and Illinois approved them, but in the deep South they stirred up a hornet's nest.[1]

Southerners — legislators, governors, and private citizens,

---

[1] Herman V. Ames, *State Documents on Federal Relations: The States and the United States* (Philadelphia, 1906), pp. 203–204.

alike — had no difficulty in seeing the danger, only slightly hidden, in Ohio's proposal. The specter that had haunted them at least since the days of the Missouri Compromise loomed again: abolition by act of Congress. If the power of the national government over slavery were ever recognized, as the Ohio legislature said it should be, then slavery was doomed. A northern and western antislavery majority, immune to coercion from planters, might someday elect a Congress that would vote for universal emancipation. The only safeguard short of secession was a resort to constitutional theory. Accordingly, southern patriots hurriedly raised the familiar standard of state sovereignty, this time as a defense of slavery and white supremacy against federal interference. They would never haul that standard down.

The South Carolina legislature informed Ohio's would-be emancipators that they had presumed too much — the legislature of South Carolina alone had power to control race relations within the state's borders. It further reassured anxious citizens that it would never allow their property "to be meddled with . . . or in any manner regulated, or controlled by any other power, foreign or domestic, than this legislature."[2] Robert J. Turnbull published letters in the Charleston *Mercury* denouncing the resolutions and a variety of other northern acts as "fanaticism" and singling out Lundy as a particular menace to southern institutions. To allow any congressional debate at all on slavery would be fatal, Turnbull warned. "Discussion will cause *death* and *destruction* to our negro property. Discussion will be equivalent to an act of emancipation. . . ."[3] Georgia's governor, George Troup, deplored the "enthusiastics and fanatics" in Ohio and elsewhere

---

[2] *Ibid.*, pp. 207–208; *Genius*, IV (February, 1825), 68.
[3] [Turnbull], *The Crisis*, p. 137.

who sought to interfere with slavery. Their philanthropy was
misplaced and worse than useless, he asserted, for "the efforts
of others to better the condition of the negro have invariably
made it worse." [4]

Lundy was shocked by the intemperate reaction to a program he himself favored as being rational and moderate and
calculated to win support from the very men who now railed
against it. The emotional atmosphere generated by the Ohio
resolutions so dismayed him that he advised his Quaker antislavery friends in Philadelphia to send no more antislavery
memorials to Congress until tension had decreased. [5] Such
counsel was typical of the conciliatory mode of operation
abolitionists had usually followed. But as time passed, it would
become far less characteristic of Lundy and of others as well.
Their caution and manifest desire to pacify the sensitive
South would soon be dissipated, largely by the acts of slaveholders themselves, but also in part by a revolutionary twenty-
four–page pamphlet published in London in the very year
southern statesmen raged so furiously against the evidences
of growing antislavery concern. [6]

Elizabeth Coltman Heyrick, a Quaker of Leicester, England, wrote *Immediate, Not Gradual Abolition* out of moral
indignation at the perpetuation of slavery within the British
Empire. Although she wrote only about her own country,
the urgency she expressed and the policy she advocated could
as easily be applied to the American situation. Philadelphia
Quakers who received the work a few weeks after it was pub-

[4] *Genius,* IV (January, 1825), 55.
[5] Lundy to Isaac Barton, March 8, 1825, Pennsylvania Abolition Society
Manuscript Collection, vol. IX.
[6] Elizabeth Coltman Heyrick, *Immediate, Not Gradual Abolition; or,
an Inquiry into the Shortest, Safest and Most Effectual Means of Getting
Rid of West Indian Slavery* (London, 1824).

lished recognized its pertinence at once and arranged to issue
an American edition before the year had ended; Lundy reprinted the pamphlet serially in the *Genius* during the fall
and winter of 1826–27. Thus most American abolitionists had
the work available to them in one form or another by the end
of the decade. Its argument became the basis for much of
the abolitionist activity of the 1830's.

All programs aimed at gradual emancipation — that "very
master-piece of Satanic policy" — were useless, Mrs. Heyrick
declared. According to her argument abolitionist efforts to
conciliate slaveholders by consulting their interests only com-
pounded their arrogance and tightened the grip with which
they held their slaves. It was a delusion, she said, to suppose
the planters would ever voluntarily relinquish their property,
however gradual an emancipating process might be proposed.
They reacted just as vociferously against programs of gradualism as against immediatism. Therefore all concern for
expediency should be abandoned. The only proper course,
she insisted, was to advocate immediate emancipation on the
ground that it was morally just, and to rely for its accomplishment not on government but on Divine guidance. She
emphasized the moral grandeur of individual action and commitment in support of a just cause. This constituted the main
theme of her essay. No room was left for a middle position on
slavery, Mrs. Heyrick insisted. One either absolutely opposed
slavery, or one favored it.

Lundy found several aspects of Mrs. Heyrick's argument
appealing, especially its moral absolutism (Lundy had long
used as the motto for the *Genius*, "Let justice be done though
the heavens should fall"), its emphasis on individual responsibility, and its forthright statement of both the problem and
its solution, all expressed in language (as he said) very "unlike the milk-and-water style of some writers on this side of

the Atlantic." [7] Although Lundy himself could not relinquish faith in political action or abandon efforts to work out an antislavery program acceptable to southerners, he recognized the validity of the Heyrick analysis. In particular her observations about the intransigence of slaveholders and the uselessness of addressing humanitarian appeals to them accorded perfectly with his own experience. Even though he could not altogether abandon his old views, he was receptive to new ideas such as Mrs. Heyrick's, and he helped make them available to others.

Even so strong an argument as hers, of course, would have been ignored in America had not the situation been prepared for its favorable reception. Lundy's work and the activities of antislavery and colonization societies had created strong antislavery sentiment, but at the same time the inability of abolitionists to make tangible accomplishments toward ending slavery had produced frustrations which invited extreme programs. More than anything else it was the stubborn refusal of slaveholders and their legislators to take any antislavery action whatever that led Lundy and other abolitionists to give sympathetic hearing to such arguments as Mrs. Heyrick's.

It is true that most of the antislavery societies then in existence were located in the slaveholding states.[8] Yet their membership remained small and their power slight. Furthermore, they were not scattered evenly throughout the South. Most of them operated among the small farmers of North Carolina and Tennessee. Georgia, South Carolina, and the new cotton states of the Southwest apparently had none at all. Even in the upper South few influential men joined them. With minor exceptions only Quakers and other inconspicuous persons,

---

[7] *Genius*, IV (December, 1824), 34.
[8] *Genius and Courier*, I (December 10, 1825), 117.

commonly regarded as eccentrics, still agitated in the South for the ending of slavery.[9]

Even the American Colonization Society, which some northerners claimed protected slavery, soon became suspect among slaveholders who had earlier endorsed its program. In South Carolina and Georgia great prejudice developed against the society as the belief spread, despite all official denials, that it aimed to end slavery.[10] Still sharper hostility arose against avowed antislavery groups. A member of the North Carolina legislature in 1826 introduced a motion to suppress and destroy "by indictment" the manumission society of that state.[11] By the end of 1827 an agent of the American Colonization Society could report from North Carolina that "the Quakers, & everything connected with emancipation & colonization is [sic] unpopular in the state." [12] Proslavery sentiment became ever more strident in the South. Both the ambitions and the anxieties of many southern whites had become irretrievably entangled with the Negro and his status as a slave. Neither Lundy nor any other abolitionist would find it possible, however great the effort, to reach the minds and hearts of persons who found slavery profitable, convenient, and satisfying.

But the certainty of failure did not prevent their trying, nor did it halt their development of new and ever more extreme methods of antislavery action. In August 1825 in a

---

9 "We have an 'Emancipation' society in this county (Maury). It consists, I believe, of only 3 men all brothers, — own no slaves — & are very unpopular, on account of the society, as well as other excentricities [sic]." Lyman D. Brewster to R. R. Gurley, June 26, 1828, American Colonization Society Papers.

10 Samuel K. Talmadge to R. R. Gurley, May 29, 1828, ibid.

11 Genius, II n.s. (December 2, 1826), 85.

12 James Nourse to R. R. Gurley, December 29, 1827, American Colonization Society Papers.

Baltimore schoolroom Lundy and a group of his associates
organized the Maryland Anti-Slavery Society with Daniel Raymond as president and Lundy as corresponding secretary.[13]
It had a purpose altogether different from practically all
earlier societies with similar names. Most societies had intended to spread antislavery ideas, to memorialize legislatures and Congress, and in various ways to aid free Negroes.
The chief aim of the Maryland Anti-Slavery Society, on the
other hand, was to inaugurate political antislavery action, a
course Lundy had long advocated. Its purpose, as Lundy explained it, was to influence the legislature "to alter and
amend the laws, and make them more favorable to manumission, colonization, and emigration." [14] But this statement of
modest aims did not adequately describe his intent. On another occasion he had expressed his purpose more accurately.
Having discovered that "slaveholders, in general, will do nothing to aid the cause of emancipation . . . and not withstand-
ing the very door is unhinged which they have said it was
necessary to open for this purpose," he was now prepared
through political action to force them to free their slaves.
"THE BALLOT BOX MUST BE RESORTED TO . . .
this will be the ONLY means, I repeat it, by which slavery
can be annihilated without commotion, rapine, and indescrib-
able woe." [15] But even though, so far as he could see, the
ballot box offered the only hope for a peaceful end of slavery, he doubted the pacific outcome of a resort to politics.
Lundy recognized the danger that might result from the growing division over slavery. "Parties are organizing for and
against the further toleration of the anti-Christian practice,"
he wrote, " — they will inevitably come into collision — and

---

[13] *Genius*, IV (August, 1825), 161.
[14] *Genius and Courier*, I (September 6, 1825), 12.
[15] *Ibid.* (September 24, 1825), p. 37.

severe will be the contest. . . . It will be as impossible to prevent this state of things as to stop the sun in its course." [16]

Despite these misgivings a full-fledged political antislavery
movement under Lundy's direction was soon underway in
Maryland. At first, according to a local newspaper, the public viewed the new society "rather with indifference than contempt" or fear,[17] but indifference turned to apprehension
when the society nominated Daniel Raymond to run for the
general assembly on a platform advocating gradual emancipation. Two groups found reason to resist the new development. City leaders recognized that a growing antislavery sentiment within Baltimore might imperil the city's influence in
the state legislature.[18] More numerous were those persons, un-
concerned about politics, who nonetheless worried that success of the movement would endanger white supremacy, encourage social disorder, and foster economic competition from
a growing free Negro population. It was this element that
provided most of the active opposition which soon rose against
the antislavery society and its candidate for the general assembly.

At one ward meeting "a gang of rosy-faced" fellows packed
the room to interrupt Raymond's speech and adjourn the
meeting.[19] Generally, however, the opposition expressed itself by words rather than by such aggressive action. On September 28, 1825, citizens hostile to the new antislavery society met at Hayes' Tavern to draw up a formal statement
against its program. Particularly disturbed by Lundy's condemnations of slavery as a moral evil, they began by passing
resolutions denying personal responsibility for the continu-

---

16 *Genius*, II n.s. (September 16, 1826), 5.
17 Fredericksburg (Md.) *Citizen* cited in *Genius*, IV (January, 1826), 2.
18 Baltimore *American*, September 20, 27, 28, 30, 1825.
19 *Genius and Courier*, I (October 16, 1825), 60.

ance of slavery. Slavery, they said, was a national evil "entailed" on the present generation by their ancestors; neither individuals nor the state should be held accountable for its existence. Repeating words often heard in the South in earlier days, they declared their desire to see slavery ended if this could be accomplished "without an interference with legally recognized private rights. . . ." Then they condemned the new antislavery society, which they recognized to have coercion as its goal, "as productive of civil commotions and domestic broils — as injurious to the happiness and interests of the unfortunate objects of their care — and as an unconstitutional interference with the rights of property. . . ." To free the slaves, they warned, would be to create "an idle, dissolute and abandoned free black population with which our streets are already too much infested." Consequently, they endorsed the American Colonization Society's proposal to remove Negroes to Africa as a happy alternative to Lundy's emancipation plans. The colonization society's promise to end slavery "without endangering the existence of civilized society" catered to their conviction of the Negro's unalterable inferiority. Since the prospect of the two races living on equal terms was unbearable to them, they seized upon the society's assurance that this need not happen. Its promise to create a white America provided the only satisfactory alternative to slavery that they could envision.[20]

The men who met at Hayes' Tavern professed to dislike slavery as much as Lundy did. Other Baltimore citizens, however, defended it as a permanent necessity. The day before the election one of that group posted handbills signed "Self-Preservation" along the city streets to warn voters of the hazards they faced from the emerging "philanthropic fanati-

---

[20] Baltimore *American*, September 30, 1825.

cism." Lundy, Raymond, and their antislavery society, the handbill charged, wished "to turn loose a depraved and ignorant black population to overrun the country. . . ." It made no distinction between gradual and immediate emancipation for the very good reason, as Mrs. Heyrick had observed, that most slaveholders now saw none. One plan of emancipation was just as objectionable to them as another. They had become unwilling to accept plans to end slavery at even a remote time. The object of the new antislavery society, warned the handbill, "is to liberate the slaves, and whether it is done now, or a century hence; whether simultaneously; or gradually, still they will be setting at large a corrupt and ignorant population to infest the country. . . . Nature herself has implanted such marked differences in the two races as render it [a]bsolutely impossible that they can exist tranquilly, together, on an equality." For that reason, they said, they had determined to oppose emancipation even if it were scheduled to occur at a date far after their own deaths. Even if Lundy should succeed in his efforts to demonstrate the economic advantages of free labor, they would still be left unconvinced and unwilling to free their slaves. To them slavery had become a social necessity irrespective of its possible economic inutility.[21]

The sentiments expressed in the preelection handbill appear not to have been opposed by the majority in Baltimore, for on election day Raymond received only 624 votes out of 10,711 cast. This massive defeat did not discourage Lundy, for he had never expected early victory. As soon as the results were in, he gave "timely notice" that an antislavery ticket would "hereafter be supported in the city until it succeeds." "The laborers will neither faint nor fear during sun-shine or

[21] *Genius and Courier*, I (October 29, 1825), 75.

storm," he said. "They have resolved that the work shall go on — and it will go on." [22]

Despite the failure he thought he could see important gains resulting from the campaign. Agitation had "carried the subject of slavery into every parlor and kitchen," arousing thought and discussion among people who never before had subjected the institution to examination. Furthermore, the election results seemed to prove that Baltimore already contained the nucleus of an antislavery party. Some 600 men had dared to vote for an antislavery candidate in the face of widespread popular disapproval which had been reinforced by the declared opposition of civic leaders and, as Lundy said, by "the frowns of our great southern neighbors." [23]

One of the most formidable spokesmen for Maryland's "great southern neighbors" had been James Barbour of Virginia, Secretary of War in John Quincy Adams' cabinet. In a speech delivered at Albemarle, Virginia, shortly before the Baltimore election, Barbour condemned abolitionists for their "wild or incendiary projects," which, he charged, threatened to dissolve the Union, and he characterized such newspapers as Lundy's *Genius* as the "croakings of the distempered, who seek to establish a character for philanthropy at the expense of others. . . ." [24]

Lundy claimed to detect something new in Barbour's speech, though in fact he could have found much the same ideas expressed in southern responses to the Ohio resolutions of 1824. As Lundy pointed out, Barbour demanded silence from those who would ask Congress to end slavery and insisted that no one except slaveowners should venture to discuss the subject at all. Furthermore, his speech constituted a

22 Baltimore *American*, October 4, 1825; *Genius*, IV (September, 1825), 180; *Genius and Courier*, I (November 26, 1825), 107.
23 *Ibid.*, pp. 108–109.
24 *Ibid.*, pp. 112–113.

frank avowal to perpetuate slavery. In commenting on Barbour's statement, Lundy remarked the truth which few had hitherto suspected "that the principles of liberty were rather losing than gaining strength in the slave region." [25] Most abolitionists, Lundy sometimes among them, fondly had imagined that the progress of reason would eventually cause the slaves' shackles to fall peacefully and with the consent of all. He now knew better. Lundy saw as quickly as anyone and far sooner than most that slavery would indeed end, and that if slaveholders did not voluntarily end it, it would be destroyed by force. An essay Lundy selected for inclusion in the *Genius* ascribed responsibility for the impending violence, which he had come to consider practically inevitable: "The spirit of inquiry is on the wing. Her tale will be told. The purifying will then be commenced. — Dream as you will, the shame of our country *shall not* 'continue.' The cry of judgment will be heard; and this work of purification will be begun: it may be by fire . . . and it will be the guilt of the south if it is." [26]

In the summer of 1826 the Maryland Anti-Slavery Society again nominated Raymond to run for the general assembly. He began his campaign at once by announcing his intention to propose a plan for gradual emancipation. "By the laws of God and nature," he said, "a child born in the United States is as much entitled to liberty, as one born in Africa." As though in defiance of Secretary of War Barbour's statement commanding silence on slavery, Raymond declared that "sacred as [the subject] may appear in the eyes of some," he intended to investigate and discuss it publicly.[27]

Raymond attempted to split the nonslaveholding voters in Baltimore from their tacit alliance with slaveholders and

[25] *Ibid.* (December 17, 1825), p. 121; (December 24, 1825), p. 129.
[26] *Ibid.* (December 17, 1825), p. 121.
[27] *Genius*, II n.s. (September 16, 1826), 1–2.

planters by demonstrating that the two groups shared no
common interest. Not one Baltimore voter in twenty owned
slaves, he pointed out. Urban mechanics and laborers could
have no economic interest in slavery. Most slaveowners themselves acknowledged their property to be a burden, Raymond
asserted. Why, then, should an ordinary voter cast his ballot
in support of slavery? [28]

All of Raymond's arguments may have been valid, yet they
were not very effective, for what he had not taken into account was the stubborn racial prejudice held by most men,
whether they owned slaves or not, and the fear among city
workers of economic competition with free Negroes. In his
effort to meet opposition stemming from such notions, Raymond compromised his antislavery principles by appearing
before a meeting of Baltimore mechanics to emphasize his
support for plans to colonize Negroes in Africa or Haiti. At
the same time he attempted to widen his popular appeal by
advocating the establishment of a public school system and
state sponsorship of internal improvements. These various
campaign arguments and issues proved only slightly effective.
This time Raymond received 974 votes out of the 13,312
cast.[29] Moreover, no further gains could be anticipated, for
the growing interest in national politics engendered by Andrew Jackson's rising popularity overshadowed the local slavery issue. Lundy noted that "the din of party strife" threatened to induce abolitionists to abandon their platform as no
longer having much appeal to voters caught up in the contest
between Jackson and Adams. Since three other candidates
favorable to Adams presented themselves for election in Baltimore in 1827, Raymond withdrew his candidacy in order not
to split the vote hopelessly.

---

[28] *Ibid.*
[29] *Ibid.*, p. 12; (September 30, 1826), p. 20; (October 7, 1826), p. 28.

Lundy, sanguine as usual, declared that Raymond's generosity in leaving the contest would "secure him many friends." Next year, Lundy predicted, Raymond would "receive the support of the administration party, generally, as well as that of the friends of emancipation." This did not happen. So overwhelming was the movement toward Jackson that Raymond chose not to run at all in 1828. The local slavery issue had become submerged in the presidential contest. Jackson's supporters included a few abolitionists, Lundy observed, "but the number of reflecting, substantial men among them is small. . . ." The Jacksonians triumphed in Maryland in 1828, with slavery being scarcely an issue in the campaign. Months before the election took place, the antislavery political movement in Baltimore had practically disappeared. Thus another of Lundy's antislavery projects, launched with great hopes and high enthusiasm, had collapsed from a fatal combination of opposition and apathy.[30]

Before Lundy had quite abandoned hope that an antislavery political party might yet succeed in Baltimore, he was given indisputable, personal evidence of the lengths to which opposition to antislavery efforts might go. While Lundy had been living in Ohio and east Tennessee, slavery and its incidents had rarely come under his direct observation. They remained for the most part horrid events that occurred in states and counties far from his home. But his move to Baltimore took him into the midst of the institution he was attempting to abolish. He now lived surrounded by slaves and slaveholders. Maryland slaveholders still profited grandly from selling their excess slaves to the emergent cotton kingdom, and as in earlier days Baltimore served as a principal emporium for the domestic slave trade, whose cruelties had first awakened Lundy

---

[30] *Ibid.*, VII (October 13, 1827), 118; [Earle], *Life*, pp. 216–217, 227.

to the iniquities of slavery.[31] In Baltimore Lundy could not have avoided daily confrontation with the institution in its varying manifestations. But it was the slave traffic that especially appalled him. The *Genius*, true to its editor's early principles, doggedly criticized the trade and all who engaged in it. Beginning with the first issue of the *Genius* published at Baltimore, members of the Woolfolk family, of whom at least six made their living from that business, had been the targets of Lundy's sharpest comments.[32] One anti-Woolfolk article, in particular, was to bring Lundy to grief.

In January 1826 when Austin Woolfolk, perhaps the dean of Maryland slave traders, was transporting twenty-nine slaves from Baltimore to Georgia on the *Decatur*, the slaves mutinied, threw the captain and mate overboard, and steered the ship toward Haiti, a haven, as Lundy had taught, for American Negroes. But another ship overtook the *Decatur* and conducted it to New York. There the slaves escaped — all except William Bowser, who was tried and convicted of mutiny and murder. According to the New York *Christian Inquirer*, Bowser made a farewell speech from the gallows, addressed particularly to Austin Woolfolk, who was said to be present. He forgave Woolfolk for having set in motion the train of events that had led to murder and his impending execution. Woolfolk, the newspaper reported, answered with angry profanity. In a few seconds the trap was sprung, and Bowser died, with Woolfolk's blasphemy the last words he heard on earth.[33]

Lundy reprinted the story and added his own comments on "the character of that monster in human shape, the Ishmaelite, Woolfolk," who was himself "the cause of the death of the

---

[31] Bancroft, *Slave-Trading*, pp. 37–43.
[32] *Ibid.*, pp. 31, 39–41.
[33] *Genius and Courier*, II (January 2, 1827), 109–110.

Captain and Mate of the Decatur, and also of the poor, unfortunate Bowser. . . ." Woolfolk, long resentful of Lundy's
frequent strictures against him and his relatives, hotly denied
that he had been present at Bowser's execution. It soon became evident that he was as outraged by Lundy's article and
comments as Lundy was by the slave trade itself.[34]

Late in the afternoon of January 9, 1827, after closing the
first form of the *Genius*, Lundy walked from his shop toward
the Baltimore post office. There on the street Austin Woolfolk accosted him with the charge of having libeled and insulted him with articles printed in the *Genius*. Lundy denied
that he had printed anything except the truth. After badger-
ing Lundy for a few moments and getting no response that
satisfied him, Woolfolk threw Lundy, a much smaller man,
to the pavement and beat him about the head until bystanders
eventually pulled him off. Lundy, severely injured, made his
way to a magistrate where he secured a writ charging Woolfolk
with assault. Upon the advice of a physician he then went
home and stayed in bed for two days and in his room for
nearly a week.[35]

On February 20 Woolfolk's trial was held without a jury
in Judge Nicholas Brice's court. Lundy engaged Daniel Raymond to aid the state's attorney; his only witness was his physician. Woolfolk pleaded guilty to assault as charged, but his
three lawyers presented in his defense the extreme provocation Lundy's articles had given. They read extracts from the
Genius in which Lundy had denounced the slave trade as
"barbarous, inhuman and unchristian" and called Woolfolk
a "soul seller" who was "equally guilty in the sight of God
with the man who was engaged in the African slave trade." [36]

---

[34] *Ibid.*, p. 110.
[35] *Ibid.*, pp. 118, 125.
[36] *Ibid.* (February 24, 1827), pp. 142–143.

Judge Brice found Lundy's rhetoric extremely distasteful. He could hardly acquit Woolfolk of the charges Lundy had brought, but in fining him only one dollar and costs, he observed that he "had never seen a case in which the provocation for a battery was greater . . . [and that] Lundy had received no more than a merited chastisement for his abuse of the traverser. . . ." Furthermore, said the judge, Lundy had been in error in condemning the domestic slave trade as an evil institution; on the contrary, it was economically beneficial to Maryland and otherwise useful because "it removed a great many rogues and vagabonds who were a nuisance in the state. . . ."[37]

With the encouragement of Judge Brice, Woolfolk then brought charges of libel against Lundy, although as it turned out the grand jury refused to return a true bill. Lundy interpreted the dismissal correctly as a great victory over those who sought "to muzzle the Press in this republican country, and in this age of free inquiry. . . ."[38] Nonetheless, his optimism remained limited. The entire incident had sharpened his understanding that antislavery victory would not come through the benevolence of time and the consent of slaveholders. Woolfolk's assault and the ordeals in the courtroom combined with other recent defeats to lead Lundy to attempt new approaches against slavery. He would accept Elizabeth Heyrick's counsel to assume less conciliatory modes of operation. The rising proslavery sentiment in the South persuaded him, too, of the wisdom of attempting to develop support in the free states, a region he had hitherto largely ignored. In particular, he hoped to enlist northern humanitarians in a new movement to flood Congress with antislavery petitions.

---

[37] *Ibid.* (March 31, 1827), p. 174.
[38] *Ibid.* (March 3, 1827), p. 150.

CHAPTER VIII

An Appeal to the North

Antislavery groups had long followed the practice of petitioning state legislatures and Congress to act against slavery. Sometimes they simply addressed memorials to their lawmakers deploring its existence. More often they asked for such specific measures as laws against the foreign slave trade, the domestic slave trade, and against slavery itself. As a participant in nearly all phases of the antislavery movement Lundy had taken a conspicuous part in earlier petition campaigns, helping to promote them on many occasions since 1816 when his Union Humane Society had endorsed the wisdom of applying pressure on lawmakers. But before 1827 most such efforts had been rather desultory and not very well organized. Relatively little had been attempted by that means at the national level since the abolition of the foreign slave trade; in fact, probably antislavery groups had sent more memorials to some of the state legislatures than to Congress, for the good reason that Congress itself had discouraged antislavery petitions when it early placed strict limits on the results petitioners might expect from their efforts. During its first session

Congress had declared that it exercised no jurisdiction over slavery within the states.[1]

Although its area of potential antislavery action was thus sharply limited, congressional authority over the territories and the District of Columbia presumably still reigned supreme. The inciting problem of slavery in the territories, which had had its first terrifying hour in 1820, for the moment lay quiescent. Slavery in the District of Columbia, on the other hand, remained a constantly live issue, daily assaulting the consciences of eastern humanitarians. Its existence in the district implied national support for an institution which some Americans had come to deplore and which most southerners insisted belonged solely to local jurisdiction. There national authority preserved, regulated, and perpetuated it. Accordingly, waves of protesting petitions had reached Congress from those to whom this situation constituted a moral reproach. As antislavery sentiment grew bolder and antislavery groups less confident of achieving success within the South, their petitions became more numerous and more insistent.

Early in January 1827, a few days before Lundy fell to the Baltimore pavement under Woolfolk's assault, he drafted, with the aid of his lawyer, Daniel Raymond, a new memorial to Congress asking for gradual abolition in the District of Columbia. Neither the memorial itself nor its request was novel, yet a discerning reader might easily have detected new elements in its rhetoric. Its highly condemnatory tone and note of urgency had rarely appeared in such documents before. Furthermore, although Lundy and Raymond sought con-

---

[1] *Annals of Congress*, 1 Cong., 2 Sess., pp. 1473–74; *Genius*, I (October, 1821), 57; II (February, 1823), 114; Alice Dana Adams, *The Neglected Period of Anti-Slavery in America, 1808–1831* (Boston, 1908), pp. 48–50, 87, 185–191.

gressional action only against slavery in the district, their memorial presented a comprehensive indictment of slavery everywhere. Slavery, they charged, warred with the fundamental republican principles of the United States, promoted idleness and encouraged vice, conflicted with Christianity, and otherwise weakened the nation.[2]

During the first week of January Lundy published the memorial in both the *Genius* and the Baltimore *American*. The resulting uproar in Baltimore was considerable — it may even have contributed to Woolfolk's attack on Lundy.[3] Slaveholders and slave traders understandably resented the sentiments expressed in the document, but even some men who enjoyed an antislavery reputation likewise took alarm. Colonizationists in particular, many of whom claimed to favor the eventual ending of slavery, worried that the Lundy-Raymond attack on slavery would be taken as representing colonizationist views and thus cost them support in the South. Undiscriminating readers might suppose that all antislavery people concurred with Lundy, whereas in fact, as colonizationists well knew, distinct lines had already been drawn between proponents of African colonization and the abolitionists. Colonizationists hastened to exploit that fact. They let the citizens of Baltimore know that they did not share Lundy's and Raymond's extreme antislavery views and their call for congressional action.[4]

The American Colonization Society's agent in Baltimore, who declared the memorial "one of the most indiscreet productions of this memorializing era," saw in its publication a

---

[2] *Genius*, VI (January, 1827), 103, 133; Providence (R.I.) *Investigator*, June 5, 1828.

[3] Baltimore *American*, January 5, 1827; Baltimore *Gazette*, January 4, 1827.

[4] Baltimore *American*, January 9, 1827.

chance to bring abolitionists into further disrepute. He promised to "take particular care to saddle it upon the right horse,
that is, the abolitionists. . . ." [5] In the face of such opposition
Lundy's friends circulated the memorial throughout Baltimore and the District of Columbia. Colonizationists must
have been disappointed to learn that a considerable number
of signatures (some said more than a thousand) were collected.[6]

A month later while Woolfolk was being tried for assaulting Lundy, Representative John Barney, a Maryland Federalist, presented the well-signed memorial in Congress. South
Carolina's George McDuffie, ever a faithful watchdog against
congressional encroachment on "southern rights," led the
opposition to printing it. He was effectively supported by another of Maryland's representatives, Clement Dorsey, who
called his colleagues' attention to the only partially concealed
danger that he had perceived in the document. "It breathed
the spirit of general emancipation," he charged, "and though
its request began within this district, its ulterior purpose went
much further." Such peril, once recognized, sufficed to marshal the opposition. Lundy soon received word that the House
"by a large majority" had tabled his memorial after voting
not to print it.[7]

That repulse hardly ended the matter. Rejection simply
stimulated abolitionists to still greater and more persistent
efforts. At its autumn meeting in Philadelphia in 1827 the
American Convention, acting with unaccustomed vigor, decided to support the petition movement. It appointed Lundy
chairman of a committee to circularize every antislavery so-

---

[5] C. C. Harper to R. R. Gurley, January [5], 1827, American Colonization Society Papers.
[6] Worcester (Mass.) *Yeoman*, August 23, 1828.
[7] *Register of Debates*, 19 Cong., 2 Sess., III, 1099–1101.

ciety in the country with a plea to petition Congress for abolition in the District of Columbia.[8]

At the same time, Representative Charles Miner, a Federalist newspaper editor from West Chester, Pennsylvania, announced his intention to work in Congress for abolition in the district. He, too, called for popular support in the form of petitions addressed to Congress. Pleased at having found a resolute friend in the House, Lundy resolved to contribute all that he could to Miner's efforts.[9] He printed appeals in the *Genius* for petitions and sent letters to antislavery groups throughout the country as the American Convention had authorized him to do. "Let petitions and memorials flow into the Hall of Congress, from all quarters," he urged; "load their tables with them, Teaze the members with importunities, until they are *provoked* to deeds of justice." [10]

Not all antislavery societies approved the project. Some Philadelphia Quakers, shrinking from controversy, warned that it was a "question whether it would now be politic" to follow Lundy's urgings. Lundy himself had expressed similar doubts in 1824, when the South seethed from the Ohio legislature's antislavery resolutions. Then he had refrained for a time from sending Congress additional memorials on the ground that they might further irritate an inflamed South. Now his mood had changed. Frustration produced by continued failure to win support from slaveholders had combined with Mrs. Heyrick's message of dynamic resolution to alter permanently his strategy of conciliation. He had learned to live on intimate terms with hostility, to accept it, and to make few compromises with it. To his cautious Philadelphia

[8] *Genius*, VIII (January 5, 1828), 12.
[9] Lundy to Isaac Barton, January 30, 1828, Pennsylvania Abolition Society Manuscript Collection, vol. X.
[10] *Genius*, VIII (January 26, 1828), 22; (February 2, 1828), p. 31.

friends he addressed an impatient note: "When will it be politic?" he chided — slaveholders would always raise a commotion over any antislavery proposal whatever. "Away with this popular-calculating policy! Let us go to work — *strip to it* — and *hold on*, whatever our antagonists may say or do. If there be much excitement among them, regulate your conduct according to the dictates of wisdom — but never cease from laboring to effect your object. *Never abandon an inch of ground, after it has been taken.*" At the same time he asserted in the *Genius* expressions of the same highly doctrinaire spirit that had informed Mrs. Heyrick's essay. "Ours is the cause of Justice," he wrote; "it is the Cause of Heaven. — No earthly consideration should interfere with it." [11]

Lundy's resolution to back Miner's project led him in the first months of 1828 to make plans to travel through the northeastern states, a section he had not yet visited. There in a region he thought largely untouched by antislavery activity, he would seek to arouse support for the petition campaign. Of course, New York and New England by 1828 were not quite so void of antislavery sentiment as Lundy supposed.[12] Even while Lundy prepared to invade the Northeast, Eliphalet Gillett, a colonization agent writing from Maine, observed that a revolution in attitude toward slavery had recently taken place among settlers on that northern frontier. They had awakened at last, Gillett said, to a problem they once had hardly known existed. "Five years ago if you had spoken to them of relief to a Virginia Negro, they would have been as much surprised as if you had called upon them to aid 'the man in the moon.'" Throughout New England the venerable tradition of benevolent activity waited only for leadership to

---

[11] Lundy to Isaac Barton, January 30, 1828, Pennsylvania Abolition Society Manuscript Collection, vol. X; *Genius*, VIII (January 26, 1828), 22.
[12] Adams, *Neglected Period*, pp. 62–64, 84, 87.

direct it into antislavery channels. Amos A. Phelps, then a
student at Andover Theological Seminary but destined to win
fame as an antislavery lecturer, believed "the want of feeling
generally in most of our northern states on this subject is
owing entirely to want of information." Samuel J. May likewise attributed the indifference of northerners solely to ignorance. "They hardly seem to know there is such a thing as
Slavery in the land," he wrote. "Because we see no Slaves, we
can hardly realize that there are any." But as Gillett observed,
wherever the American Colonization Society's agents had
worked, they had proved an effective educative force against
slavery. Now Lundy planned to journey to New England to
build on the foundations laid by a decade of colonizationist
activity.[13]

His immediate goal was to organize a petition campaign
among New Englanders, but he intended also to found antislavery societies in the Northeast much as he had encouraged
them in the upper South.[14] He hoped, too, to find new subscribers for the *Genius.* His financial state had declined from
one low point to another until now he faced bankruptcy. On
July 4, 1825, under the sponsorship of the National Anti-
Slavery Tract Society, he had begun to issue a weekly newspaper, the *Genius of Universal Emancipation and Baltimore
Courier,* as a means of reaching the large Baltimore reading
public. But the venture had gone badly. Six months later
the weekly had only 340 subscribers and the monthly only
700. Since the small subscription receipts did not allow him
to hire assistants, he was forced to conduct the business sin-

---

[13] Eliphalet Gillett to R. R. Gurley, January 5, 1828, Amos A. Phelps to
Gurley, January 15, 1828, and Samuel J. May to James Dunn, July 5,
1828, American Colonization Society Papers.
[14] Worcester *Yeoman,* August 23, 1828; Providence *Investigator,* June 5,
1828.

gle-handedly. The lamp in his office burned far into the night while he wrote, set type, and performed all the other labor involved in producing and distributing two newspapers. A loan of fifty dollars from the Pennsylvania Abolition Society in January 1826, together with the society's timely order for twenty-five dollars worth of subscriptions momentarily bolstered Lundy's fortunes, but before the month ended, he decided there was no recourse but to suspend publication of the monthly *Genius*. Even that expedient did not solve the problem. Although by October 1827 subscriptions to the weekly had climbed to nearly 1,000, this still hardly sufficed to meet expenses. New patrons must be found if the *Genius* were to survive.[15]

Thus it was with many expectations that Lundy set out for the North in March 1828, leaving his newspaper in the care of William Swaim, a bookish youth he had met on his earlier travels in North Carolina. After stopping in Philadelphia to deliver a speech to Quakers interested in the free-produce movement, he proceeded to New York, where he hopefully called at the home of Arthur Tappan, the wealthy merchant-philanthropist. Although Tappan would soon rank as one of the most generous patrons of abolitionism, at that time he was not yet prepared to commit himself to the antislavery cause, and Lundy received nothing more tangible from his visit than encouragement and sympathy.[16]

At Providence, Rhode Island, he conferred with William Goodell, already a reformer of some fame, who edited the *Investigator and General Intelligencer*. The meeting brought

---

15 Lundy to Isaac Barton, January 10, 23, 1826, and Barton to Lundy, July 26, 1826, Pennsylvania Abolition Society Manuscript Collection, vol. IX; *Genius*, VII (October 13, 1827), 119.

16 [Earle], *Life*, p. 25; Garrison and Garrison, *William Lloyd Garrison*, I, 91.

a sympathetic response from Goodell, but Lundy was less fortunate in his other encounters in Providence. At the Steam Boat Hotel he met Sylvester S. Southworth, editor of the Providence *Literary Cadet*, who took a great dislike to the visitor and managed to communicate it to the public through the columns of his newspaper. According to Southworth's appraisal, Lundy was "a visionary" and "a zealot," working for a quixotic cause. Furthermore, he was self-seeking, "fond of fame," and "intellectually incapable" of the work he had undertaken.[17]

These strictures against Lundy's personality, character, and capacity may in part have been warranted. The first impression he gave to strangers and at public meetings was not particularly favorable. Below medium height, of slender frame, and diffident in manner, his was never a commanding presence.[18] Those who judged him solely by his unprepossessing appearance were thus tempted to dismiss him as a person of slight ability. That some justifiably considered him vain can hardly be doubted either. Like many another man of small physique Lundy was constantly beset by the often merited suspicion that others estimated his worth much below the esteem in which he held himself. When he imagined himself slighted in such fashion, he sometimes assumed an arrogance of manner that others inevitably found offensive.

It is likely, too, that as Southworth charged Lundy was "intellectually incapable" of the work that had brought him to New England. There is no reason to suppose that Lundy's mind was of the first rank, and certainly he possessed no special training to qualify him for his mission. His vision of human freedom always exceeded his capacity for

---

[17] Providence *Investigator*, March 13, April 1, August 21, 1828.
[18] *Liberator*, September 20, 1839.

achieving it. Yet, one finally asks, who in America *was* intellectually capable of developing plans that would succeed in abolishing slavery? If such a paragon existed, he failed to make himself known at any time before the Civil War. Lundy never claimed to be more than he was — a Quaker of humble origins and limited endowment, dedicated to expending all his energies and talents, however limited they might be, to the ending of slavery in America.

Southworth's criticism extended with still more damaging effect from an examination of Lundy's personal attributes to a questioning of his motives. Lundy had come to New England, Southworth charged, as a secret agent for certain unspecified politicians who schemed against southern interests; in fulfilling his designs, he planned to destroy the benevolently conservative American Colonization Society; furthermore, his goals were partly selfish, for he intended to raise money not to free slaves but to prosecute his recent assailant, Austin Woolfolk.

Lundy defended himself against Southworth's allegations as best he could, taking special pains to deny that he had any design against the American Colonization Society. At the same time, however, he carefully indicated the limited value he assigned that organization. Colonization, Lundy said, should be thought of only as a "powerful auxiliary" to more important emancipation programs. His estimate of the society's worth — never very high — had been further lessened by Southworth's charges, for they seemed to support the conclusion that colonizationists had broken fellowship with those whose programs focused on the ending of slavery rather than merely the transportation of Negroes.[19]

The hostile reception Southworth had given Lundy led

---

[19] *Genius*, VIII (June 7, 1828), 125; Providence *Investigator*, June 12, 1828.

him to postpone for a time any plan to hold meetings or to try to win adherents in Rhode Island. Still smarting from the unpleasantries at Providence, he proceeded to Boston, the religious center of the entire Northeast and thus for his purposes the most important city on his itinerary. There he hoped to enlist the aid of the clergy. As part of his strategy he took lodging at a boardinghouse on Milk Street run by the Reverend William Collier, a Baptist preacher and founder of the *National Philanthropist*, a journal dedicated to temperance and universal reform. Among Collier's other lodgers was William Lloyd Garrison, a twenty-two-year-old journalist who had arrived in Boston a year and a half earlier from Newburyport, Massachusetts, and who now edited the *National Philanthropist* for its new owner, Nathaniel White. Lundy imagined that at Collier's boardinghouse he would be close to men whose access to the inner circles of Boston reform would assure the prosperity of his own efforts. He soon discovered his error.

At a meeting of eight clergymen convened at Collier's home, Lundy presented his plans and asked for clerical support. There he found that association with Collier and Garrison had added little to his own limited influence. The clergy listened to his proposals skeptically and with disappointing response. All of the eight readily endorsed the *Genius* as a respectable and useful reform journal worthy of the patronage of church members, but there they stopped. They refused to commit themselves to support any specific plan of action against slavery. In particular they refused either to give public endorsement to the petition campaign or to follow Lundy's suggestion that they form an antislavery society.[20]

---

[20] [Earle], *Life*, p. 25; *Liberator*, September 20, 1838; *National Philanthropist* (Boston), March 21, 1828; Garrison and Garrison, *William Lloyd Garrison*, I, 93–94.

Regard for their own public position and a shrinking from controversy restrained them from acting. It was one thing for clergymen to assure Lundy in the privacy of Collier's parlor that they considered him a respectable reformer; it would be quite another for them to stand openly in favor of his cause and thereby risk the consequence of precipitating controversy and the loss of public esteem. Some who attended may have been inhibited by disinterested and more profound considerations. The Unitarian William Ellery Channing, for example, worried that the antislavery agitation Lundy proposed to extend to New England would lead to sectional discord, secession, and civil war.[21] Only from William Lloyd Garrison — intense, eager to commit himself to a cause, and lacking the responsibility of a congregation — did Lundy secure unqualified support.

Little informed about slavery before he moved to Boston, Garrison had undergone a rapid education in antislavery reform. This had been accomplished largely through the agency of the *Genius*, which regularly appeared as an exchange in his own newspaper office. Garrison admired the single-minded zeal of the *Genius* and had looked forward to meeting its editor. He later recalled the disappointment he experienced when Lundy appeared at Collier's boardinghouse. Imagining from his vigorous writings that Lundy must be a Hercules, Garrison found him in appearance more "like the apostle Paul . . . 'weak and contemptible.'" Although Lundy may have seemed to Garrison an unimpressive figure, his ideas admittedly were of a different order. Garrison was captivated by the older man's dedication and the clarity with which he communicated his moral vision.[22] Garrison sought a cause;

[21] William Ellery Channing to Daniel Webster, May 14, 1828, in *Works of Daniel Webster* (Boston, 1872), V, 366–367.
[22] Garrison and Garrison, *William Lloyd Garrison*, I, 92–93; *Proceed-*

Lundy had found one. The two held long and earnest conversations, with Garrison attempting to fathom the mind of a man who, though obviously poverty-stricken and plagued by ill fortune, persisted in his course. "I would not exchange circumstances with any person on earth, if I must thereby relinquish the cause in which I am enlisted," Lundy told him.[23] Such commitment could only bring admiration from Garrison. The two ran together like drops of water. Lundy's meeting with Garrison constituted one of the few encouraging incidents of his New England tour.

In his own newspaper Garrison printed a two-and-a-half–column essay praising Lundy and terming the *Genius* "the bravest and best attempt in the history of newspaper publications." Lundy had discovered a disciple. He had helped turn Garrison toward slavery as a crusading interest; the anti-slavery movement would never be quite the same again.

Lundy now hurried back to Baltimore to check on his troubled business affairs, but on the first of May he set out once again for the Northeast to complete his unfinished work. His second trip was in several respects a *tour de force*, marked as it was by long walks between towns (one day he traveled forty-five miles on foot) and a series of some forty-three public addresses delivered in nearly as many cities.[24]

Almost as soon as he left Baltimore, he began to hold anti-slavery meetings. Often his audience consisted of Quakers, and his forum was a Friends' meetinghouse, but whenever possible he spoke under other auspices. His was not a sec-

ings of the American Anti-Slavery Society at Its Third Decade Held in the City of Philadelphia, December 3rd and 4th, 1863 (New York, 1864), p. 120.
[23] Garrison and Garrison, *William Lloyd Garrison*, I, 93.
[24] [Earle], *Life*, p. 28.

tarian cause, and though he could invariably obtain a hearing from Quakers, he would have considered his efforts nearly wasted had his message reached only that group. Methodists, Baptists, Presbyterians, Congregationalists, and Unitarians —all supplied him with meeting places and audiences. In each community that he visited he tried to arrange interviews with men noted for their interest in reform or for their influence on public opinion. Thus he conferred with the great Congregational divine Lyman Beecher, and at Brooklyn, Connecticut, he lodged at the home of George Benson, a veteran antislavery advocate whose daughter Helen would soon marry Garrison. At New Haven he addressed a meeting of philanthropists, including members of the Connecticut legislature, convened to make plans to further Negro education.[25]

On June 23 he arrived in Providence once more and proceeded directly to William Goodell's newspaper office. Goodell, moving ever closer to abolitionist commitment, was eager to help Lundy conduct an antislavery campaign in the city. They hoped that by that time the memory of Lundy's sharp exchange with Southworth would have disappeared. Goodell introduced Lundy to some of the city's leading men, who he thought would be interested in his plans. But Goodell had miscalculated. Since the businessmen of Providence were for the most part engaged in the cotton trade or manufacture and otherwise maintained close economic ties with the South, Lundy got nowhere with them. Even the Providence churches refused him use of their lecture halls. Of the city's important

---

[25] *Ibid.*, pp. 26–28; Garrison and Garrison, *William Lloyd Garrison*, I, 425; Samuel J. May, *Some Recollections of Our Anti-Slavery Conflict* (Boston, 1869), pp. 11–12; [Lewis Tappan], *The Life of Arthur Tappan* (New York, 1870), p. 147; Barnes, *Antislavery Impulse*, pp. 41–42, 216.

citizens other than Goodell only Moses Brown, the elderly
Quaker philanthropist, encouraged Lundy's efforts.[26]

Lundy met with a warmer reception in other parts of New
England. After holding meetings with the Friends at Nan-
tucket, he sailed to Portland, Maine, where the Presbyterians
gave him an audience. At Portsmouth, New Hampshire, he
spoke in the Baptist Church of the Reverend Baron Stow,
recently arrived from a pastorate in the District of Columbia
and soon to become an abolitionist. At Andover he convened
a group of college students; at Salem, he spoke in the Congregational Church, and at Lynn to the Unitarians and, sep-
arately, to the Methodists.

On August 1 he began making arrangements to carry his
campaign back to Boston. Although he suspected that Boston
philanthropists were absorbed with "too many other meetings"
for his own to receive the special attention he considered its
due, he went doggedly ahead with his plans. This time he did
not rely solely on Garrison and Collier to provide him entrée
to Boston philanthropy. Instead, the Reverend Howard Malcom, the nationally known pastor of the Federal Street Baptist
Church, helped him get in touch with prospective supporters
and provided him free use of his church's lecture room.[27]

On August 7 the meeting was held with Malcom acting as
chairman. To the assembled citizens and church leaders
Lundy described the antislavery work already accomplished
in the West and the upper South. New England, he sug-

---

[26] Lundy to William Goodell, June 18, 1828, Oberlin Autograph Collection (Oberlin College Library, Oberlin, Ohio); Rinaldo R. Williams,
"Benjamin Lundy, Pioneer, Hero, and Martyr" (typescript, Illinois State
Historical Society). This was published in Chicago *Inter-Ocean*, March 7
and 14, 1897.

[27] [Earle], *Life*, p. 27; on Malcom, see *Dictionary of American Biography* (New York, 1928–58), XII, 220.

gested, lagged in support of a vital reform activity. Although many prominent Bostonians contributed to the American Colonization Society, Lundy minimized its worth. In an effort to appeal to New England moral values, he subtly denigrated the goal and mode of operation of colonizationists, whose success depended solely upon money. The antislavery societies he had helped to found, he said, had started "a moral agitation which should never rest until the shackles of the oppressed were broken 'by the will, not by the wealth, of the people.'" Lundy specifically pointed out the folly of supposing that colonization could ever abolish slavery. In the rest of his speech he described in harrowing detail the domestic slave trade as one of the more reprehensible aspects of the slave system.

When Lundy had finished his address, the Reverend Mr. Malcom arose to make some remarks of his own. As his speech indicated, he viewed the universe as benevolent and history as benign. In commenting on Lundy's criticism of the slave trade, Malcom observed that "God often overrules events in themselves evil, for the promotion of ultimate good." The sale of slaves to the lower South, he said, might make Kentucky, Virginia, and Maryland ultimately free. Slavery, he speculated, might eventually die a natural death. Malcom did not oppose Lundy or his program, but he did suggest that no action was needed, particularly on the part of men living far from the South. God in his own good time would solve the problem without the aid of Lundy or his newspaper or of antislavery societies. Having grown accustomed to both inertia and opposition, Lundy took Malcom's rebuff calmly, but Garrison was furious. As was his habit, he read malice into even moderate criticism of abolitionist tactics. He prepared an agitated letter for the Boston *Courier* in which he denounced Malcom as a slavite and proposed stepped-up anti-slavery activity to counteract such opposition.[28]

The unfortunate incident failed to inhibit Lundy's determination to carry out his plans. Four days later he held a second meeting at which a committee of twenty, including Garrison, was formed to organize an antislavery society in Boston and to circulate antislavery petitions in every town in Massachusetts. The committee was stillborn, however, for only one petition — and no antislavery society — resulted.[29]

After these not very successful efforts in Boston Lundy set out for a trip across New York, speaking in Albany, Utica, Lockport, Buffalo, and other cities along the way. At Albany he held a meeting for free Negroes in the First African Baptist Church of the Reverend Nathaniel Paul, a dynamic proponent of racial justice. At Lockport he met Lyman Spalding, a well-to-do Quaker merchant who would later provide him with valuable financial aid. Arriving back at Poughkeepsie in the middle of October, he held the forty-third — and last — meeting of his tour. On October 25 he returned to Baltimore.[30]

From one point of view the trip to the Northeast had been a failure. Lundy had not succeeded in finding enough new subscribers to the *Genius* to assure its continued publication. No antislavery societies resulted directly from his efforts, and the small number of petitions sent from New England failed to influence Congress to abolish slavery in the District of Columbia. Representative Miner did move that the House commit-

---

[28] [Earle], *Life*, p. 27; Garrison and Garrison, *William Lloyd Garrison*, I, 97–98. Malcom's version of the affair, which I have generally followed, is in Howard Malcom to William Lloyd Garrison, August 25, 1835, in *Liberator*, August 29, 1835.

[29] *Genius*, IX (September 13, 1828), 14; Garrison and Garrison, *William Lloyd Garrison*, I, 98.

[30] [Earle], *Life*, p. 28.

tee for the district be instructed to investigate the condition of slaves in the district, report any needed legislation, and state whether or not gradual abolition would be expedient. The House authorized the committee to make such an investigation, but no constructive report or recommendation ever resulted from its work.[31]

In other respects, however, Lundy's tour succeeded beyond his expectations. He had managed to carry his antislavery message into parts of the Northeast where it had been little heard before. He had talked with many men who already saw slavery as a grievous national problem and communicated to them some of his own views on the necessity for action against it.[32] The number of persons thus induced to support or at least to investigate the antislavery movement cannot, of course, be known, though it must have been considerable. But whatever Lundy's influence on New England in general it is certain that at Boston he helped make an abolitionist out of William Lloyd Garrison.[33]

Before Lundy had concluded his tour, Garrison had been invited to establish a newspaper in Bennington, Vermont. The first issue of his *Journal of the Times* appeared on October 2, 1828, to advocate, as he said, temperance, emancipation, and peace. So much attention did he give to slavery that the American Convention endorsed the new venture as a welcome addition to the short list of antislavery journals and agreed to purchase five subscriptions.[34] During the next months both Garrison and Lundy wrote admiring editorials

---

[31] *Register of Debates*, 20 Cong., 2 Sess., V, 175–187, 192.
[32] May, *Some Recollections*, p. 12; see the endorsement of Lundy's program in *New England Inquirer* (Amherst, Mass.), October 2, 1828.
[33] Garrison credited Lundy with awakening him to "the holy cause of emancipation." *Liberator*, December 1, 1832.
[34] Adams, *Neglected Period*, p. 161.

about the other's work and exchanged appreciative letters. Lundy told Garrison of his hope that "I shall not only find a valuable coadjuter in the person of my friend Garrison, but that the *'ice is broken'* in the hitherto frozen — no, no, not frozen — COOL regions of the North!" Garrison, for his part, assured Lundy that "our zeal in the cause of emancipation suffers no diminution. Before God and our country, we give our pledge that the liberation of the enslaved Africans shall always be uppermost in our pursuits. The people of New England are interested in this matter, and they must be aroused from their lethargy as by a trumpet call." [35] As it happened, however, Garrison's trumpet would first be heard not in New England but at Baltimore in partnership with Benjamin Lundy.

---

[35] Garrison and Garrison, *William Lloyd Garrison*, I, 99, 118–119.

CHAPTER IX

New Associates and New Approaches

While Garrison conducted his newspaper with indifferent success in Vermont, Lundy returned to Baltimore to confront new difficulties. He found first of all that he must cope with an immediate change in working arrangements. The freedom from editorial duties that had allowed him to make two prolonged business trips was about to end, for William Swaim, his assistant who had conducted the *Genius* throughout the summer, had decided to leave Baltimore to establish his own newspaper at Greensboro, North Carolina.[1] Again Lundy would be left to edit the *Genius* unaided. It was a troublesome prospect. He could not possibly carry on that confining work and at the same time travel in the interest of the antislavery movement as he now believed he was obliged to do.

Of far more serious concern were his deepening financial troubles. Southerners who had once supported the *Genius* now declined to do so, while northerners awoke but slowly

---

[1] Swaim announced in the first issue of the Greensborough (N.C.) *Patriot*, May 23, 1829, that his purpose was "to break the spell which has so long palsied the energies of the Southern States. . . ."

to Lundy's call for aid. So many subscribers lagged in making payments that he could not continue to meet the expenses of publication. On November 22, 1828, he issued the *Genius* on a half-sheet to save money. Still more drastic retrenchment was forced upon him when his creditors took most of his printing equipment, leaving him without the means of producing the newspaper in his own shop. Finally he was forced to announce that with the approval of the board of managers of the National Anti-Slavery Tract Society, which had undertaken to sponsor the *Genius*, he had decided to suspend publication for "10 or 12 weeks." He had no intention, however, of permanently abandoning the only newspaper in America exclusively devoted to abolition. "Types are potent implements of modern political and moral warfare," wrote Lundy. "Castles fall before them — cannons are silenced." [2]

Though unemployed and deprived of the newspaper which had absorbed his energies for so long a time, Lundy did not relax his antislavery efforts. Instead, he made plans to use his enforced leisure to learn more about slavery in the hope that greater knowledge would help him wage a more effective campaign against it. Theories about slavery existed in plenty; abundant facts about the institution in Maryland, Virginia, and other border states had long been available, but Lundy, at least, knew nothing from his own observation about slavery in the new cotton kingdom. Thus he proposed to make a grand tour of the South. Traveling in disguise and protected by an assumed name, he would walk across the South from the Carolinas and Georgia to Louisiana. His objects would be (1) to gather information about slavery *"as it now exists*

---

[2] Lundy to Isaac Barton, January 21, 1829, Pennsylvania Abolition Society Manuscript Collection, vol. X; for a contemporary account of the decline of antislavery sentiment in the South, see *Genius*, X (February 5, 1830), 170.

in the Southern States," (2) to study the internal slave trade
in the deep South, (3) "to ascertain positively" whether
slaves were still being introduced from Cuba in defiance of
the law, and (4) to "procure all the information that may be
procurable, relative to the production of Southern staples by
free labor." Friends in Wilmington, Delaware, sent him twenty dollars, and the Pennsylvania Abolition Society appropriated forty dollars to aid his project. He expected to stop
and work for additional money on the way.[3]

No abolitionist before him and none afterward ever proposed such an undertaking, unless Theodore Weld's research
which resulted in his *American Slavery as It Is, the Testimony
of a Thousand Witnesses* (New York, 1839) be regarded as a
similar enterprise. But the trip was never made. Before Lundy
had set out on the journey, Joseph Leonard Smith, a Maryland slaveowner, offered to free twelve of his slaves on condition that Lundy escort them to Haiti. Lundy agreed to Smith's
proposal as a duty and also as an opportunity to investigate
the condition of the American Negroes who had moved to the
island in earlier years. In Haiti he succeeded in making satisfactory arrangements for the twelve and at the same time induced certain Haitian landlords to reform the sharecrop system, which had proved a continuing burden to many of the
earlier emigrants.[4] All this doubtless constituted an important
service to Haitian Negroes, but it scarcely substituted for the
contribution the southern tour might have made in acquainting Lundy — and thereby many others — with the realities
of slavery. However, the choice was characteristic of Lundy.
The certain freeing of twelve slaves in the present seemed to
him more important than carrying out a project which might

---

[3] Lundy to Thomas Ridgeway, January 31, 1829, Pennsylvania Abolition
Society Manuscript Collection, vol. X.
[4] Lundy to Thomas Ridgeway, June 27, 1829, *ibid.*; [Earle], *Life*, p. 29;
Genius, X (September 2, 1829), 1–2.

contribute in an unspecified manner to the prospect of freeing all of them in some indefinite future.

By the time Lundy returned from Haiti in the middle of June 1829, he considered it too late to begin the southern tour, and suggested vaguely that he might make the trip "next summer."[5] Instead of traveling through the South, he prepared to resume publication of the *Genius*, this time with the aid of two competent associates.

Elizabeth Margaret Chandler, a young Quaker recluse, had agreed to supervise the women's section of the *Genius* from the seclusion of her Philadelphia home. Scrupulously reared by her Quaker grandmother and educated in Friends' schools, Miss Chandler had early developed remarkable sensitivity to the cruelties and injustices of the world. She could become incensed at evils as diverse as war, cruelty toward the southern Indians, discrimination against women, and mistreatment of the deaf and dumb. Like many other reformers, however, she finally decided that slavery was the source of most of the evils that afflicted American society and thus the most deserving target of her pen. When one of her antislavery compositions won third prize in a literary contest, she came to the attention of Lundy, who encouraged her to write more works in the same vein. Beginning in 1826, her antislavery essays and poems, many of them celebrating the virtues of free produce, appeared regularly in the *Genius*. After many importunities from Lundy she finally consented to edit the *Genius'* "Ladies Repository" on condition that she remain anonymous and her name never appear in print.[6]

Lundy's other new associate was less shy of publicity. Dur-

---

[5] Lundy to Thomas Ridgeway, June 27, 1829, Pennsylvania Abolition Society Manuscript Collection, vol. X.

[6] Merton L. Dillon, "Elizabeth Chandler and the Spread of Antislavery Sentiment to Michigan," *Michigan History*, XXXIX (December, 1955), 481–494.

ing the winter of 1828–29 he had negotiated with William
Lloyd Garrison, urging him to come to Baltimore and join in
editing the *Genius*. Garrison's decision to accept the invitation gave Lundy renewed hope for the future of his newspaper. In January 1829 while the *Genius* remained suspended,
Lundy reported to the Philadelphia abolitionists, who had
suspected that his editorial career was coming to an end, his
expectation "next summer, to have a very suitable partner
. . . [and to] improve the paper, both in matter and manner
of mechanical execution." [7]

Garrison for his part was no less optimistic. On March 27,
1829, when his contract with the proprietors of the *Journal
of the Times* expired, he described in a valedictory to the
people of Bennington his plans for the future and his hopes
for himself. "I trust in God that I may be the humble instrument of breaking at least one chain, and restoring one captive
to liberty," he wrote; "it will repay a life of severe toil." [8]

Garrison then prepared to set out for Baltimore, but with
the *Genius* suspended and Lundy absent on his mission to
Haiti, the young editor decided instead to stop in Boston,
find temporary work, and wait for Lundy to report that his
services were needed. Thus during the spring and early summer of 1829 he assisted William Goodell, Lundy's friend who
had recently moved from Providence, in editing the *National
Philanthropist* at Boston. It was an important season in their
lives. Both Garrison and Goodell had started their editorial
careers as comprehensive reformers, interested in a variety of
causes. But during the preceding months, partly because of
Lundy's influence, each had begun to focus his attention on
slavery. Now together in Boston they sharpened each other's

---

[7] Lundy to Isaac Barton, January 21, 1829, Pennsylvania Abolition Society Manuscript Collection, vol. X.

[8] *Journal of the Times* (Bennington, Vt.), March 27, 1829.

perception of the threat the continuance of slavery posed to the nation. Both concluded that antislavery advocates should renounce all temporizing measures in regard to slavery and urge immediate emancipation. Goodell shortly would become a leader of abolition in New York; Garrison to most of his generation would become the very personification of the antislavery movement.[9]

In the middle of the summer Lundy sent word to Garrison that he was ready for him to come to Baltimore and help prepare for the resumption of the *Genius*. The young New Englander found the atmosphere in Baltimore conducive to concentrating his attention on slavery to the exclusion of everything else. The partners moved into a boardinghouse kept by two Quaker sisters and patronized chiefly by antislavery Friends. Among their other close associates were some of the leaders of Baltimore's free Negro community, especially William Watkins, Jacob Greener and his sons — all outspoken opponents of the American Colonization Society — and Hezekiah Grice, who would shortly help found the Negro convention movement. Such men were hostile to all schemes which implied Negro inferiority or required their expulsion from the United States, and they opposed slavery with a fervor few residents of New England could experience. Both Garrison and Lundy caught some of the contagion of their spirit. Garrison in particular adopted their attitudes toward slavery and colonization.[10]

On September 2, 1829, the first issue of the new and enlarged *Genius*, now a weekly, appeared. The subscription rate had been raised to three dollars, the typework was improved,

---

[9] Garrison and Garrison, *William Lloyd Garrison*, I, 124, 140; Goodell, *Slavery*, p. 401.
[10] Garrison and Garrison, *William Lloyd Garrison*, I, 145; Aptheker, *Documentary History*, p. 100.

the content expanded. A new plan of operation had been worked out by Lundy. He announced that he expected to spend most of his time traveling to organize antislavery societies, secure subscriptions, and otherwise gain support for his work, while Garrison would remain in Baltimore as resident editor of the newspaper. Since both men would be writing for the paper and since both were seasoned editors in their own right, each agreed to sign his own articles. The decision thus to identify their contributions was not made because they detected any important disagreements in their views toward slavery but rather from recognition that each was an equal member of the partnership.[11]

The partnership on the whole proved a happy one, although Lundy scorned Garrison's orthodox religious views, and the editors diverged considerably in their approach toward the antislavery cause. It was not in their views on slavery that they differed, however. The chief point of contrast was that Garrison chose to deal exclusively in words — in arguments, theories, condemnations. Lundy had passed through that stage nearly a decade earlier. Files of the *Genius* contained almost every argument that could be advanced against slavery. But Lundy for some time had been ready to move beyond argumentation, censure, and proclamations of his own commitment. He had long been prepared to put into operation plans that he hoped would free some slaves immediately. Although this constituted an important difference between Garrison and Lundy, it did not signify disagreement or conflict over principle. Rather, it indicated differing temperaments and differing stages in the maturity and experience of the two men.

Garrison had mastered a flamboyant rhetoric. Now left in

---

11 Garrison and Garrison, *William Lloyd Garrison*, I, 140, explain this arrangement as resulting from their disagreement over immediatism.

immediate charge of the *Genius*, he set out at once to declare his position on slavery in the sharpest, most effective language he could command. Garrison belonged to that species of liberal to whom discussion is action. For him, declarations of commitment constituted ends in themselves. He could never resist the temptation to issue pronouncements and declarations of personal faith. Each of his statements appeared as though in testimony to recent conversion from error. A doctrinaire quality, largely absent in Lundy, pervaded nearly everything that Garrison wrote. Ideas that Lundy had presented as speculation and programs that he had broached tentatively were promoted as doctrine by Garrison. It was, then, a difference in style rather than in the substance of their thought that distinguished the two men.

Garrison decided that his first obligation in his new post was to make clear his recently developed position on the American Colonization Society. Although he commended the society's Liberian colony, he expressed doubts about the usefulness of the society that had sponsored it. "The work of colonization is exceedingly dilatory and uncertain," he wrote. "Viewed as an auxiliary, it deserves encouragement, but as a remedy, it is altogether inadequate . . . if we depend alone upon the efforts of colonization societies, slavery will never be exterminated. . . ." [12] There was nothing at all revolutionary in any of this. Indeed, so far as Lundy was concerned, it was orthodoxy, for he had long adhered to exactly the same view.[13] Neither did Garrison disapprove of efforts of the sort Lundy had made to help free Negroes emigrate to Haiti. He would soon join his name with Lundy's in an advertise-

[12] *Genius*, X (September 2, 1829), 5.
[13] See, for instance, *ibid.*, VII (September 29, 1827), 103; (December 8, 1827), p. 182; *Genius and Courier*, I (January 7, 1826), 149.

ment asking for twenty to fifty slaves to be transported to Haiti, and even after his partnership with Lundy had ended, he would support some of Lundy's emigration projects.[14]

After defining his position on colonization, Garrison then announced that he would advocate immediate rather than gradual emancipation.[15] Here the partners diverged somewhat in policy. As a matter of theory Lundy accepted immediatism as right — after all, it was he who had first published in the United States Mrs. Heyrick's essays, which urged such a program, and he had repeatedly admitted other calls for immediatism to his newspaper columns. But as a matter of policy Lundy remained a gradualist because he believed that gradualism was the only program which had any chance of acceptance in the South. Garrison reasoned otherwise. Sometime in the late summer of 1829, while associated with Goodell in Boston, Garrison had decided "that no valid excuse can be given for the continuance of the evil a single hour."[16] He called for immediate emancipation not by act of Congress but by the states. He qualified the apparent extremism of his demand, however, by explaining that he did "not advocate total and instantaneous abolition, without at the same time urging the duty of the states to make liberal provisions and suitable regulations, *by law*, for the maintenance and government of the emancipated blacks."[17]

There was nothing at all new about the substance of Garrison's doctrine or his demand. Articles advocating similar policy and action had appeared before in the *Genius* as well as in other publications, and every consistent reader of Lundy's

---

[14] *Genius*, X (November 10, 1829), 75; Greensborough *Patriot*, November 21, 1829; *Liberator*, January 25, 1831, May 12, 1832.

[15] *Genius*, X (September 2, 1829), 8.

[16] *Ibid.*

[17] *Ibid.* (September 25, 1829), p. 19.

newspaper would have been familiar with Garrison's argument.

Although the peremptory tone of Garrison's message and his supreme self-confidence had seldom been heard from earlier abolitionists, the quality of extremism in his writing, which aroused such fears among slaveholders and among the timid everywhere, struck a note peculiarly in keeping with the times. The resurrected *Genius* appeared at a moment when growing impatience characterized participants in the antislavery movement. In New England young men in particular, who were less concerned than their elders with fears of rending the web of society, had begun to speak against slavery as an evil no longer to be temporized with. Gradualism had had its day. With increasing frequency demands for immediate action had been heard. The same spirit of moral urgency that had moved Mrs. Heyrick in England now agitated some Americans. In September 1828 Lundy had published a letter from Connecticut exploring the subject. "The only obstacle to immediate Emancipation, is the *expediency* of the measure," wrote the New England abolitionist. "But what have we to do with the question of *expediency*, if it be made to appear plainly that it is our *duty*?" [18]

In many quarters reformers expressed persistent doubts both about the utility of the American Colonization Society as a means of ending slavery and about the morality and the necessity of expatriating Negroes. Even in North Carolina, where white men lived surrounded by slaves, the president of the state manumission society addressed these questions to the society's branches: (1) "Is it practicable for this government to colonize all its colored population in Africa?" (2) "Will it ever be possible to seperate [*sic*] the African

---

[18] *Ibid.*, IX (September 6, 1828), 7; (September 28, 1828), p. 21.

race from among us in any way?" (3) "Is such entire separation absolutely indispensable to every course of gradual emancipation?" [19]

A few speculative minds even rejected the all but universally held fear of racial amalgamation. "Our feelings are seldom critical judges of what is right and what is wrong," reasoned one writer. "The argument [against emancipation], if it be an argument at all, arising out of the apprehension of a mixture of the two races, is certainly addressed more to the feelings than the judgment." [20]

At the same time that older ideas about the means of abolishing slavery were thus being questioned, interests friendly to slavery and its perpetuation appeared to dominate the federal government. Antislavery petitions had achieved no important results in Congress. Andrew Jackson, whom Lundy had condemned as "nothing more nor less than a SOUL-SELLING, SLAVE-DRIVING, SOUTHERN COTTON-PLANTER," had replaced John Quincy Adams as President.[21] South Carolina statesmen were threatening to nullify federal law and even to break up the Union, while slavery continued its unimpeded spread into the Southwest, and the domestic slave trade flourished. "Our State is known to be a nursery, on which these disturbers of the human family prey," wrote Lundy, "and our city is about to become the grand depot; and ere long, last Sunday's exhibition of twenty-seven men, women, and children, chained and hand-cuffed, being driven through our streets may be an every day occurrence." [22] The declining strength of the antislavery impulse could be measured in still other ways. When Daniel Raymond ran for

[19] *Ibid.*, VIII (April 12, 1828), 100.
[20] *Ibid.*, IX (December 6, 1828), 73.
[21] *Ibid.* (September 6, 1828), p. 6.
[22] *Ibid.* (October 4, 1828), p. 29.

the Maryland House of Delegates in 1829, he received only 186 votes to his opponents' 7,769. At the twenty-first meeting of the American Convention held at Washington in 1829, no antislavery society south of the District of Columbia was represented, and only a few delegates from other regions appeared.[23]

Colonization offered no hope, and gradualism had failed to make any measurable headway in the campaign against slavery. Slavery was a far stronger institution in 1829 than it had been in 1820. No plan of operation yet devised had succeeded in impeding its growth or security. Apparently nothing less than a revolution could ever dislodge slavery from the United States, and in the 1820's there appeared to be few revolutionaries. No effort at reasonable persuasion had sufficed to free the slaves; no warnings that slavery violated natural law had accomplished it; no rationale of slow progress had provided the means to end it. Moderate ideas and programs had proved inadequate to provide either the intellectual justification or the technique for revolution. Yet while all programs had failed, the need for abolition seemed greater than ever. The times thus were conducive to louder, more insistent voices advocating stronger, less conciliatory programs. The strident demands that now emanated from the *Genius* were perfectly in accord with contemporary urgency. In particular, they coincided with new religious movements.

It was left to evangelical Christianity of the sort spread by the great revivals of the late 1820's to supply to reformers the particular attitude toward social change that fostered an unyielding campaign against slavery. The rationalists who had dominated the antislavery movement before 1830 had assumed this to be an orderly, closely articulated universe which

---

[23] *Ibid.*, X (October 9, 1829), 37; (December 25, 1829), p. 121.

runs by natural law. It could be adjusted and its flaws, such as slavery, removed in the interest of making the mechanism operate more efficiently. But it must in every instance be dealt with gently and with restraint lest chaos result. Men holding such views shunned the prospect of discontinuity and radical change.[24] Thus the abolitionists before 1830, under the sway of liberal religion, hoped to remove slavery by degrees and through their own benevolent efforts and without serious disruption of the social order.

The orthodox Christianity preached by the revivalists was not like that. Their Christianity was full of violent disjunctions. It presumed the presence of discontinuity in history. Above all, it did not posit continuous progress throughout infinite time. Neither did it suppose that the earthly city could be transformed into the city of God through efforts made by men, however good their will. In the life of the individual it sought the event of conversion. That event was sudden and devastating, marking radical change in the individual's relation to God and to society.[25] Its theology described creation out of nothing. It forecast judgment upon man and all his works; it anticipated the end of the world.

From beginning to end orthodox Christianity was characterized by the irrational, the violent, the incoherent. It spoke in tongues of flame and burning bushes; its spirit was that of violence and avenging swords. If for the gentle-hearted there was blessed assurance in the revivalists' Christianity, there was for others the harsh knowledge of certain retribution, imminent judgment, and the ultimate end of the world. Therefore, within the heart of orthodox Christianity there lived a spirit friendly to radical change, a spirit that could under-

---

[24] See, for instance, the views of Samuel J. May's father as reported in May, *Some Recollections*, pp. 23–24.
[25] Goodell, *Slavery*, pp. 135, 387–388.

stand revolutionary thought and action because it did not shrink from violence. It was itself a philosophy acquainted with sudden, irrational change and informed with the inevitability of retribution, death, and destruction. Its apocalyptic vision was itself a prophecy of cosmic revolution.

The revolutionary spirit that marked American religious life in the decade after 1825 came also to mark its most influential reform movement. The abolitionists who responded to Garrison's agitated voice when it was first heard through the *Genius* did not expect to end slavery slowly and by degrees. They had little hope that by gentle persuasion they could convince slaveholders to part with 3,000,000,000 dollars worth of property. They had few illusions about the ability of reason and appeals to natural or moral law to counteract the economic interests of the planters or to neutralize their deep-seated fears and anxieties. Few abolitionists could seriously have believed that slavery would be ended without violence. And they reconciled themselves to that bitter knowledge.[26]

The abolitionists condemned slavery as a sin. Slavery to them was not simply a moral wrong or an economic handicap or a political evil. It might be all those things, but above all else it was a sin against God. God, they said, does not ask of His people the gradual end of sin; He requires its immediate abandonment. He does not ask whether it will be convenient for His people to relinquish sin or whether it will disturb their temporal interests to do so; rather He requires that sin be given up immediately, regardless of temporal consequence.

The new abolitionists — of whom Garrison rapidly became the best known among thousands — demanded the immediate ending of slavery irrespective of the result. They did not

---

[26] May, *Some Recollections*, p. 27.

discuss how this could conveniently be done without disrupting southern economy and society, without destroying the southern way of life in every aspect. Earlier antislavery men, under the spell of the Enlightenment's liberal religion and its respect for institutions, would have done so. The abolitionists did not ask this question any more than the orthodox Christian expected God to inquire of them whether *now* would be a convenient time to destroy the sinful world. They knew very well that the judgment they had proclaimed against slavery would ruin the plantation South, but since only in that manner could slavery be ended, they did not shrink from the South's destruction. There was nothing in orthodox Christian thought to make them suppose that deep-seated evil could ever be extirpated without causing pain and bloodshed. The implications of this new doctrine were not lost on slaveholders and their friends.

Lundy denied to the end of his life that any distinction could properly be made between the antislavery movement of the 1820's and the "modern abolitionism" (as contemporaries called it) of the 1830's. "What is incendiary about current anti-slavery papers?" he asked in 1835. "They have taken no new ground. . . . They have denounced the system of slavery in no stronger terms than many others have done before them." The real cause of complaint against the later abolitionists, he concluded, was simply that by the mid-1830's there were more antislavery workers, more writers, more newspapers, more facts published about slavery, more adherents to the antislavery cause, and thus the "oppressors of their species perceive that 'their *craft* is in danger.' " [27] There is much truth to Lundy's view about the essential continuity of the antislavery movement. Certainly slaveholders had found "grad-

---

[27] *Genius*, XIV (November, 1835), 119; see also *ibid.*, XVI (March 29, 1839), 14.

ualism" quite as objectionable as "immediatism." They tolerated the one no more than the other. It was the prospect of abolition rather than the particular mode of its accomplishment that distressed them.

The small number of abolitionists in the 1820's made them easy to ignore. They could not be ignored a decade later when their newspapers, pamphlets, books, and agents made them important everywhere. Their danger to southern interests lay less in changes in doctrine than in their growth in numbers and influence which a changed intellectual atmosphere had helped make possible.

The *Genius'* new theme of mingled orthodox religion and abolitionism predictably aroused antagonism in both North and South. On the other hand it also received approval from many. Free Negroes, naturally enough, welcomed Garrison as a dynamic spokesman for their interests, and from widely separated parts of the country communications endorsing immediatism soon reached the office of the *Genius.* A writer in Sadsbury, Pennsylvania, speculated that "had the British parliament advocated the gradual abolition of the slave trade, it would not yet have been accomplished, for by the same reasoning that slavery could be proved to be right for a single day, by the very same reasoning it could be proved to be right for a year, or forever. . . ." And, he continued, "supposing . . . that somebody must suffer in consequence of the liberation of the blacks, then I would say, let the whites suffer, for the blacks have suffered long enough." [28] At Bennington Seminary in Vermont in October 1829 a student oration on "The Claims of the Slave" advocated immediate emancipation and the abandonment of "expediency." A correspondent at Salem, Ohio, declared that he had "long been of the mind, that the advocates of emancipation were injuring the

---

[28] *Ibid.,* X (October 16, 1829), 41.

cause, by arguing that the blacks were not in a fit situation to have their liberty, and that emancipation must be a gradual work. Can anyone who believes in 'a God who judges in the earth,' argue that there is danger in doing justice, regardless of the consequence?" From western Virginia a writer asserted that it "is not our province to reason whether we shall obey the commands of justice, or not — but it is our bounden duty and high privilege to comply immediately, reckless of consequences. Justice is a sure paymaster. . . ."[29]

While thunderous calls for immediate abolition rolled across the land, Garrison at the *Genius'* office in Baltimore also dealt with local and specific issues. He revived "The Black List," a catalog of atrocities chargeable to slavery which Lundy had earlier introduced and then abandoned.[30] In particular Garrison continued and even stepped up the intensity of the long feud Lundy had waged with the Woolfolk family over their slave-trading enterprises. Once again Austin Woolfolk found himself the target of an editorial barrage. Garrison condemned him as the largest shipper of slaves to the markets of New Orleans. "May God have mercy on his soul!" intoned the young editor. He also castigated the Baltimore *American* for carrying Woolfolk's advertisements.

When Garrison heard that the thin-skinned Woolfolk resented the *Genius'* renewed campaign against him and attributed it to Lundy, he issued Woolfolk a challenge exuding youthful arrogance. "If he wishes to discuss the subject of slavery, or to complain of any slander of his character, I shall be happy to see him at my boarding-house, No. 135, Market-street. . . . Let me assure him . . . that I am not to be in-

29 *Ibid.* (March 5, 1830), p. 202; XI (September, 1830), 86.
30 Thomas, *The Liberator*, p. 108, mistakenly credits Garrison with originating this feature.

timidated by the utterance of any threats, or the perpetration of any acts of violence. *Dieu defend le droit.*" [31]

Garrison scattered his shot even beyond Baltimore. Hearing that the *Francis*, a ship owned by Francis Todd, merchant of Newburyport, Massachusetts, and captained by a Yankee skipper, Nicholas Brown, had cleared Baltimore harbor for New Orleans with some seventy-five slaves aboard, Garrison prepared an article hot with condemnation of the slave trade and of New Englanders who engaged in it. The voyage, he said, was an instance of "domestic piracy" illustrative of "New England humanity and morality." Such men as Todd should be "sentenced to solitary confinement for life; they are the enemies of their own species — highway robbers and murderers. . . ." To make certain that Todd did not miss these comments, Garrison, in a gesture of bravado, sent him a copy of the newspaper in which they appeared.[32]

The result was the indictment in Baltimore court of both Garrison and Lundy for "a gross and malicious libel upon Francis Todd and Nicholas Brown." When the indictment was returned, Lundy was absent from the city on his travels through the countryside trying to persuade persons he suspected of sympathizing with the antislavery cause to subscribe to the *Genius*. When he returned to Baltimore, he was brought before Judge Nicholas Brice, where he gave bail to appear at the June term of city court. The suit against him then was quashed on the ground that he had borne no responsibility for the offending article. Garrison, however, stood trial and was sentenced to pay a fifty-dollar fine and costs. Since he had no money and Lundy could not raise any for him, he was sentenced to serve six months in jail. With

---

[31] *Genius*, X (October 16, 1829), 43; (October 28, 1829), p. 51; (November 6, 1829), p. 70.

[32] *Ibid.* (November 10, 1829), p. 75; (November 20, 1829), p. 83.

Garrison thus unable to share in conducting the *Genius*, his friend Isaac Knapp hurried down from Boston to help Lundy publish the newspaper.[33]

Many years later the Quaker poet John G. Whittier remembered that he had appealed to Henry Clay, whose American System both Garrison and Lundy had supported editorially, to use his influence to secure his friend's release from jail, and that Clay had promised to request Hezekiah Niles, publisher of the *Register*, to intervene; but before any help materialized from that quarter, Arthur Tappan of New York sent Lundy his draft for one hundred dollars which set Garrison free after he had spent forty-nine days in the Baltimore city jail. Tappan also offered to contribute a like sum to help support the *Genius*, which he said was much needed "to hold up to American freemen, in all its naked deformity, the subject of slavery." [34]

While the libel suit was still pending, Lundy announced the dissolution of his partnership with Garrison. Again Lundy would issue the *Genius* by himself; again it would be a monthly sold at one dollar a year, its editorial matter "confined to the subject of Universal Emancipation." In parting from Garrison, Lundy printed generous testimonials "to his strict integrity, amiable deportment, and virtuous conduct. . . ." To allay suspicions that the partners had quarreled, he assured readers that "we have ever cherished for each other the kindliest feelings, and mutual personal regard." The partnership

---

[33] *Ibid.* (January 8, 1830), p. 141; XI (June, 1830), 34; William L. Garrison, *A Brief Sketch of the Trial of William Lloyd Garrison for an Alleged Libel on Francis Todd, of Newburyport, Massachusetts* (Boston, 1834), *passim*; Garrison and Garrison, *William Lloyd Garrison*, I, 168–171.

[34] Garrison and Garrison, *William Lloyd Garrison*, I, 189–191; *Genius*, XI (June, 1830), 35; John G. Whittier to Lewis Tappan, May 2, 1870, in [Tappan], *Life of Arthur Tappan*, p. 167.

had ended not because of ill will or disagreement, but simply because the experiment of publishing an antislavery weekly had once again proved a financial failure. Although expenses had totaled at least fifty dollars a week, subscribers had not remitted more than that amount during a four-month period. The popular demand for a weekly antislavery newspaper in the South seemed too limited to support a partnership. As Lundy explained it, instead "of being placed in circumstances that would enable us to act independently — which is all we have asked — and which a proper advocacy of our cause requires — we are compelled to struggle (harder than nature will long endure) for existence itself." [35]

Many years later Garrison would imply that the weekly had failed because his extremism had antagonized subscribers who approved of Lundy's moderation.[36] This was not strictly true. Garrison in his old age exaggerated the extent of the differences in doctrine and mode of expression that had existed between himself and Lundy. Although Lundy was never as doctrinaire as Garrison, he had upon occasion been quite as extreme in condemning slavery and slaveholders, and even during their partnership some of the articles bearing his signature had reflected a dedication and zeal hardly surpassed by Garrison. Insofar as Garrison and Lundy disagreed in 1830, it was not over immediatism versus gradualism but over the wisdom of mingling antislavery doctrine with orthodox religion. Lundy, a Quaker of measured religious views, had little patience with the enthusiastic sectarianism that Garrison then accepted.[37] But Lundy certainly did not charge Garrison's religious extremism with alienating subscribers.

---

[35] *Genius*, X (January 25, 1830), 158; (March 5, 1830), p. 205.
[36] *Proceedings of the American Anti-Slavery Society at Its Third Decade*, p. 121.
[37] *Genius*, X (September 25, 1829), 27; XV (October, 1837), 64.

Garrison had little effect on the fortunes of the *Genius*. The truth was that the newspaper had failed once before under Lundy's editorship when financial stringency had forced him to suspend it for eight months in 1829. Now after a brief effort to revive it, it had failed again. Slaveholders and those under their sway had found Lundy's condemnation of slavery no more palatable than Garrison's. Indeed, they could scarcely distinguish between them. They would not patronize an anti-slavery newspaper no matter who edited it.

As though to demonstrate still further that he held Garrison blameless in the newspaper's declining circulation, Lundy planned with him a joint effort to resume publication. Freed from prison on June 5, 1830, Garrison headed for New York and New England, partly to collect information for his defense in the forthcoming civil suit for damages that Todd had brought against him, but partly also to seek support to re-establish the *Genius* as a weekly journal. He carried with him a manuscript prospectus dated June 7, 1830, written by Lundy and addressed "To the Friends of the Anti-Slavery Cause."

"The undersigned and his late partner, W. L. Garrison [it began], propose to make another effort to continue the weekly publication of the 'Genius of Universal Emancipation.' We believe that our cause is fast gaining ground; and that *one* such periodical, at least, faithfully and fearlessly devoted thereto, is absolutely necessary, to expose the enormities of the slave system . . . and acquaint the advocates of Emancipation with the progress of events in relation to it." Lundy promised that though he and Garrison would continue to "pursue the straight-forward path of *duty*, regardless of every earthly consequence," they would at the same time "aim to preserve a proper dignity of style, and extend a becoming liberality towards our opponents." And, he added, "the work will partake somewhat more of a *literary* character than formerly." [38]

All appeals for funds failed, however. When Garrison returned to Baltimore in July to await trial, he reported to Lundy that he had not found enough financial support to justify an attempt to resume the weekly *Genius*. He decided to sever all connection with Lundy and his newspaper and make his own way in the antislavery movement. Before his case came to trial, he had left Baltimore. At the October 1830 term of the Baltimore county court the jury found for the plaintiff 1,000 dollars damages, which, needless to say, was not paid. Garrison's lawyer, whom Lundy had engaged for him, offered no defense; Garrison himself ignored the entire proceedings. "This was wrong," said Lundy. Though Garrison "walked forth in conscious innocence, and thought himself secure, he should know that *any cause*, however just, depends for its success upon *vigilance* and *activity*." [39]

Lundy did not need to feel concern that Garrison had turned into a lamb. Having engaged with Lundy in the turbulence of abolitionist journalism and having suffered a species of martyrdom for his efforts, he felt prepared to strike out on his own dynamic course. In a series of fervid lectures delivered in Philadelphia, New York, and Boston during the late summer and early fall of 1830, he proclaimed a crusade against the American Colonization Society and launched a campaign to raise funds to found his own newspaper, the *Liberator*.[40]

While the youthful Garrison stood at the threshold of a

[38] "To the Friends of the Anti-Slavery Cause," William Lloyd Garrison Papers (Boston Public Library); see also *Genius*, XI (May, 1830), 17.
[39] *Ibid.* (October, 1830), pp. 97–100; (November, 1830), p. 114.
[40] *Ibid.* (December, 1830), p. 129; Garrison and Garrison, *William Lloyd Garrison*, I, 203–204, 212–216.

spectacular career, Lundy at the age of forty-one tried to restore momentum to what appeared to be a flagging course.
Perhaps using the money Tappan had offered him, he bought
new type and again printed the *Genius* in his own shop. "My
spirits are so, so, and my health is excellent," he wrote. "My
coat is off, my sleeves rolled up, and I am working away." [41]

As an auxiliary enterprise he opened a free-produce store
in Baltimore, but it proved short-lived, and subscriptions for
the *Genius* lagged as before.[42] In October he announced his
decision to move the newspaper to Washington to an office
at the corner of Pennsylvania Avenue and 11th Street West.
His new location, he explained, would allow him "to become
more generally acquainted with intelligent and influential
men, from every part of the Union, and thus to increase the
facilities of collecting and disseminating important information. . . ." [43]

Since Garrison in September had published his plans to
establish the *Liberator* at Washington, it is tempting to specu-
late that Lundy announced his move in order to forestall the
establishment of a vigorous rival so near his own location.
But if such were the case, Garrison bore him no apparent resentment, and the two editors remained on the friendliest of
terms. Garrison kept Lundy informed about the lectures he
was delivering in northern cities, and Lundy publicly admired
his efforts. "The language which he uses is warm, energetic
and bold," he wrote. "Nothing but this will reach the adamantine hearts of slavites," or, he added, our own *"humane
ones."* [44]

Lundy admitted, however, that he could not "wholly ap-

---

[41] *Genius*, XI (June, 1830), 33; (July, 1830), p. 51.
[42] *Ibid.* (August, 1830), p. 65.
[43] *Ibid.* (October, 1830), p. 97.
[44] *Ibid.* (December, 1830), p. 129.

prove of our friend Garrison's sweeping denunciation of the American Colonization Society." He concurred with Garrison's indictment at most points; for example, the society's view that the Negro could not live as a free man in the United States Lundy too found "monstrous," and with Garrison he objected to the society's "timid, half-way measures." But he was not prepared to reject it altogether as an ally in the war against slavery. "I am clearly of the opinion," he wrote, "that *every effort* that is made to exhibit to public view the deplorable condition of the colored race, must have a *tendency* to mitigate it," while he still urged "the adoption of more efficient measures for the consummation of our great and philanthropic undertaking." [45]

As for Garrison's doctrine of immediatism, Lundy approved it, although characteristically he insisted on spelling out exactly what the term would mean if the principle were to be put into effect. Set the captives free with suitable restrictions by law, he urged; end the domestic slave trade; end slave punishments; train the young. *"This* you may *immediately* do. . . ." [46]

On January 1, 1831, Garrison issued the first number of the *Liberator* at Boston, and Lundy became its subscription agent at Washington. He commended the newspaper as "a warm, 'enthusiastic' advocate of the total, immediate, abolition of slavery" and urged that "every one subscribe for it that can spare *two dollars a year.*" After four issues had appeared, his views had not changed. "Instead of giving it a dry old-fashioned 'puff,'" he advised, with an attempt at humor, "every friend of our cause to *immediately* subscribe for it." [47]

Lundy was pleased that antislavery work had been extended

---

[45] *Ibid.,* p. 130.
[46] *Ibid.*
[47] *Ibid.* (January, 1831), p. 150; (February, 1831), p. 161. Italics added.

in so vigorous a form to New England, where his own influence had been limited. He took understandable pride in Garrison, who, in turn, freely acknowledged his ideological debt to Lundy. Lundy had come to think of himself as the elder statesman of the antislavery movement, initiating younger men into its mysteries and inducting them into the cause. Garrison was his disciple in the North; William Swaim in more muted tones conducted the antislavery *Patriot* in Greensboro, North Carolina. They "performed, each, a brief *apprenticeship* with me, at different periods, a few years since," he wrote. "They were fine lads. Striplings, as they were, they had clear heads, stout hearts, and brawney arms. . . . These philanthropic ex 'apprentices' of mine are now full grown men. Each stands at the helm editorial of a 'fearless' Press of his own. And they are severally entitled to great praise, for the abilities with which they perform the duties *of the station*." [48]

All this naturally was gratifying to Lundy; yet in spite of the multiplying sources of antislavery expression, for which he could take much credit, he constantly reminded himself that for all his efforts and sacrifices he had discovered no means to put an end to slavery.

---

[48] *Ibid.*, XIII (January, 1833), 40.

CHAPTER X

Emigration Plans Renewed

While Garrison in Boston sent forth ringing appeals for adherence to the abstract principles of justice, Lundy doggedly continued his search for ways to weaken slavery immediately and to give tangible aid to free Negroes. Their need appeared great, for as Negro population increased in northern border cities, a fury of persecution assailed them. So bitterly did opposition rage in the late 1820's that some Negroes who had stubbornly resisted all efforts to send them to Liberia now sorrowfully concluded that new homes outside the United States might yet be preferable to continued oppression within its borders.[1]

As a long-time champion of American Negroes, whether slave or free, Lundy could not now ignore their worsening condition. His Union Humane Society in Ohio and the Humane Protecting Society in Tennessee had aimed to protect free Negroes against outrages at the hands of kidnappers and others who refused to recognize their rights as free men.

---

[1] *Genius*, XI (August, 1830), 69.

He had made two trips to Haiti in their behalf, and he had continued to search for ways to ameliorate their condition in America. But he had always recognized those activities as auxiliary to his main concern, the destruction of slavery. Now in the new emergency he temporarily allowed his campaign against slavery to become subordinate to his efforts in behalf of free Negroes.

Immediate aid seemed essential. In the western states complaints against the attempts of free Negroes to settle on free soil had led to the passage of restrictive laws and to the expression of intractable prejudice. "For the purposes of legislation, it is sufficient to know, that the blacks in Ohio, *must always exist as a separate and degraded race*," asserted a select committee of the Ohio legislature, "that when the Leopard shall change his spots and the Ethiopean his skin, then, *but not till then*, may we expect that the descendants of Africans will be admitted into society, on terms of social and political equality." [2] Sometimes racial prejudice took the form of economic discrimination, as in Maryland, where the residents of Baltimore presented a memorial to the House of Delegates requesting it to prohibit Negroes from being licensed to drive hacks, carts, and drays.[3] Often prejudice led to organized violence. During the fall of 1831 mobs in Providence, Rhode Island, tore down Negro houses; shortly afterward Negro homes were wrecked at New Haven, Connecticut, in riots set off by plans to establish a Negro college.[4]

But the worst assaults of all took place in the winter of 1829–30 in Cincinnati, Ohio, where mobs drove much of the free Negro population from the city. Some of the refugees found uneasy sanctuary in Indiana, some in other parts of

---

[2] *Ibid.*, VII (November 3, 1827), 139; *Liberator*, February 4, 1832.
[3] [Earle], *Life*, p. 221; *Genius*, VIII (January 26, 1828), 23.
[4] *Liberator*, October 4, 22, 1831; *Genius*, XII (September, 1831), 78–79.

Ohio. Many chose to leave the United States altogether and settle as a colony in the Huron Tract of Upper Canada under the leadership of James C. Brown, a Cincinnati Negro, who had negotiated with the governor of the Canadian province for asylum. With free Negro organizations in Philadelphia and Boston joining white Quakers in support of the settlement, Wilberforce, as it was known, soon became the mecca for free Negroes in widely separated parts of the country.[5] The Canadian colony appeared to prosper, and Lundy predicted that within one year this "self-created independent settlement" would be larger than the American Colonization Society's colony of Liberia after twelve years of nationwide effort.[6]

Garrison fully shared Lundy's view of the wisdom of supporting the Negro settlement in Canada. Though it has commonly been asserted that Garrison differed from Lundy in his doctrinaire opposition to all colonization plans, the facts are otherwise. Garrison enthusiastically endorsed the Canadian colony even after he had left his partnership with Lundy and founded the *Liberator*.[7]

Free Negroes did the same. Although they generally held only scorn for the American Colonization Society's plans to return them to Africa, they felt differently about the Canadian project. On September 20, 1830, Negro delegates from several eastern states met at the Bethel Methodist Church in Philadelphia to hold the first of a series of Negro conventions. One of their first acts was to organize the "American

---

[5] *Ibid.*, X (September 2, 1829), 6; William H. Pease and Jane H. Pease, *Black Utopia; Negro Communal Experiments in America* (Madison, Wis., 1963), pp. 46–62; Fred Landon, "Wilberforce, an Experiment in the Colonization of Freed Negroes in Upper Canada," *Transactions of the Royal Society of Canada*, XXXI, third series, section II (1937), 69–71.

[6] *Genius*, X (March 5, 1830), 201.

[7] *Liberator*, June 25, July 2, 1831.

Society of Free Persons of Colour, for Improving Their Condition in the United States; for Purchasing Lands; and for the Establishing of a Settlement in Upper Canada." The next summer the delegates convened at Philadelphia again, this time with Lundy, Garrison, Arthur Tappan, and other white abolitionists present as observers. After passing a resolution commending Lundy and Garrison as "tried friends, and fearless advocates of our rights and promoters of our best interests, [who] are entitled to a prominent place in our affections," the delegates agreed to encourage Canadian emigration, while at the same time they opposed the projects of the American Colonization Society as "an immense and wanton waste of lives and property. . . ." [8]

Although Lundy gave the refugees at Wilberforce all possible aid and encouragement, he still had some reservations about Canada as a site for large-scale emigration. He decided that he ought to inspect conditions there for himself in order to learn whether he could conscientiously recommend emigration to the considerable number of free Negroes who had expressed eagerness to leave the United States "if they could 'go a-foot.' . . ." [9] Lundy's Baltimore associate Hezekiah Grice was already preparing for publication a map of the Wilberforce colony showing routes to Canada for the aid of prospective settlers. Lundy feared that aided by such charts many would soon undertake the long journey with little knowledge of the conditions they might face when they arrived.[10]

Lundy knew enough about the climate and geography of Canada to make him doubt that settlers from any region

[8] *Ibid.*, October 22, 1831; *Genius*, XI (October, 1830), 103–104; XII (January, 1832), 136.
[9] *Ibid.*, XI (May, 1830), 18.
[10] *Ibid.* (August, 1830), p. 69.

south of Virginia would find its winters congenial. Already another, more attractive site for emigration had come to his attention. In an article published in the *Genius* in October 1831, he announced that the "time has come, when we think it proper to say: That of all the places ever mentioned as suitable for the emigration of our *southern* colored population [Texas] is the most inviting, and the most desirable." [11] Recalling the Mexican government's antislavery policy, he predicted that Texas ("that fine region where the rigors of winter are unknown, and where man, without distinction of color or condition, is looked upon as the being that Deity made him — *free and independent*") ultimately would *"present an asylum for hundreds of thousands of our oppressed colored people. . . ."* [12] The Wilberforce colony, he suspected, would prove of limited attraction when compared with the Mexican province. Accordingly, he hoped that on his trip to inspect the Canadian settlement he could interest philanthropists in supporting a project that would open a way for many Negroes to move to Texas.

In the fall of 1831 he left Baltimore to begin the long trip to Wilberforce. He had laid out a zigzag route for the journey that would take him through parts of Pennsylvania, New York, Michigan, and Ohio, as well as Upper Canada. He would visit relatives and friends along the way, he would inspect a small tract of land he had recently bought near Columbus, Ohio, and he would make an effort to collect the many debts owed him by subscribers, a continued obstacle to the successful operation of the *Genius*.[13]

---

11 *Ibid.*, XII (October, 1831), 87.
12 *Ibid* (supplement, December, 1831), p. 114.
13 Lundy to Lydia S. Wierman, May 29, 1831, Benjamin Lundy Papers (Ohio Historical Society, Columbus); Lundy to Elizabeth M. Chandler, April 2, 1831, Chandler Papers; *Genius*, XI (April, 1831), 193.

He especially looked forward to visiting his editorial associate, Elizabeth Chandler, who in the summer of 1830 had moved with her brother Thomas from Philadelphia to Michigan Territory. Since Lundy had little money to finance the trip, he expected to work as a journeyman saddler along the way. He decided too that he would have the *Genius* printed wherever he could on the tour. He would carry his office with him, so to speak, and at convenient locations arrange with local printers to do the work. "Thee will, no doubt, smile at the idea of an *itinerant editor!*" he told Miss Chandler, "and, probably, laugh outright, to think of an *itinerant periodical!!* — But never mind. — I have often conned the *negro maxim*: 'continuous half work, massa.' I will 'continue' many schemes, before I abandon a purpose that I have once resolved on." [14]

After conferring with Quaker antislavery workers in Philadelphia, he traveled on to New York City. There he called on William Goodell, in whose print shop an issue of the *Genius* was prepared, and obtained from him a letter to Gerrit Smith, whose home had already become a mecca for proponents of all kinds of humanitarian causes. Lundy too hoped to share in the financial bounty Smith dispensed to those reformers whose projects won his favor. On December 7 when he reached Peterboro in the western part of the state, he presented Goodell's letter to the wealthy philanthropist and requested permission to acquaint him with his plans. He did not receive a sympathetic audience. Although he left Smith copies of recent issues of the *Genius* and a long letter detailing his accomplishments and future plans, they proved ineffectual. Smith soon would become an abolitionist, but at the time Lundy met him, he still supported the American Colonization Society and deplored the doctrines that appeared in the

---

[14] *Ibid.*, XVI (August 30, 1839), 43; Lundy to Elizabeth M. Chandler, April 2, 1831, Chandler Papers.

Liberator. Some might appraise Lundy as a gentle Quaker whose program was moderate and safe. Smith thought otherwise. "He is too much akin to Garrison to suit me," the cautious philanthropist admitted. He soon relented, however. Within a few months he had sent Lundy money for a two-year subscription to the *Genius* and engaged him to perform a small item of business in Washington. Before long he would join the abolitionist ranks.[15]

At Lockport Lundy had more immediate success. There in a conference with Lyman Spalding, a fellow Quaker whom he had met on his earlier trip through New York, he disclosed his hopes to found a Negro settlement in Texas. Spalding lent him 250 dollars, a princely sum in Lundy's eyes, and promised further aid as the project developed.[16]

On January 13, 1832, Lundy entered Canada. He traveled by stage, and, in order to miss nothing, "rode the whole day on the outside, standing all the while. . . ." Proceeding in a westerly direction, the stage passed through "a beautiful and exceedingly fertile country, partly clothed with a thick forest and partly chequered with fine farms. . . ." The land, he thought, would produce fine crops, for he saw stacks of "very fine timothy hay, by the road side, and the corn stalks were large. . . ." But soil fertility was not his main concern, nor would rich soil be the chief desire of Negro settlers, who longed rather for a free atmosphere. In this respect Canada, it appeared, might prove a disappointment, for a recent petition signed by 121 white residents of Upper Canada had requested the assembly to prevent the settlement of more

15 William Goodell to Gerrit Smith, November 24, 1831, Smith to R. R. Gurley, December 9, 1831, and Lundy to Smith, February 2, 1833, Gerrit Smith Papers (Syracuse University Library, Syracuse, N.Y.).
16 "Agreement Between Benjamin Lundy of Washington and Lyman Spalding of Lockport, New York, January 8, 1836," Lundy Papers.

Negroes in the province. After talking with as many white
and black settlers as he could, Lundy was compelled to admit
that, as he had feared, "the white emigrants from the United
States retain all the prejudices here that they formerly held
against the coloured people in their native country. And the
latter, being admitted to equal privileges with them under
this government, are accused of being 'saucy.' " [17]

In company with a Negro from the village of London
Lundy traveled to the Negro colony of Wilberforce, where
on January 20 he attended a meeting of nearly all the male
residents assembled to welcome the visitor as a great proponent of Negro freedom and equality. But the meeting soon
degenerated into a display of the factionalism that had nearly
rent the settlement. Lundy found that he had got in the middle of an internal quarrel among the leaders of the colony,
and concluded with some of them that the colony's agent,
Israel Lewis, was a scoundrel. The internal dissension shocked
him. His reports to his friend Lyman Spalding brought Spalding's advice to colony leaders to settle their differences lest
the disputes cause a loss of support from United States philanthropists.[18]

In spite of these evidences of discord and the remnants of
racial prejudice Lundy prepared a generally favorable account of the colony and of Upper Canada for publication in
the *Genius*. Clearly, he had decided to endorse the settlement

---

[17] Fred Landon (ed.), *The Diary of Benjamin Lundy, Written During
His Journey Through Upper Canada, January, 1832* (Toronto, 1922),
pp. 10, 12, 13–14 (the diary first appeared in the *Genius*); *Liberator*,
April 2, 1831.
[18] Landon (ed.), *Diary*, p. 16; Austin Steward to William Lloyd Garrison and Isaac Knapp, March 12, 1833, and Lyman Spalding to Steward
and Benjamin Paul, February 4, 1832, in Carter G. Woodson, *The
Mind of the Negro as Reflected in Letters Written During the Crisis,
1800–1860* (Washington, D.C., 1926), pp. 186, 625.

of American Negroes in Canada. But now increasingly sensitive to the criticism that many abolitionists and free Negroes alike directed toward anyone who ventured to suggest that Negroes ought to be compelled to leave the United States, he carefully defined the limits of his support for emigration: "I would not urge, I would not ask a single free man to go, who is not so disposed. My business is to give him information. If he can profit by it I shall rejoice, if he neglects to pay attention to it he but exercises a perfect right which it would be highly improper for me to question him about. . . . I shall be amply rewarded for the hardship and expense of my cold and toilsome journey, if I can be successful in laying it, generally, before them." [19]

After inspecting the Wilberforce colony, Lundy crossed into the United States at Detroit and proceeded by wagon and sleigh to "Hazlebank" in Lenawee County, Michigan Territory, the log-cabin home of Thomas and Elizabeth Chandler, from which the *Genius'* Ladies Repository had been edited since the summer of 1830. Although most of Michigan still remained a wilderness, the community along the Raisin River where the Chandlers had settled already possessed some of the amenities and much of the intellectual ferment common to the East. Upon Lundy's recommendation Garrison had supplied Miss Chandler with a complimentary subscription to the *Liberator*; the Adrian Library Company was being organized just as Lundy arrived in the settlement; and a temperance society had been formed in 1830. The settlers refused even to accept the material deprivation the West ordinarily imposed on its residents. The Chandlers' rich neighbor, Darius Comstock, whose wife was a distant relative of Lundy, rode about the neighborhood's primitive roads in a "close

---

[19] *Genius*, XII (March, 1832), 153–156; (April, 1832), pp. 169–172; (May, 1832), pp. 185–191; Landon (ed.), *Diary*, p. 24.

carriage . . . that would be called 'stylish' even in Philadelphia. . . ." Miss Chandler had reported to her Philadelphia relatives, who feared she lived among savages, "The character of the people here is decidedly intelligent, and that in no very trifling degree." And, she added, *"bumpkins* are very scarce. . . ." [20]

Lundy discussed recent events in the antislavery movement with these receptive men and women, and persuaded some of them to subscribe to his newspaper. Miss Chandler, anticipating important results from Lundy's visit, hoped that a more general circulation of the *Genius* among her neighbors would be "the means of extending the Emancipation Spirit," which, she said, already prevailed "in a very good degree" through the settlement.[21] Lundy did not attempt to organize an antislavery society in Michigan before he continued his travels into Ohio. Instead, he left that task to his editorial associate. Miss Chandler, shrinking from contact with society, waited all summer before taking any decisive action. Then, during the first week in October 1832 at the Friends' meetinghouse, a group of Quakers under her leadership founded the first antislavery society in Michigan Territory.[22]

From Michigan Lundy proceeded into Ohio, where he encountered traveling conditions so bad as to cause him to question the wisdom of the undertaking and his ability to complete it. "The worst travelling ever experienced," he wrote in his journal; "but one house in 20 miles . . . swale & swamp. Had to wade from half leg to knee deep more than 20 times while snow falling fast & it was *freezing* rapidly!! . . . cloak, coat, pantaloons, stockings, all a glare of ice. feet benumbed!!

---

[20] Elizabeth M. Chandler to Jane Howell, February 29, June 20, [September 30], December 13, 1832, Chandler Papers.
[21] Elizabeth M. Chandler to Jane Howell, February [12], 1832, *ibid.*
[22] Ruth Evans to Jane Howell, October 22, 1832, *ibid.*

—nothing to strike a fire!!! — no house, nobody knew where!!!! — jump, and stomp, and run — nearly dark a *house* in the extended view . . . go 1½ miles farther — *nearly* exhausted." [23]

The rest of the trip through Ohio proved easier and more agreeable, though on the steamboat from Marietta to Cincinnati a mildly unpleasant encounter with a Louisville planter and his nephew momentarily distressed him. Never able to discipline himself to look upon slaveholders dispassionately, Lundy took an immediate dislike to the younger man — an "ignorant drowsy eyed lump of vegetation. . . ." Yet, he reflected, "this worthless creature will lord it over many a naturally noble minded man and amiable woman, calling them his 'property' !!!" [24]

After two weeks in Cincinnati Lundy walked to the large Quaker settlement at Richmond, Indiana, and then in early May returned to Cincinnati, having obtained at one place and another along the way some 200 new subscribers to the *Genius* and at least the verbal assurances of tangible support for his antislavery work.[25] Lundy's prolonged stay in the West was occasioned, however, not so much by his obvious need to add to his subscription list as by his decision to seek backing for a daring, imaginative, and highly speculative venture. He decided not to delay taking preliminary steps to effect his plan to colonize Texas. He would make a whirlwind trip to Mexico to investigate the possibility of establishing a colony of free Negroes in that country.

As he had made his way through the West, he found more interest than he had anticipated for such a project. Spalding's financial support had encouraged him that he could obtain

---

[23] Journal, Lundy Papers.
[24] *Ibid.*
[25] *Ibid.*

the necessary backing. But it was the interest free Negroes expressed in such a plan that led him to conclude he must make every effort to plant a colony in Mexico. Just before he arrived in Cincinnati an assembly of Negroes in the city had resolved that "we will never remove to Africa, but should any of our brethren wish to emigrate, we recommend Canada or Mexico, as countries far more congenial to our constitutions, and where our rights as freemen are secured." [26] A Negro woman in Philadelphia wrote that though she "would not be taken to Africa, were the Society to make [her] queen of the country," Mexico might provide a suitable retreat; "where is that country to which we may remove, and thus become free and equal?" she asked, and supplied her own answer — "I believe that country to be Mexico." A correspondent signing himself D. U. E. wrote in the *Liberator* that all of Texas and the territory north and east of the Gila River to the Gulf of California could be obtained from Mexico as a refuge for Negroes "by the Jeffersonian mode of acquiring territory." "A Colored Citizen of Brooklyn," observing the emigration of Negroes to Canada, commented: "Thus you see that the Lord is opening a way for us to pack up and march off, without crossing the seas, to Canada, and I hope soon, to the Texas, or some neighboring province." Lundy's trip to Mexico was prompted by his desire to make it possible for these vague hopes of the free Negroes to be realized. [27]

The arguments in favor of establishing a settlement far from the United States appeared unassailable. It would serve as a refuge for American Negroes whose lives were made wretched by discrimination and oppression. With few exceptions white society refused to accept their presence or their services in any other role than that of menials rigidly isolated

[26] *Liberator*, February 4, 1832.
[27] *Ibid.*, January 28, February 25, April 7, 1832.

from meaningful contact with the dominant white group. Even in New England, where, as Garrison had written, "the curse of slavery" had long ago been removed, "the curse of deep-rooted prejudice" remained.[28] Even some confirmed opponents of slavery, squeamish about contact with Negroes, experienced difficulty in ridding themselves of the notion that nature had permanently relegated black men to a lowly rank in creation. Lundy did not share their view. Inferiority, he insisted, was not inherent; it had been created by white men in history for their own selfish ends. "I believe that the more we investigate the matter we shall find that 'human nature is all in all,' " he had written. "The odious distinctions between white and black, &c. have all been created by tyrants and their co-adjutors for the express purpose of acquiring and preserving their *usurped authority*. This is the Alpha and Omega of it." [29] He never veered from that faith in human equality and that view of the source of prejudice. All other true abolitionists agreed with him that the conditions imposed by slavery were responsible for the apparent inferiority of American Negroes. Free the slaves, educate them, cease oppressing them, and they would prove as capable of achievement as other men. Duty, as Lundy knew, bound a philanthropist to argue against prejudice and attempt to destroy it; yet the fact remained that prejudice did flourish, and its end was nowhere in sight; therefore, he reasoned, whatever could be done to help the Negroes then living to escape its blighting effect ought to be done.

Lundy believed that a Negro settlement located far from the power of whites to repress and humiliate would serve two immediate purposes. By removing some oppressed men from

[28] *Genius*, X (November 27, 1829), 91.
[29] Lundy to Isaac Barton, March 8, 1825, Pennsylvania Abolition Society Manuscript Collection, vol. IX.

an intolerably cruel situation, it would serve a noble, humanitarian cause. At the same time it would demonstrate to white Americans the capacity of Negroes to improve themselves. Freed from oppression, Negroes soon would advance in enterprise and virtue. Thus racial prejudice would be lessened and one of the chief objections to emancipation would be removed.

A Negro colony would provide still another argument for emancipation. It would further the free-produce movement. Lundy hoped that free Negroes could be settled in a warm climate where they would raise cotton, tobacco, sugar, and rice — the same commodities slave labor presently produced in the South. His long-standing interest in free produce had continued. At the American Convention in 1827 he had been instrumental in having a committee appointed to study the relative advantages of free and slave labor and to investigate experiments that had been made in producing cotton by free labor. In the spring of 1831 he had addressed the Colored Men's Free Produce Society of Pennsylvania and induced them to give ten dollars to be added to a premium to be offered for free-labor rice.[30]

Lundy was confident that Negroes would work harder and more efficiently as free men than as slaves. Their success as independent husbandmen would prove to southern planters the superiority of free labor. Some planters, confronted with such evidence, might then be induced to manumit their own slaves and hire them as free workers. But even if this should not happen on a large scale, the production by free Negroes of such staples as cotton would destroy the near monopoly southern slaveholders presently enjoyed. If given the choice, Lundy believed, many Americans would buy free-labor goods

[30] Ruth Anna (Ketring) Nuermberger, *The Free Produce Movement, a Quaker Protest Against Slavery* (Durham, N.C., 1942), pp. 16, 19, 21; *Genius*, X (December 11, 1829), 105.

as a matter of principle. Southern planters who chose to continue to use servile labor would find themselves unable to compete with their more efficient rivals. At the same time they would lose their market as increasing numbers of customers shunned slave-grown products. Planters then would have no recourse but to substitute free for slave labor. Economic coercion, Lundy predicted, would work where moral argument had failed.

A great many Quakers agreed with Lundy on this point, and free-labor stores had been opened to satisfy their scruples; free-labor associations operated to persuade the public to abstain from the consumption of slave-produced goods. In Richmond, Indiana, C. W. Starr reportedly had founded a spinning mill which used only cotton grown in Indiana and Illinois.[31] Garrison, fully convinced that the free-produce movement offered an efficient weapon against slavery, had endorsed the movement, listing as one of the main points in his antislavery program the establishment of free-produce societies which, he said, would "strike at the root of slavery." [32]

Lundy's encouragement of the Haitian emigration plan, in part motivated by such considerations, had not been very successful, and he had continued to search for a more suitable emigration site. Texas had come to seem the ideal location. He had probably known about its attractions for many years. When he lived in Missouri from 1819 to 1821 his home had been Herculaneum, which was also the home of Moses Austin and his son Stephen, who during those same years obtained grants from Mexico to plant a colony in Texas.[33] In any event,

---

[31] *Ibid.*, XI (August, 1830), 72; Lundy opened a free-produce store in Baltimore. *Ibid.*, p. 65.

[32] *Liberator*, March 26, 1831.

[33] Eugene C. Barker (ed.), *The Austin Papers* (Washington, D.C., 1928), II, part I, 300, 316–319, 324–327, 329–330.

as Texas colonization progressed during the decade, Lundy would have been given ample opportunity to develop interest in the area. The possibilities of Texas became even more evident to him when a friend in Liverpool sent him a copy of Ward's *Mexico in 1827*, which contained an account of the production in Mexico of cotton and sugar by free labor.[34] Furthermore, as all humanitarians knew, the Mexican government by a decree of September 15, 1829, had abolished slavery.[35] Apparently the region had been designed for the very program Lundy envisioned.

Lundy of course also knew that the Mexican government by the Law of April 6, 1830, had prohibited the further settlement of North Americans in Texas, but he probably hoped that the humanitarian nature of his project would induce Mexican officials to make an exception to their colonization ban. That result, which certainly would have to be preceded by delicate negotiation, could hardly be achieved simply by correspondence or through the efforts of representatives. Lundy realized, moreover, that before proceeding far with his own plans he should personally investigate the opportunities Texas offered for free Negroes. He would have to visit Texas himself.

Thus in the spring of 1832 he put his papers in safe hands in Cincinnati and prepared to make the trip. As he described it, the venture partook of melodrama. Fearing that his antislavery reputation would endanger his life should his identity be revealed, he "put on a rough dress, procured a knapsack, adopted the cognomen of 'J. Dynul,' and plunged into the

---

[34] Henry George Ward, *Mexico in 1827* (London, 1828); *Genius*, XII (May, 1831), 6.
[35] Eugene C. Barker, *The Life of Stephen F. Austin; a Chapter in the Westward Movement of the Anglo-American People* (Nashville, Tenn., 1925), pp. 243–245.

'lion's den' of slavites, slave traders, and all the devils in human shape that infest those 'nether regions,' the slave golgothas of the South!"[36] Thus disguised — and prepared for the worst — he traveled uneventfully to Nashville and Columbia in Tennessee, where he obtained funds from antislavery sympathizers. From Nashville he sailed by steamboat as a deck passenger to New Orleans and thence to Nacogdoches in Texas. On the steamboat in Louisiana he imagined that the other, more elegant passengers — "every *gemman* — and *lady* too —" looked upon him "with quite as much contempt as they did upon the Negroes and even the *dogs*." But he welcomed their scorn, for it spared him, as he said, "the unwelcome task of conversing with many of them. . . ."[37]

As he approached Nacogdoches, he carefully recorded in his journal his impressions of the country, probably for the benefit of prospective settlers. "In no part of America have I seen better corn than in this section of country," he wrote; and, again, the "citizens generally are very kind, social and hospitable." These pleasant observations were soon interrupted, however, for as he neared the town, he heard disquieting news. Revolutionists, it was said, planned an imminent attack upon the fort at Nacogdoches. Considering his mission too important for delay, Lundy proceeded in spite of the rumors, and on July 1 arrived in the town. He found the citizens in great confusion. Predictions of an approaching attack were heard everywhere, and Indians armed and equipped for battle paraded through the streets. In this military atmosphere the pacifist Quaker called on José de las Piedras, the commandant of the fort, who through an interpreter reassured him and welcomed him to Texas.[38]

---

[36] Lundy to Elizabeth M. Chandler, September 6, 1832, Chandler Papers.
[37] *Ibid.*
[38] *Genius,* XII (August, 1832), 205–207.

Only momentarily disconcerted by the possibility of war Lundy stayed six days in Nacogdoches. He used the time to ask as many citizens as possible about conditions in the region and to talk with as many influential persons as he could meet. Juan Antonio Padilla, former secretary of state of Texas, encouraged his project, and a free Negro assured him of his own satisfaction with life in Mexico. Naturally all of this pleased Lundy. He even developed a benign interpretation of the political and military strife in Mexico, evidences of which he saw in the warlike atmosphere that surrounded him: ". . . the contest is between the Democracy and the Aristocracy of the country . . ." he wrote with assurance, and "the former must eventually, and speedily, unite the moral with the physical power, and rule the nation." The military skirmishes that had just occurred were directed, he thought, by lovers of liberty against the tyrannical and arbitrary actions of the Mexican commanders of the Texas garrisons. Devotion to freedom would become so general, he predicted, that few slaveholders would settle in Texas in the future, and free Negroes would be welcomed.[39]

He had not been mistaken, he concluded, in believing Texas the best spot in North America for a Negro colony. Before leaving Nacogdoches, he petitioned the governor of Coahuila and Texas to help him obtain permission to colonize 400 families "of respectable industrious free colored people . . . either in the tract of country lately granted to Frost Thorn, on the Trinity River . . . (and recently forfeited by him) or on such other fertile and suitable sections as may be designated." He assured the governor, who was by now worried about the secessionists in Texas, that only settlers "known to be positively in favor of maintaining the integrity of the

---

[39] *Ibid.*, p. 205.

Mexican Republic against every encroachment" would be per-
mitted in the colony.[40]

The first steps had been taken. Lundy had found the land
good, and he had initiated proceedings with the government
for obtaining a colonization grant. Having accomplished this
much, he returned on foot to Louisiana to begin the long
journey back to Washington, there to wait for the slow proc-
esses of government to do their work. His next step must be
to collect money and to organize support for a project of
whose soundness he was now convinced.

---

[40] Lundy to Elizabeth M. Chandler, September 6, 1832, Chandler Papers; Lundy to the Governor of the State of Coahuila and Texas, July 5,
1832, Lundy-Vickers Collection.

CHAPTER XI

Negotiations in Mexico

If Lundy imagined that his colonization plan would receive widespread support from eastern abolitionists, he soon was to be disappointed. Garrison wished Lundy's project well — "May success attend his benevolent mission," he had written; yet at the same time he seemed to berate its significance while magnifying the importance of his own efforts in the abolitionist cause.[1] Few other antislavery leaders went even that far in endorsing the Texas colony. Most ignored it. The new abolitionist vanguard could become only casually interested in a free-labor experiment designed to take place in a distant, foreign country. They were willing to encourage the production of staples by free labor; they conceded the utility of aiding free Negroes in the manner Lundy proposed; and they respected his efforts as the work of a dedicated humanitarian; yet they had themselves become so absorbed in argumentation, so obsessed with words, and so fascinated with dogma that they minimized the worth of any antislavery ac-

[1] *Liberator*, May 26, 1832.

tivity which did not have as its object demands for commitment to the doctrine of immediate emancipation. A battle
was raging in the North for men's minds. Opponents of slavery underwent emotional upheaval and soul travail in the
early 1830's as they struggled to achieve their own total commitment to the abolitionist creed and then to win others to
similar conviction. Their concern had become ideological.
Lundy moved in more earthly realms.

As he traveled through the upper South and the Ohio River
Valley, he found that his Texas plan, generally ignored by
fellow workers in the East, stirred the imagination of white
men and free Negroes alike.[2] On the way back to Washington
he stopped to visit his old friends in Mount Pleasant, Ohio,
and painted for them a glowing picture of the Southwest. He
told them that he had seen "the finest cattle in that country
he ever saw . . . they do not have to provide any thing to
feed their cattle through the winter . . . the snow has been
known to lay all day in the shade of fences . . . but such oc-
currences are seldom." To men about to face the blasts of another winter in the Appalachian foothills, the attractions of
Texas as he described them seemed irresistible. Jesse Thomas, Jr., son of the harnessmaker who had taught Lundy his
trade, declared that if Mexico repealed its law against further
settlement of United States citizens he would move to
Texas.[3]

Such evidence of enthusiasm was encouraging, but at this
early stage of the project Lundy concerned himself more with
making business arrangements than in enlisting potential
settlers. At Cincinnati he engaged Samuel Yorke Atlee,
younger brother of the antislavery veteran Dr. Edwin Atlee of

---

[2] [Earle], *Life*, pp. 32, 110–112.
[3] Jesse Thomas, Jr., to Nathan M. Thomas, November 21, 1832, Thomas
Papers.

Philadelphia, to superintend publication of the *Genius* during his future absences from Washington. Atlee would not be a partner — Lundy had had enough of partners — but would instead be paid a salary for his labors, a combination of editing, traveling to sell subscriptions, and delivering antislavery lectures. "I hope much from his co-operation," Lundy wrote, "if, indeed he do not (like all the rest . . .) quit me at the end of *six months,* or sooner!"[4] Lundy then hurried to Lockport, New York, for another interview with his benefactor, Lyman Spalding. His optimistic account of Texas led Spalding to advance another 250 dollars to aid his plans.[5] With so much arranged to his satisfaction, Lundy returned to his office at Washington.

He took little part in the winter's mounting debate between "immediatists" on the one hand and "gradualists" and "colonizationists" on the other. While Garrison and other New England abolitionists maintained constant verbal warfare with the supporters of the American Colonization Society and with all others who disagreed with them, Lundy remained outside both camps. His sympathies lay with the Garrisonians, whose moral indictment of slavery coincided with his own, but he differed with them in not sharing their belief that they and they alone had found truth. This does not mean that he thought them rash or believed they should temper their antislavery attack or proceed any less swiftly in their campaign. "There is no danger of going on too fast . . ." he said. He thought most of the objections that had been raised to Garrison's doctrine irrelevant. "What would be the consequence of effecting an immediate emancipation. . . . This is the cry of every unreflecting dunce in the land. . . . Indeed,

---

[4] Lundy to Elizabeth M. Chandler, September 6, 1832, Chandler Papers.
[5] "Agreement Between Benjamin Lundy of Washington and Lyman Spalding of Lockport, New York, January 8, 1836," Lundy Papers.

nobody knows — and *nobody will know* for THIS WILL
NOT BE DONE." [6] Lundy could not believe that the combined action of all the men and women who had yet joined
the antislavery movement would avail much against so well
entrenched an institution as slavery. Therefore, unlike Garrison's followers, he welcomed all honest efforts to the cause,
and he refused to denounce those whose mode of antislavery
operation differed from his own. "It is not to be expected that
this grand reformation can be accomplished by any *single*
system of operations," he wrote. "The evil of Slavery is one of
immense magnitude, and will require the *combined efforts*
of all the wise and virtuous in the nation to eradicate it."
Differences in opinion as to the best plan of operation should
be minimized rather than fought over, he thought, and every
effort to achieve abolition encouraged. He made but one proviso — the essential demand made by all abolitionists: ". . .
one important principle must be adhered to — the one great
object must be kept constantly in view — namely: Christianity
requires, and Justice *demands*, the prompt advocacy and
IMMEDIATE ADOPTION of measures, that shall break the
fetters of the slave, and *prepare him* for the enjoyment of
perfect freedom." [7]

For his own part he continued to publicize his colonization
plan, thinking of it as a complement rather than an alternative to Garrison's program. Texas, he advised the readers of
the *Genius*, surpassed all other proposed sites for Negro colonization because of (1) its pleasant and healthful climate,
(2) the ease and cheapness of reaching it, (3) the opportunity
it offered "for extending agricultural and commercial enterprise," (4) "*the opportunities it will give the philanthropists
of the present generation* TO MAKE EXPERIMENTS REL-

---

[6] *Genius*, XIII (April, 1833), 89.
[7] *Ibid.* (November, 1832), p. 1.

ATIVE TO THE VALUE OF FREE LABOR . . . *by the side of our southern slaveholders,*" and (5) "the speedy means it will afford the man of color to become wealthy, and rise above the degradation that slavery and prejudice has [sic] imposed on him, thereby FURTHER PROVING to the people of this nation, that *here, in America — the land of his birth and his natural home* — he may be fitted for freedom and self-government with perfect ease and safety." [8]

After waiting all winter in vain for word that his petition to admit settlers to Texas had been granted, he realized that he would have to make a second trip to Mexico. At that time of quickening activity in the antislavery movement, an abolitionist of such long standing as Lundy might well hesitate to absent himself from the country. Nothing but matters of the greatest importance, he explained, "could induce him to leave his post, at this interesting period. . . ." [9] He hoped that he would need go no farther than the capital of Coahuila and Texas, but if the law excluding United States citizens from settling within Texas could not be repealed he was prepared to go to Mexico City to plead his cause. [10]

By the spring of 1833 his preparations for the return trip were nearly complete. He had secured a substantial amount of money, part of it borrowed from Spalding and part received as gifts from the Free Produce Society of Philadelphia and from many individuals. [11] The acting committee of the American Convention lent him 100 dollars to aid in conducting the *Genius* during his absence. [12] He would need sizable

---

[8] *Ibid.*, p. 7.

[9] *Ibid.* (April, 1833), p. 81.

[10] Lundy to Elizabeth M. Chandler, March 30, 1833, Chandler Papers.

[11] *Ibid.*

[12] Acting Committee Minutes (1827–37), March 21, 1833, Papers of the American Convention for Promoting the Abolition of Slavery (Historical Society of Pennsylvania).

resources, however, since this trip, which he believed might take four or five months, was to last a year.

While Lundy busied himself with plans for his return to Mexico, Garrison with much fanfare was collecting money to finance a trip to England, ostensibly for the purpose of raising funds to establish a Negro college.[13] Lundy watched the well-publicized proceedings with distaste. "What does thee think of our friend Garrison's *ostentatious parade*, in *begging money* to go to England?" Lundy asked Elizabeth Chandler. "For my part it pains me to see it. . . . I fear they will *spoil him*. He is naturally vain and egotistical; and to add to this *public begging*, is too much to be endured. I like *modesty* in such matters." Lundy contrasted his own method of raising money with Garrison's: "If I *must* procure means through such a medium, I would say to the generous donor: 'When thou doest thine "alms," let it be done *in secret*.'"[14]

Lundy's remarks hinted at the breach that was developing between himself and his former partner. It was prompted by Garrison's needling criticisms rather than by any displeasure Lundy may have felt with Garrison's doctrine. Lundy had reprinted from another newspaper a proposal that the federal government allocate part of the treasury surplus for the purchase and emancipation of slaves. Garrison berated the suggestion and at the same time called Lundy to account for what he appeared to consider the offense of heresy. It did not matter to Garrison that the proposal Lundy advanced might free some slaves; the important consideration to Garrison was that the plan seemed to recognize property rights in slaves and to advocate something less than the principle of immediate emancipation. It thus violated Garrisonian orthodoxy.

---

[13] Garrison and Garrison, *William Lloyd Garrison*, I, 325–347; Thomas, *The Liberator*, pp. 155–157.

[14] Lundy to Elizabeth M. Chandler, March 30, 1833, Chandler Papers.

When Lundy attempted a clarification of his endorsement of the scheme, agreeing that "no man can, in justice, hold another as a slave for a single moment," Garrison refused to accept it, and repeated his earlier criticism.[15] It was hardly surprising, therefore, that Lundy should feel resentment toward the dogmatism and intellectual arrogance of the young man whom he had recently introduced to abolitionism. Garrison's carping, of course, did not halt Lundy's plans to return to Mexico, and by the spring of 1833 his preparations for the trip were nearly complete.

He left his newspaper in charge of Evan Lewis, a trusted Quaker associate (Atlee had remained with him no longer than his earlier assistants), and on May 7, 1833, set out from Philadelphia.[16] Anxious that his zeal for colonization in Texas not be misconstrued as a racist effort to exile American Negroes, he carefully explained his purposes before he left. "The Africans have a *right* to be free on the soil of their nativity, and no impression can ever be made on their numbers, by colonization," he said. Although the Texas colony would open a "door of relief to a few persecuted . . . and an asylum . . . for a small number of liberated slaves . . . the great mass of the Africans must forever remain on the soil of their birth, and there be restored to their rights." [17]

From Nashville he dispatched an explanatory note to the American Convention of the Free People of Color, about to meet in Philadelphia. He called their attention to such asylums as Canada and Mexico, which might serve as a refuge "until prejudice and tyranny of custom and law shall be re-

---

[15] The controversy may be followed in *Liberator*, March 3, July 7, 14, September 15, 1832, and *Genius*, XII (August, 1832), 208.

[16] Lundy to Elizabeth M. Chandler, March 30, 1833, Chandler Papers; [Earle], *Life*, p. 31.

[17] *Genius*, XIII (May, 1833), 97.

laxed, modified, or extinguished. . . ." But his primary object, he assured them, was not the creation of a white America. He aimed at nothing less than "total and unconditional
abolition." Pending abolition he intended to work for the
amelioration of the Negroes' lot, and after they had been
freed he would seek to establish their perfect equality of privilege with the whites. The success of his colony, he told the
convention, would help persuade voters in both North and
South that slavery should be abolished. They would then use
"the potent medium of the *ballot box*" to decree "that '*slavery shall exist no longer.*' " [18]

With these assurances given, Lundy proceeded with his travels. He stopped to deliver antislavery lectures in towns along
the Ohio River, where he thought support might be won
for his project, he visited old acquaintances who might be
persuaded to contribute to the cost of the expedition, and he
met with groups of free colored people whose aid he wished to
enlist. At last after an especially long delay in Tennessee occasioned by his illness from cholera, he boarded a steamboat
bound for New Orleans. It was a tediously slow vessel, and
Lundy became impatient. "To relieve the irksomeness of the
delay," he wrote, "I study Spanish." He never succeeded in
learning the language, however, and found when he arrived
in Texas that he could converse with Mexican officials only
through the aid of interpreters.[19]

On July 21 he reached Brazoria, where he expected to find
transportation to carry him and his heavy luggage toward
San Antonio de Béxar and Monclova, the seat of government.
But no transportation was available. After waiting five days,
he set out in company with two young Kentuckians to walk
the distance. At San Felipe de Austin on the Brazos, the first

---

[18] *Ibid.*, pp. 118–120.
[19] [Earle], *Life*, pp. 32–33.

important settlement on the road, Lundy stopped to rest from his travels. There in Stephen F. Austin's colony he found himself in a society decidedly hostile to the critics of slavery. Perhaps he met men in San Felipe who had known him in Missouri or elsewhere; perhaps he imprudently criticized the local practice of indenturing Negroes for long periods in circumvention of the Mexican law prohibiting the introduction of slaves. Whatever the explanation his efforts to conceal his identity as an abolitionist failed, and for the first time in Texas he encountered threats of violence. However unpleasant the experience may have been, no physical harm resulted to Lundy, and after a few days he continued his journey without further opposition.[20] The incident in itself was no doubt a trivial thing, yet it must have had its effect in confirming his suspicion of some of the members of Austin's colony. As he left San Felipe, he carried away with him the conviction that the motives of some Texans in regard to slavery were irretrievably evil, that they plotted to undo the Mexican antislavery laws, even that they were agents of southern imperialism. The benign view he had previously held about the Americans in Texas began to disappear.

Lundy arrived in San Antonio eighteen days after leaving San Felipe. His hope that he would find the governor in residence in that city was not realized. It would be necessary to travel farther. For the moment, however, he had no choice but to stop in San Antonio, for the next part of the journey to Monclova presented great problems. His money was nearly gone; there were reports too of Indian troubles in the region that might make travel hazardous. Though he lacked nothing in bravery, he did not feel that without companions he could continue the journey, and no one else in San Antonio seemed

---

[20] *Ibid.*, pp. 37–40.

to be going in that direction. Accordingly, he settled down in the city for the rest of August and September. During the interval he again met Juan Antonio Padilla, whose acquaintance he had made the summer before at Nacogdoches. Padilla introduced him to various local officials, who, Lundy thought, might prove helpful in the future. Lundy then rented a room which would serve both as a place to live and a workshop and proceeded to carry on his trade as a leather worker. He made and repaired suspenders and after exhausting the demand for that service fashioned shot bags out of panther skins and deer hides. Not until the end of the first week in October did he leave for Monclova in company with a merchant from St. Louis.[21]

When they reached Monclova two weeks later, Lundy found that he could get no speedy action on his request for land. Because of the ravages of a recent cholera epidemic, "everything seem[ed] to be 'out of joint,' relative to public business," he reported. But at last he managed to present Santiago del Valle, the secretary of state, with a letter of introduction from Padilla, and a few days later visited the secretary in his home. Del Valle was not enthusiastic about Lundy's plan to colonize free Negroes, whose degraded condition, the secretary thought, would generally make them unfit for Mexican citizenship; nor did he offer any hope that a land grant would be forthcoming until Congress had repealed the restrictive Law of April 6, 1830, a most uncertain event.[22]

None of this was encouraging, but after investing so much time and effort, Lundy could not afford the luxury of gloom. With unwarranted optimism he drafted a petition to the governor in the expectation that the law preventing the emi-

---

[21] *Ibid.*, pp. 47–56.
[22] *Ibid.*, pp. 62–63; Lundy to Evan Lewis, October 23, 1833, in *Genius*, XIV (March, 1834), 37.

gration of United States citizens soon would be repealed,
and on November 4 he visited the governor himself. He was
not received sympathetically, because, Lundy explained, the
governor believed him to be one of the "rash Texas schemers."
Whether Lundy's apprehension was correct or not, the analysis nonetheless revealed much about his own growing distrust
of the settlers in Austin's colony. The Texas leaders, Lundy
was convinced, plotted civil disturbances in order to further
their plans to perpetuate slavery. If the governor suspected
Lundy of belonging to their company, he soon changed his
mind, and three days later in a second interview assured him
that he would eventually receive a land grant and predicted
that the state legislature soon would ask the National Congress to repeal the restrictive Law of April 6, 1830.[23]

This was cheering news, but its effect lasted only a few
days. Lundy soon found himself thwarted once more. The
secretary of state reported that the Congress probably would
defer action on the law until its January session. There was
nothing to do but wait. The frequent delays proved both
irksome and expensive. Although Lundy had earned some
money in Texas, it was not enough, and before he left Monclova, he was reduced to selling all his disposable goods in
order to buy food and lodging. A less sanguine and resource-
ful man might have been tempted to give up after so many
disappointments. Lundy, however, was inured to frustration
from long experience, and he used the new delay to good
advantage. He filled the weeks by meeting as many persons
as he could and by investigating the life and manners of the
Mexicans. He "went to see the gamblers," he attended a ball,
and he visited the bullfights, which he watched with fascina-
tion, though (good Quaker that he was) he glanced occasion-

23 [Earle], *Life*, pp. 64–66.

ally at the skies, hoping that rain would "put a stop to the barbarous amusement." [24]

On December 3 news reached Monclova that the Law of April 6, 1830, had at last been repealed, the repeal to take effect six months later. Lundy thought he could now expect speedy action on his request for land. But action was neither as fast nor as favorable as he hoped. Five days passed before the governor sent him a printed copy of the repeal and scheduled an interview. When, in order to speed the negotiations, Lundy requested the secretary of state to provide him with the printed form he should use to apply for the land, the secretary refused on the ground that nothing could be done until the law actually had gone into effect. Lundy's hopes of a few days earlier faded still further when the governor let it be known that he agreed with the secretary — there could be no action for six months.

Lundy could not wait six months. Already he had been in Mexico far longer than he had planned; his funds were exhausted; his friends in the United States supposed him dead. "What shall I do now?" he wrote despairingly in his journal. But in the same spirit that had hitherto dominated his antislavery efforts, he added a note of determination. "I will not yet give over all hopes." [25]

He resorted to various vain expedients. He sent a portrait of George Washington to Santa Anna, the President of Mexico, supposing perhaps that this implied flattery would in some way win official favor.[26] He attempted to negotiate with

---

[24] *Ibid.*, pp. 73–74, 76–77.

[25] *Ibid.*, pp. 78–80; Jane Howell to Thomas Chandler, January 7, 1835, Chandler Papers; Lucretia Mott to J. Miller McKim, April 8, 1834, Lucretia Mott Papers (Friends Historical Library, Swarthmore College, Swarthmore, Pennsylvania).

[26] [Earle], *Life*, p. 82; Lundy to Antonio López de Santa Anna, December 30, 1833, Lundy Papers.

Henry Egerton, a land speculator from New York, who offered to sell him the land he was about to receive from the Mexican government, a grant which included the tract Lundy had intended to request. Lundy, of course, had no money to make such a purchase. "It is very provoking to be thus tormented by heartless speculators," he wrote. Resentful over Egerton's success Lundy visited the governor for the last time and used the occasion to condemn the activities of land speculators in Texas who, he charged, used the generosity of the Mexican government not to populate the region as had been intended but for their own personal profit. This was perhaps merely pique on Lundy's part. He never forgot, however, that land speculation by Americans flourished in Texas, nor did he relinquish his earlier impression that some Texans from the United States flouted the Mexican government's restrictions on slavery. Both of these conditions were later to prove telling arguments in his antislavery campaign.[27]

Before Lundy's interview with the governor had concluded, the governor promised that he could take over any land grant that might be forfeited and assured him that he would receive a grant in his own name as soon as one could legally be arranged. Having secured all that officials were then willing to concede, Lundy prepared to return to the United States. Before leaving Monclova, however, he put into operation another plan which might allow him to receive land even if the Mexican officials failed to act in his favor. He made an agreement with J. Blackaller, a British subject, to whom the Law of April 6, 1830, did not apply. Blackaller would obtain two grants of land, which he would share with Lundy upon his return to Mexico.[28] For the present, however, Lundy must

---

[27] [Earle], *Life*, pp. 85–87, 89–90.
[28] *Ibid.*, p. 90.

go back to the United States to raise money and to seek public
support for his project.

His financial need could hardly have been more desperate.
He was quite destitute and obtained steamboat passage only
on promise to pay when he arrived at his destination. But
the ebb in his personal fortunes did not affect his general
optimism. On April 9 word reached the boat that the legislature of Antigua had voted for the immediate abolition of
slavery. The "glorious news" uplifted his spirits as he reflected
that the "days of American slavery are numbered — glory be
to God." Free Negroes on the boat, learning his identity, lent
him money and cheered him further by the eagerness they
expressed to migrate to a free-labor colony in Texas. "The
coloured people are every where my best friends," commented
Lundy.[29]

Arriving in Cincinnati in the middle of April 1834, he attended lectures at the African Methodist Church delivered
by Lane Seminary students, who only a few weeks earlier had
distressed the school's officials by endorsing immediate emancipation. Shortly afterward Lundy himself spoke in the same
church at an antislavery meeting attended by a dozen Lane
students, and later he visited the seminary, where he found
"some warm friends." [30]

He decided not to take time to travel farther east. Instead,
he dispatched letters to Lyman Spalding in New York and
to Quaker abolitionists in Philadelphia, informing them of
the state of his land-grant proposals. To secure more general
publicity, he persuaded his old associate Charles Hammond,
then editor of the Cincinnati *Gazette*, to print an article that
he had written about Texas.[31] As soon as Lundy returned to

---

[29] *Ibid.*, pp. 109–110.
[30] *Ibid.*, pp. 110–111.
[31] *Ibid.*, p. 111; Cincinnati *Gazette*, April 22, 1834.

Nashville he prepared a printed letter which he sent all over the country as an attempt to maintain contact with other abolitionists by relating his enterprises to theirs. He congratulated them on their contributions to the "wonderful and extremely favorable change in public sentiment, which has at length taken place." But at the same time he reminded any who might have forgotten of his own services to the anti-slavery cause during that "long, dreary, and stormy night of persecution and toil — every moment of which it was necessary to guard with the most intense care the flickering lamp which I had placed upon the 'hill' of public observation. . . ."

"My heart is with you," he told his eastern associates, "and although I may be individually absent from my post for a season, I trust that Divine Providence will, ere long, enable me to return to the charge, and labor with you shoulder to shoulder, until the horrible 'Bastile' of American slavery shall be prostrated in the dust. I never can abandon the cause until this arm becomes nerveless, and this heart ceases its pulsations." [32]

But he had no intention of immediately rejoining his eastern co-workers. Instead, at Nashville he busied himself with financial arrangements for returning to Mexico. He was unable to secure a loan as he had hoped, but a group of free Negroes proposed to raise one hundred dollars for his support, and his friends Thomas Hoge, Jr., and William Bryant agreed to collect funds for him and otherwise to act as his agents in Tennessee. Late in May 1834 he left Nashville on a steamboat bound for New Orleans.

On the way a fellow passenger acquainted him with the terms the Mexican government had offered earlier impresari-

---

[32] Lundy to "Esteemed Friend," May 9, 1834, a printed circular in Smith Papers.

os. There he learned, apparently for the first time, that grantees were "entitled to all the surplus lands in their grants, after they had accommodated the number of settlers that they agreed to introduce. . . ."[33] A new dimension was thus added to Lundy's enterprise. He had thus far developed his colonization plan in a spirit of selflessness. Now he saw before himself the possibility of its making him a rich man. His project, which until then had had as its exclusive aims helping free Negroes and hastening the end of slavery, now also became the vehicle for promoting his own fortunes. Of course, there was nothing necessarily reprehensible in this. Given Lundy's long record of perseverance in the antislavery cause with no prospect whatever of gain, there is no reason to suppose that his determination to carry out his Texas plan was strengthened by the prospect it now appeared to offer to make him rich. Lundy could hardly have been poorer. Except for the tract of undeveloped land in Ohio which he may still have owned, he possessed nothing. A year and a half earlier on his forty-fifth birthday he had expressed his situation in verse:

> The adage says, "At forty wise,"
> But adages I fear are lies.
> Wise men their business should contrive,
> To have a home at forty-five.
>
> But I have had a work to do
> That kept me rambling to and fro,
> And conscience doth not chide and strive
> Within my breast at forty-five.
>
> Now let this rhyming bagatelle
> Go forth — and, journeying ill or well,
> I pray that all who me survive,
> May fare no worse at forty-five.[34]

---

33 [Earle], *Life*, pp. 111–112.
34 *Ibid.*, p. 84.

Although his spirits may generally have been high, as the verse suggested, his material circumstances unquestionably were wretched. He may therefore be excused for welcoming that glimmer of wealth as an unanticipated accompaniment to his humanitarian venture.

When Lundy reached Texas once more, he got in touch with R. M. Williamson at San Felipe, agent for Benjamin R. Milam, a Texas land speculator, and received from him a certificate entitling him to locate one league of land west of the Colorado River in Milam's colony.[35] Lundy was hedging in the event that he should fail to receive his grant from the Mexican government.

He expected now to resume negotiations with the government and also to take possession of the land which he supposed Blackaller would have secured for him in his absence. Apparently the prospect of success gave him increased confidence, for this time he did not travel incognito as he had thought necessary on earlier trips, and his manner of travel was more comfortable. At Nacogdoches he bought a Cherokee pony, which he loaded with his baggage, a luxury he had not before allowed himself.

When he arrived at San Felipe on August 8, he met with Colonel Juan N. Almonte, a commissioner from the Mexican government sent to Texas to investigate provincial affairs. The two became fast friends. Almonte sympathized with Lundy's colonization plan — in fact the Mexican government had authorized him to consult with Negroes in Texas to find out whether they would be willing to move into a colony — and he may also have shared Lundy's distrust of the motives of some prominent Americans in Texas. Almonte's official reports were favorable to the Texans,[36] yet his loyalty to Mex-

---

[35] Certificate #275, July 31, 1834, Lundy Papers.
[36] Juan N. Almonte, "Statistical Report on Texas," *Southwestern Historical Quarterly*, XXVIII (January, 1925), 177n., 207.

ico and his opposition to slavery suggest disagreement with
the ambitions of at least some members of Austin's colony.
Later when the Texans had established their independence,
Almonte would supply Lundy and other abolitionists with
information designed to halt efforts to annex the region to
the United States.[37]

By the time Lundy reached San Felipe, Almonte had completed his official mission and was about to return south of
the Rio Grande. They decided to travel together to Monclova. Before they could leave San Felipe, however, Lundy
was given occasion to remember his earlier unpleasant experience in that city. Again he found some of its leading citizens hostile to his presence. Rumors spread that he was to be
tarred and feathered as an abolitionist, and officials sum-
moned him before the *alcalde* to explain his plans. He apparently satisfied his inquisitors that his project involved no
harm to their interests, and he was allowed to leave the
town unmolested, although he claimed later that only the
presence of the influential Almonte had saved him from violence.[38]

Two days later Almonte rode away from San Felipe accompanied by Spencer H. Jack and Peter W. Grayson, local lawyers who were on a mission to Mexico City to attempt to secure the release of Stephen F. Austin, then held by Mexican
authorities. Illness prevented Lundy from traveling with the
party except occasionally, but he saw enough of Jack and
Grayson to develop a dislike for them as representatives of
interests he believed evil. They were, he noted, only his "*soi-
disant* friends." And when they separated from him and Almonte to take the road to Mexico City, Lundy perhaps recalled
the observation he had recorded in his diary shortly before:

[37] Juan N. Almonte to Lundy, September 24, 1835, in Armstrong, *Lundy
Family*, pp. 387–388.
[38] [Earle], *Life*, p. 122; *Genius*, XIV (November, 1835), 119.

"There is many a wolf in Mexico, from our country, in the guise of a sheep." [39]

As soon as Lundy reached Monclova, he called on Blackaller, expecting to find that his grant had been secured. But to his "great surprise and extreme mortification," he discovered that Blackaller had failed to get the land. The governor had refused to act, Blackaller explained, because he had learned that the Congress was about to pass new laws prohibiting such grants. "Thus, after all my hardships and perils," Lundy lamented, "I am completely baffled in my attempts to establish colonies in Texas." For once he succumbed to despair. All his "toil, privation and peril had been wasted," he wrote, and he could see in the future nothing but "total disappointment, conscious poverty, and remediless despair." [40]

He talked the problem over with Almonte. Why not abandon the effort to secure favors from Coahuila and Texas, Almonte suggested, and try instead to obtain a grant from Tamaulipas, the state bordering Texas on the south, where the restrictions against settlement by United States citizens did not apply. Both Almonte and Padilla, the former secretary of state who happened also to be in Monclova, advised Lundy to proceed at once to Matamoras at the mouth of the Rio Grande, where he might be able to conduct the necessary negotiations. Both men promised to help speed the process. With his customary optimism thus restored, Lundy prepared for a further attempt to obtain land. [41]

Upon reaching Matamoras, Lundy could find no responsible official in the city willing to act on his proposals. Learning, however, that the governor of the state would soon visit

[39] [Earle], *Life*, pp. 89, 126.
[40] *Ibid.*, pp. 127–128; Lundy to Thomas Chandler, August 6, 1835, Chandler Papers.
[41] [Earle], *Life*, p. 130.

the city, he resigned himself to another period of waiting. He lodged and boarded with Henry Powell, a Negro from Louisiana who promised to join the projected colony. With Powell's help Lundy soon became acquainted with other members of the large group of free Negroes who had settled in the region. During the ensuing weeks he spent many hours conferring with them, enlisting their support, and learning the advantages Mexico offered members of their race.

He also met Richard Pearce, an emigrant from New England who for a time had been a southern planter and now lived near Matamoras. Pearce agreed to join Lundy's colony, where he would establish a sugar plantation operated by free labor. Lundy found time, too, to earn much needed money by engaging in his old trade of repairing harness, saddles, and carriages — all the time "feeling like a fish out of water," he wrote, "for I am conscious that I ought to be doing something else." But there was nothing else that could be done until the governor arrived. In preparation for that occasion Lundy composed a letter to present to him and a formal petition for a land grant.[42]

Weeks passed, and the governor did not appear. Finding further delay intolerable, Lundy borrowed twenty dollars from Negro friends and accompanied by Nicholas Drouet, a Negro brickmaker who also hoped to obtain a land grant, traveled to Victoria, the capital of the state. There he presented Richard Pearce's letter of introduction to the government printer, Samuel Bangs, a native of Boston, who provided valuable help in the ensuing negotiations.[43] After long delays and numerous complications the governor and council finally granted Lundy a tract of 138,000 acres between the Rio

[42] Ibid., pp. 142–154.
[43] Ibid., pp. 149, 154, 161; Lota M. Spell, Pioneer Printer, Samuel Bangs in Mexico and Texas (Austin, Tex., 1963), pp. 86–89.

Grande and the Nueces (the exact location was to be selected by Lundy) and permission to colonize 250 families within two years. On March 10, 1835, he signed a contract with the governor completing the arrangements.[44] He then left Victoria, exultant that at last his mission had succeeded.

Back in Matamoras he took lodging again with his Negro friend Powell and spent several days trying with little success to raise money to finance the return trip to Washington. During his stay the free Negroes of the city held a meeting under the chairmanship of Powell in which they passed resolutions pointing out the lack of racial prejudice in Mexico and favoring the establishment of a free-labor colony as the most effective means of "extinguishing the system of slavery upon pacific principles." [45]

These satisfactory developments were soon interrupted by disturbing news. A letter from Bangs in Victoria reported that the governor of Tamaulipas had ruled Lundy could not locate his grant until he had actually brought part of the settlers into the state. Moreover, two-thirds of his contract must be fulfilled within two years, or the grant would lapse. These requirements necessitated speedier action than Lundy had anticipated. Accordingly, he hurried back to the United States to gather his first party of emigrants.[46]

As soon as the boat had dropped anchor at the mouth of the Mississippi, Lundy wrote a note to Lyman Spalding to tell him the jubilant news. "Tho I had to surmount difficulties and dangers, and endure hardships without number, — my efforts are, at last *crowned with success*," he announced. Tamaulipas, he said, was "one of the most beautiful, and

---

[44] [Earle], *Life*, pp. 162–168; "Treaty Between Benjamin Lundy and Francisco Vetal Fernandez, March 10, 1835," Lundy Papers.
[45] [Earle], *Life*, pp. 172–174; Armstrong, *Lundy Family*, pp. 384–386.
[46] [Earle], *Life*, p. 172.

healthy [regions], with the finest climate, and the most fertile soil" he had ever seen. He recounted to Spalding the terms under which he had received the grant, and promised to put him "in the way of realizing a splendid fortune in a short time by comparatively little effort. . . ." [47]

All this was a dream not to be accomplished. No colony for free Negroes would ever result from all Lundy's exertions in Mexico; neither would he or Spalding ever profit from the land grant. But Lundy's enterprise finally would contribute to the abolition cause in a far different way than he had planned or imagined.

---

[47] Lundy to Lyman Spalding, April 16, 1835 (photostat in private possession of Fred Landon, London, Ontario); Lundy to Joseph Lundy, April 15, 1835, Lundy-Vickers Collection.

CHAPTER XII

A Lost Cause

Lundy's exertions and privations in Mexico had left him physically exhausted. Nothing in his life as editor had prepared him for the variety of hardships the journey brought, hardships that ordinarily were endured only by western hunters and trappers. He had traveled on foot much of the way, and before buying his Cherokee pony, he had been burdened with a twenty-five-pound knapsack. When, as was often the case, he had not been able to find lodging in that sparsely peopled country, he had slept outdoors on the damp ground with insufficient covering. His diet had been poor and scanty, and periodic attacks of cholera had further impaired his strength.[1] So debilitating was the experience that he would never recover his former health.

By the time he arrived in Nashville on May 4, 1835, he had fallen desperately ill. R. P. Graham, who subscribed his name at the head of the list of settlers for the projected colony,

---

[1] [Earle], *Life,* pp. 40–41; Lundy to Evan Lewis, September 8, 1833, in *Genius,* XIII (October, 1833), 180.

lodged him at his home and arranged for a physician to attend him. But even in his illness Lundy did not desist from activity in behalf of his emigration plan. He roused himself from his sickbed to prepare a broadside addressed "To American Philanthropists, and Men of Capital, Industry, and Enterprize, Generally," which repeated his well-rehearsed arguments to win public support. The Mexican settlement, Lundy wrote, would afford a chance for Negroes to elevate themselves economically and socially, besides proving the superiority of free labor; it would thus provide an easily understood and incontrovertible argument against slavery. This kind of demonstration, he asserted, had prepared the way for the ending of slavery in the British Empire. G. V. H. Forbes, editor of the *Western Methodist*, who aided Lundy in various ways, printed the message and distributed it widely.[2]

As soon as Lundy had recovered from his illness, he engaged agents to enlist prospective settlers — Ira Robinson of Jeffersonville, Indiana, Samuel Yorke Atlee of Cincinnati (his onetime assistant), and William Bryant of Nashville. Then aided by money obtained from Arthur Tappan of New York, he resumed his journey.[3]

With his broadside message preparing the way, Lundy returned to the East to seek aid and support from other abolitionists. It was a hopeless prospect. His two-year absence in Mexico had isolated him from the main stream of antislavery development. Most abolitionists, now resolutely defending

---

2 [Earle], *Life*, pp. 180–181; *Western Methodist* (Nashville, Tenn.), May 8, 1835.

3 [Earle], *Life*, p. 182; Benjamin Lundy, *A Circular Addressed to Agriculturists, Manufacturers, Mechanics, etc. on the Subject of Mexican Colonization; with a General Statement Respecting Lundy's Grant in the State of Tamaulipas: Accompanied by a Geographical Description, etc. of That Interesting Portion of the Mexican Republic* (Philadelphia, 1835), p. 6.

their own civil rights as well as the rights of Negroes, showed
no interest in colonization in whatever form or for whatever
purpose, except to oppose it. While antislavery organization
had proceeded and abolitionists across the North had fought
spectacular battles, Lundy's solitary enterprise had kept him
far from the view of abolitionists and slaveholders alike. To
most of them he had come to seem irrelevant, a relic from
some other era.

He had shared in no way in the events that had marked
recent antislavery progress. He had not been present, for example, at the Philadelphia convention in December 1833 that
founded the American Anti-Slavery Society, although the delegates had taken due note of his absence and had acknowledged his importance by appointing him to the society's board
of managers. Lewis Tappan, with whom Lundy had conferred
in the interest of antislavery as early as 1828, took care to
have entered into the convention's minutes his hopes that "the
name of Benjamin Lundy will not be forgotten. It is a name
dear to everyone engaged in the cause." And William Goodell,
likewise an acquaintance Lundy made on his New England
tour, had introduced a resolution that "the early, disinterested
and persevering labors of BENJAMIN LUNDY, in the cause
of emancipation, deserve the lively gratitude of this Convention, and of the friends of human rights throughout the
world." [4] But generous as these tributes were, they resembled
eulogies for a dead hero rather than praise for an active com-
rade in arms. Unless Lundy's career were to take some un-
expected turn, it appeared that he would no longer occupy
an influential place in the antislavery movement.

While he made his way toward Philadelphia, belittling
criticism of his emigration project emanated from Boston and
New York. Goodell, who now edited the New York *Emanci-*

---

[4] *Liberator*, December 21, 1833.

pator, minimized the importance of Lundy's proposal, although he gave no reasons for his stand. Garrison in the *Liberator* was explicit. He had "never perceived the utility" of the project, he explained, and had "therefore given it no countenance. . . . We ask in relation to it, — so far at least as the abolition cause is concerned, — *cui bono?*" Lundy read the comment and sent his jaunty answer: "*Nous verrons.*" [5] The exchange of exotic tags was not play, however, for it imperfectly disguised both Garrison's scorn and Lundy's sense of outrage. He dispatched a sharp letter to Garrison, who then replied lengthily in his newspaper. After chiding Lundy for writing "somewhat hotly" against him, Garrison explained in detail why he thought Lundy was "probably laboring in vain, and spending his strength for nought. . . ." [6]

Lundy's plan, Garrison said, was colonization and therefore objectionable for that reason alone, even if it did not suffer from other flaws. Negroes, Garrison claimed (with much exaggeration), opposed "every scheme of this kind. . . ." He raised other valid objections to the project: Settlement in Mexico would be accompanied by "great uncertainties, unavoidable perils, real privations . . . loss of life, and considerable expense"; the colony's success would depend upon "the permanency and character of the Mexican government," both of which were then in doubt. Finally, Garrison said, even if all those shortcomings could in some way be removed, the fact remained that the experiment was "too limited, and will be too slow in its results, to aid essentially the anti-slavery cause; and if it were otherwise, it is not needed to establish either the safety or pecuniary advantages of emancipation."

Garrison's main criticism, however, was more fundamental than any of those points. Even if he had been convinced

---

[5] *Genius,* XIV (November, 1835), 120; *Liberator,* May 2, 1835.
[6] *Ibid.,* June 13, 1835.

that Lundy's scheme would contribute in some important way to the ending of slavery, he still would have opposed it because it placed emancipation upon the ground of policy rather than principle — slaveowners were to be shown not that slavery was wrong but that it was unprofitable. Therefore, Garrison found the plan, in his phrase, "highly objectionable." Slavery, said Garrison, would "be destroyed by holding it up as a flagrant sin against God," in the manner which he believed had succeeded in England.[7]

Lundy replied at length and in doing so took several gibes at his critic. "It is true," he wrote with unaccustomed sarcasm, "that I set up no pretensions to infallibility, in judgment or opinion; but I have had some experience in the work of Emancipation, and am unwilling to yield to any in sincerity and devotion to the cause." He advised Garrison to be less censorious toward those abolitionists with whom he differed. "I would suggest to friend Garrison, as well as to others, the propriety of endeavoring to preserve union and harmony among themselves. It is probable that we shall have our hands full, a while at least, in combatting the enemies of our cause."

Lundy judged Garrison mistaken, "so far as a great portion of the American people" was concerned, in thinking it unnecessary to emphasize any argument against slavery except its immorality. "A large portion of the human race are extremely careless in regard to the duties of religion," he observed, "and there are many interested *knaves* who make it their business to deceive them." He pointed out that a majority had never been moved to any course of action simply by appeals to conscience; never in all Christian history had the majority been made to feel so excessively burdened by the weight of any sin as to cast it behind them. He could not

---

7 *Ibid.*

imagine that the entire American population or even most of
it could now be made sensitive enough to religious obligation
that it would consent to abolish slavery on such ground
alone.

Lundy divided the antislavery community into four classes:
(1) the truly religious who treated slavery exclusively as a sin,
(2) the moralists who viewed it as it affected social relations,
(3) the politicians who were concerned with its effect on the
safety and welfare of the state, and (4) those enterprisers who
considered its economic consequence and nothing else. Each
of those groups, Lundy believed, would welcome the end of
slavery for its own reasons, even though it might remain deaf
to the claims of others. The aid of no group should be scorned
on the ground that its antislavery policy proceeded from
ignoble motives.

If slavery were to be abolished "by a resort to the *ballot-
box*" (as Lundy always assumed it must be), then the support
of a majority of voters must be sought. Abolitionists should
endeavor to influence all classes of potential opponents of
slavery by varying their appeals. "Were not only the preachers,
but also the moralizers, the political orators, and even bankers
and planters engaged in discussing the question," said Lundy,
"I believe more proselytes would be made to our cause, and
the ballot-box would be sooner enlisted in its favour." Finally,
Lundy denied the validity of Garrison's interpretation of recent British history. The British antislavery movement, Lundy
insisted, had not triumphed solely because of religious argument; rather, the success of free labor in the West Indies and
in Mexico, as publicized by Henry George Ward, had done
much to sway British opinion.[8]

Lundy's complex analysis made Garrison appear naive as
well as doctrinaire; yet, for all his discernment Lundy had

---

[8] *Genius*, XIV (November, 1835), 120–122.

not broken the bank of the future. If Garrison's vision of universal religious awakening as the vehicle of emancipation
seemed utopian, it was hardly more so than Lundy's forecast
of a great American consensus in which all voters would con-
verge by different routes toward the common goal of abolition.

There the matter rested. Garrison could derive satisfaction
from again standing on lofty principle, but Lundy for his
part gained little advantage from having analyzed the issue
acutely. He soon realized that neither the Garrisonians in
New England nor their western counterparts, who also expected to achieve emancipation through religious revival,
would give more than incidental aid to his emigration plan.

He seemed to face a bleak future. Upon returning to Philadelphia, he found that the *Genius*, which had served the antislavery movement for fourteen years, had practically expired.
Evan Lewis, the faithful reformer in whose charge he had
left the newspaper, had moved it from Washington to Philadelphia. There on March 25, 1834, Lewis died, whereupon
Edwin P. Atlee became editor. Published only occasionally
during the next year, the *Genius* had lost most of its subscribers by the time Lundy returned, and was burdened with
a large debt besides.[9] Lundy, himself nearly penniless, seemed
helpless to revive it. Shortly after arriving in Philadelphia,
he apparently tried without success to raise funds for that
purpose among philanthropists in New York and elsewhere.[10]
But even if he had maintained the *Genius*, it seems doubtful
that it could have competed successfully against the numerous antislavery journals which had recently sprung up in the
eastern states under the sponsorship of the new abolition so-

[9] *Ibid.* (February, 1834), p. 53; Jane Howell to Thomas Chandler, January 7, 1835, Chandler Papers.
[10] "Chronological Resume of Lewis Tappan's Life," entry for July 13,
1835, Lewis Tappan Papers (Library of Congress).

cieties. Even one of Lundy's most loyal Quaker supporters, who hoped he could revive "his useful paper," predicted that it would "not be read by his subscribers with the same interest, it has been for some years past —." [11]

As though to compound these difficulties, one of his creditors obtained a judgment of 300 dollars against him in the district court of Philadelphia. Unable to pay this sum, he was ordered confined in the debtor's apartment of the county prison.[12] ". . . dire misfortune sits like an incubus upon me, and holds my body in the most unpleasant 'durance,'" he wrote from his prison cell. But he added a stoic note: "We meet with many obstacles in the pursuit of happiness; and they are most likely to attain it, who submit in quiet resignation to the will of an unerring Providence."[13] At the end of a week he was released, presumably after friends had contributed to pay his debt.[14] Upon leaving prison, he soon suspended the *Genius*. No issue appeared between November 1835 and August 1836.

While financial disaster thus hovered over him, he was confronted with personal sorrow. Shortly after returning to Philadelphia, he had called on Ruth Evans, a devout antislavery Quaker and aunt of Elizabeth Chandler. From her he learned of his assistant's death in Michigan Territory on November 2, 1834. As he read the letter detailing the event, "He shed many tears . . ." said Miss Evans, "and paced the room for sometime." To Miss Chandler's brother he sent his condo-

[11] Ruth Evans to Jane Howell, March 5, 1835, Chandler Papers.
[12] District Court of Philadelphia, Appearance Docket, June term, 1835, no. 646 (Department of Records, Philadelphia); *Liberator*, October 8, 1840.
[13] Lundy to Lucretia Mott, September 19, 1835, Charles Smith Ogden Papers (Friends Historical Library).
[14] District Court of Philadelphia, Execution Docket, September term, 1835, no. 263 (Department of Records, Philadelphia).

lences, and remarked that *"I, too,* am thus deprived of the dearest sister I had upon earth." [15]

The Chandler family had considered engaging Garrison to prepare a memoir and an edition of Miss Chandler's works, but deciding finally that sentiment in Philadelphia against Garrison's views of racial equality had become so strong that he should not be allowed to undertake the project, they sought a less controversial editor. Lundy, anxious for reasons of his own that the task not be assigned to Garrison, offered to write the book himself. By July 1836 he had completed the manuscript. It was finally published by subscription, for Lundy discovered that hostility to abolitionists was so severe in Philadelphia that no publisher would venture to put his imprint on a book filled with extreme antislavery expression.[16]

None of the misfortunes that afflicted Lundy upon his return to Philadelphia — poverty, the death of friends, the opposition of co-workers — deterred him from persisting in his colonization plans. While work on the Chandler memoir proceeded, he made preparations to return to Mexico to plant his colony. In November 1835, in the last issue of the *Genius* to appear before its suspension, he printed an appeal for aid from antislavery humanitarians: ". . . it is my sincere wish to do what the means at command shall enable me, in hastening the downfall of that system of oppression which has corrupted tens of thousands of our citizens, reduced millions to a cruel bondage, and endangered the very existence of our institutions." [17]

---

[15] Ruth Evans to Jane Howell, July 29, 1835, and Lundy to Thomas Chandler, August 6, 1835, Chandler Papers.

[16] Lundy to Thomas Chandler, February 16, 1836, Ruth Evans to Jane Howell, December 21, 1834, July 29, 1835, and Jane Howell to Ruth Evans, January 21, 1835, *ibid.*

[17] *Genius*, XIV (November, 1835), 127.

He also prepared a sixteen-page pamphlet on Tamaulipas for the information of potential settlers. In particular he hoped that it would "induce men of capital to engage extensively in the culture of sugar, cotton and rice" through the use of free labor.[18] The fact that the pamphlet was addressed to white investors and did not dwell on the humanitarian aspects of the project does not mean that Lundy had betrayed his antislavery purpose. He had come to realize, however, that large amounts of money would be required to move free Negro families so great a distance and to establish them in Mexico. A letter from Richard Pearce of Matamoras had advised him on the essentials for the colony. At every point Pearce had emphasized the need for capital and for skilled direction of the settlers. He had even recommended that Lundy furnish the colony with a ninety-ton vessel of shallow draft for trading with New Orleans! [19] Philanthropy alone appeared unlikely to supply funds in such quantity; ambitious businessmen conceivably might do so.

On January 8, 1836, Lundy signed a contract with Lyman Spalding as his co-partner in the Tamaulipas project. Lundy pledged himself to settle the lands as soon as possible; the partners agreed to share expenses equally after Lundy had repaid the 500 dollars Spalding had lent him. They would hold the land jointly, with Lundy having the responsibility of allotting land to settlers. Spalding would have sole right to purchase a site for a city. In exchange for six city lots Lundy agreed to prepare a plan for the city, lay it out, and name it.[20]

This was a blueprint for business enterprise at least as magnificent in concept as any designed by other southwestern pro-

---

[18] Lundy, *Circular Addressed to Agriculturists*, p. 3.

[19] [Richard Pearce] to Lundy, March 31, 1835, Lundy Papers.

[20] "Agreement Between Benjamin Lundy of Washington and Lyman Spalding of Lockport, New York, January 8, 1836," *ibid.*

moters, and early in 1836 prospects still looked favorable for its success, in spite of the small support it had received from other abolitionists. Although the revolution in Texas proceeded on its confused course, Lundy informed Spalding that as yet he had no fear that the disorders would significantly hamper their plans. He imagined the Texans to be extremely weak and guilty of sending out false reports which magnified their military achievement. "Why have not the rebels *long since* taken General Cos?" asked Lundy. "After capturing Cos, *twice*, the news-manufacturers have *condescended* to let him remain *half-captured*!! — and General Austin is dispatched to the U. S. for men and money and guns!!!" [21]

The prospect that the rebels might persuade the United States government to attempt to purchase Texas from Mexico did not disturb Lundy either. He corresponded with Juan Almonte, who positively assured him that Mexico would never part with the territory. "We know too well to appreciate good things," he said, "and not only that but the sale of Texas would produce a revolution in Mexico." Almonte reported further that, as Lundy suspected, "everything goes on smoothly" with the war.[22] Lundy also conferred several times in Philadelphia with the Mexican chargé d'affaires, who promised to facilitate his operations in Tamaulipas and flattered him by ordering several volumes of the *Genius* to send to the President of Mexico.[23]

But the greatest cause of all for optimism was the decision

[21] Lundy to Lyman Spalding, January 13, 1836, Lyman Spalding Collection (Regional History Collection, Cornell University, Ithaca, N.Y.).
[22] Juan N. Almonte to Lundy, September 24, 1835, in Armstrong, *Lundy Family*, pp. 387–388.
[23] Lundy to David Lee Child, January 25, 1835 [1836], Lydia and David Child Papers (Boston Public Library); Lundy to Lyman Spalding, January 13, 1836, Spalding Collection.

made by two important Boston abolitionists, David Lee Child and his wife, Lydia Maria Child, to join Lundy's expedition to Mexico.[24] Unlike most other New England abolitionists, Mrs. Child still saw utility in Lundy's free-labor argument and resolved to use her considerable influence to gain support for it.[25] At about the same time, George Kimball, a New Hampshire lawyer, also agreed to go, and Mrs. Child reported that others among her friends, including a cotton manufacturer, might decide to join the colony. Lundy could not resist gloating over these important accessions, for they seemed to indicate that his ideas and programs had not been altogether rejected as had appeared and as Garrison claimed they deserved to be. More than that, Lundy was not blind to the irony of the fact that, as he said, the Childs were Garrison's "particular friends, and among the most active and influential of the New England abolitionists." His elation as he imagined Garrison's chagrin was understandable. "How our friend Garrison, and a few others will relish it, I do not know," he wrote.[26]

Child, anxious to improve his declining economic situation, proposed that Lundy make him a partner in the enterprise. Although Lundy informed him this was impossible on account of his prior agreement with Spalding, he promised Child that "when I can *see thee*, I will inform thee, more particularly than I have yet done, how thee may acquire ample means to realize something handsome, in a comparatively short period." Lundy promised him a half-league of land as soon as the first fifty settlers had arrived and additional

[24] [Earle], *Life*, p. 188.
[25] Lydia Maria Child to Ellis Gray Loring, January 30, 1836, The Loring Papers (The Women's Archives, Radcliffe College, Cambridge, Mass.).
[26] Lundy to Lyman Spalding, January 13, 1836, Spalding Collection.

amounts if he employed eight or ten laborers. Eventually, Lundy said, he might hold 11,133 acres.[27]

Child resigned a mission to England for the American Anti-Slavery Society in order to accept these luring arrangements. Both he and his wife felt an urgent need to settle in a new country, especially if it offered the prospect of riches. Although Mrs. Child dreaded thus exiling herself from Boston, she took consolation from the fact that moving to so remote a region need not mean isolation from the antislavery movement for her any more than it had for Elizabeth Chandler when she left Philadelphia for the Michigan backwoods; ". . . be assured we shall labor for this cause, let us be where we may," she wrote. "One thing that reconciles me to this Mexican project, is the reasonable prospect of being extensively useful to the oppressed." Besides, she said, she could continue to write antislavery books wherever she might be.[28]

Early in the spring of 1836 Lundy proposed that he and Child disguise themselves and travel at once to New Orleans and thence to Matamoras, there to make preparations to receive the first group of settlers. Mrs. Child discouraged this plan on account of the peril she feared both would face. "But your danger will be a hundred fold greater than his," she warned Lundy. "I do beseech you not to be so rash as to think of running this great risk. . . . I pray you do not go by way of N. Orleans. Having survived so many dangers, do not hazard all on one throw, just as the way seems open for the final accomplishment of your wishes." [29] Although Mrs. Child's womanly plea did not sway Lundy, her husband was per-

[27] Lundy to David Lee Child, January 25, 1835 [1836], Child Papers.
[28] Lydia Maria Child to Ellis Gray Loring, January 30, 1836, Loring Papers.
[29] Lydia Maria Child to Lundy, March 14, 1836, in Armstrong, *Lundy Family*, pp. 391–392.

suaded to remain at home, and Lundy decided to delay his own departure until Child could accompany him.

Mrs. Child attempted to reconcile Lundy to the delay by speculating that the revolt in Texas would soon be put down and travel in that region made less hazardous. "It seems to me that the Texas traitors are now going down hill to destruction as fast as the greatest sinners need to . . ." she said. "The Mexican nation and government have been so long harassed, irritated, and insulted by these insolent desperadoes that they will, I doubt not, make thorough work with them now." [30]

Later news reports dashed these hopes. Men, arms, and money had poured into Texas from the United States, and on April 21, 1836, the Texans' victory at the Battle of San Jacinto altered the prospect. All Mexican troops then withdrew south of the Rio Grande, and Texas extended its authority southward to that river. In consequence, Lundy's grant lay in Texas, not in Tamaulipas, and Texans, as Lundy knew, would not tolerate an abolitionist scheme. But even had the boundary not been changed, it seemed unlikely that the Mexican government, smarting from its experience with United States settlers in Texas, would have allowed new colonies of North Americans to be planted within her territory.

By early June 1836 Lundy had concluded that the project in Tamaulipas was "finished" and that he must soon place himself in "an attitude to do *something else*." [31] He would never have his grant with its opportunities for his own wealth. He would never accomplish his plan to establish a free-labor colony and thus bring nearer the end of slavery. His disap-

---

[30] *Ibid.*
[31] Lundy to John Quincy Adams, June 9, 1836, The Adams Family Papers (all references are to the microfilm edition).

pointment must have been bitter in the extreme as he sur-
veyed the ruin of his hopes. The project in which he had invested years of his life lay shattered. All his privations and
sacrifices and exertions seemed to have availed nothing. Yet
Lundy rarely was given to despair. He did not surrender to
misfortune, and within the next year he had succeeded in
converting this great defeat into a victory for the antislavery
cause and thereby brought himself back into the main line of
antislavery developments.

CHAPTER XIII

Texas Repulsed

From the days of Aaron Burr and the filibusterers to those of Stephen F. Austin and Sam Houston, some Americans had covetously eyed Texas. If Burr's plans for possessing the area failed to develop and remain mysterious to this day, others succeeded in writing their ambitions unmistakably into the historical record. Although the United States' claims to Texas had been surrendered in the Adams-Onís Treaty of 1819, highly placed men soon afterward began to propose reacquiring the region both for its strategic value and as a means of promoting the national interest. However justified such objects may have been, they could not in those fevered years remain unentangled with the issues of slavery and sectional power.

Shortly after Garrison joined Lundy in Baltimore in 1829, the new Jackson administration started negotiations to purchase Texas from Mexico. It did not act in secret. Instead a great public relations campaign launched the venture, with articles in favor of the purchase appearing simultaneously in

administration newspapers throughout the South and West.[1]
Lundy reacted at once, recalling in particular that Senator
Thomas Hart Benton of Missouri, author of the pro-Texas
articles signed "Americanus" and "LaSalle," had successfully
opposed his own efforts nine years earlier to bar slavery from
Missouri. Now Benton's "avowed design," Lundy charged,
was to make Texas a slave territory within the United States.[2]
Lundy, on the other hand, had already begun to think of
Texas as a potential refuge for free Negroes. "Let the public
sentiment be expressed," he urged. "Let the moral influence
of the people — (the honest yeomanry of the nation —) be
heard. . . ." As Lundy knew and as Benton's articles suggested, the issue involved not just the extension and perpetuation of slavery but also the increase of southern political
power. "We cannot longer disguise the fact," Lundy wrote,
*"that the advocates of slavery are resolved, at all hazards, to
obtain the territory in question* . . . FOR THE AVOWED
PURPOSE OF ADDING FIVE OR SIX MORE SLAVE
HOLDING STATES TO THIS UNION!!!"[3]

To northern voters, who had recently marked the defeat
of John Quincy Adams by a slaveholding planter and observed the obstructionary tactics of southern congressmen, the
prospect seemed intolerable. Newspapers in New York and
Pennsylvania as well as in New England soon joined the
Genius in opposing the purchase of Texas. Garrison, writing
in the *Genius*, rejoiced to observe that "the free states generally are decidedly inimical to the purchase." And why, he
asked, should they not be? "To them it is a question of life
and death — honor and shame — liberty and oppression." He

---

[1] John Bach McMaster, *A History of the People of the United States
from the Revolution to the Present Day* (New York, 1924), V, 543.
[2] *Genius*, X (September 16, 1829), 14; (September 25, 1829), p. 17.
[3] *Ibid.* (September 16, 1829), pp. 13–14.

advised northerners to take a belligerent, uncompromising stance in the crisis. "We know that they have borne the insults and aggressions of the south with meekness approachable to pusillanimity . . . they cannot, they will not, they should not submit to the dictates of imperious southrons. Let a separation follow, if the latter desire it, sooner than add another foot of slave territory to the republic. . . ."[4] Thus nearly twenty years before the Wilmot Proviso abolitionists began to hew the free-soil plank that they would eventually insert into the platform of the Republican party.

Lundy, realizing that he had scant power to influence the policy of the Jackson administration against acquiring Texas, ventured instead to appeal directly to the humanitarian impulses of Mexican officials. On November 20, 1829, he addressed a letter to the President of Mexico to inform him that the intended purchase would lead to "the extension and perpetuation of the horrible and oppressive system of African Slavery." American advocates of slavery dared urge the measure, he explained, only because of Jackson's election. "Flushed with recent success, in elevating to the chief magistracy of the Union a man who is a slaveholder himself, and will unquestionably throw the weight of his influence in the scale of their party, they feel secure of strength sufficient to effect their purpose. . . ."[5]

The Mexican government's rejection of the United States' offer to buy Texas temporarily allayed abolitionist fears. But Lundy's suspicions of the ultimate aim of certain southern leaders remained. Their ambition, he charged, still was either to annex Texas or to establish *"its independence, with the view of extending the system of slavery therein. . . .* It will

---

[4] *Ibid.* (December 4, 1829), p. 101.
[5] Lundy to Vicente Guerrero, quoted in Lundy to John Quincy Adams, July 13, 1836, Adams Papers.

as surely be attempted, ere long, as that the *Territory exists. . . ."* [6]

According to a District of Columbia writer whose views Lundy publicized, southern leaders, aware of the growth of northern population and the spread of antislavery sentiment, had reached a point of desperation; "there is but one device which they imagine will defeat the cause of liberty — and that is, by *dissolving* the *union*, and *setting* up for themselves — purchase or take Texas, and scatter their slaves *throughout those vast western and southern regions.* There is no doubt in my mind but that *this* is the *true ground* of all the southern excitement about state rights, the tariff, &c. . . ." [7]

Lundy accepted such charges as the truth. Circumstantial evidence supported his belief that men from the slave states had conspired to perpetuate slavery in Texas. When the state of Coahuila and Texas abolished slavery, the Texans instituted an indenture system to circumvent the law. Although shortly afterward the Mexican government abolished slavery throughout the republic, it soon found it politic to make an exception for the Texans, some of whom had brought slaves with them and insisted upon maintaining their power to exploit the labor of others in order to enhance their own prosperity and comfort. [8]

Lundy had discovered for himself that antislavery views were hardly tolerated in Austin's colony; indeed, some Texans had proved highly sensitive on the point. When Lundy visited the area in 1833 and 1834, he had been rudely treated and threatened on more than one occasion. [9] Although such prominent revolutionists as James Bowie and Oliver H. Jones

---

[6] *Genius*, XI (March, 1831), 185.

[7] *Ibid.*, XII (August, 1831), 51.

[8] Barker, *Life of Stephen F. Austin*, pp. 243–245.

[9] [Earle], *Life*, pp. 40, 122; *Genius*, XIV (November, 1835), 119.

conversed civilly with him when the three met on the streets
of Monclova, he heard rumors that other Texans had formed
an organization to work against his plan to found an antislavery colony in their midst.[10] His own apprehensions were
reinforced by Richard Pearce's advice that the projected colony in Tamaulipas should be planted as far as possible from
the Texas boundary; for, Pearce warned, there "are spirits in
Texas hostile to your enterprise. On the Nueces, they can an-
noy you, on the Rio Grande, they can not." [11]

Lundy felt no sympathy at all for the Texas rebels. In his
view Mexico had granted the American emigrants the most
liberal of concessions. Their legitimate grievances were few
and trivial, yet they remained ungrateful for those favors and
plotted rebellion against fancied oppression. Americans had
taken advantage of Mexican generosity and forbearance both
by establishing slavery in contravention of Mexican policy
and by speculating in Mexican lands.[12] Lundy's frustrating
experiences with land speculators in Texas had appeared to
confirm some of his worst suspicions.[13] Furthermore, he knew
that certain Texas grants had come under the control of a
New York firm, the Galveston Bay and Texas Land Company,
in whose management Aaron Burr's protégé, Samuel Swart-
wout — a strong supporter and favorite of Andrew Jackson
— played a large role.[14] The aged Burr, perhaps reviving his
earlier dreams of empire, had invested in one of the company's
Texas schemes and encouraged Jane McManus, a lively New

---

[10] [Earle], *Life*, p. 130.

[11] [Richard Pearce] to Lundy, March 31, 1835, Lundy Papers.

[12] Benjamin Lundy, *The War in Texas: A Review of Facts and Circumstances, Showing That This Contest Is the Result of a Long Premeditated Crusade Against the Government* . . . (Philadelphia, 1836), p. 3.

[13] [Earle], *Life*, pp. 86–87, 90.

[14] Lundy, *War in Texas*, pp. 35, 40.

York adventuress, to conduct emigrants to Texas in 1833. As the revolutionary movement unfolded, Miss McManus returned to New York to encourage speculators to aid the rebels whose victory might bring riches to herself and to many like-minded Americans who had never seen Texas.[15]

Lundy understood, just as the Texans and their American supporters did, that both the success of land speculations and the security of slavery would be enhanced if the state were independent from Mexico. He placed no credit whatever in the protestations of the rebels that their sole motivation was the desire for liberty from Mexican oppression, the name they gave to the centralizing tendencies within the Mexican government.[16] Texans opposed centralization, he supposed, for the same reason that their United States counterparts had espoused nullification and states' rights doctrine, that is, to safeguard slavery. Oppression, Lundy insisted, had never been felt by the Texans, but the profits to be realized from slavery and land speculation remained a constant attraction for them and their advocates within the United States.[17]

In the spring of 1836 the Texas rebels made good their claim to independence and in so doing created a moral and political crisis within the United States. Within a few months the Texans sought annexation, a goal which abolitionists and other northerners feared the Jackson administration would be only too ready to help them attain. Opponents and advocates of the measure prepared for battle. Lundy, having aban-

[15] Aaron Burr to Judge James Workman, November 16, 1832, Moses Austin Bryan Papers (Eugene C. Barker History Center, University of Texas, Austin); Jane McManus to Joseph D. Beers, October 29, 1835, Samuel M. Williams Papers (Rosenberg Library, Galveston, Tex.); Walter Flavius McCaleb, *The Aaron Burr Conspiracy* (New York, 1903), p. 305; James Parton, *The Life and Times of Aaron Burr* (Boston, 1892), p. 663.
[16] Lundy, *War in Texas*, pp. 17–20.
[17] *Ibid.*, p. 13.

doned all hope of establishing a free-labor colony in Mexico, now turned to the new contest. He was in an unparalleled position to help arouse northern opinion against annexation, for probably no other American citizen could claim to be so well informed about Texas affairs as he. Moreover, his considerable literary skill and experience combined with moral fervor to give him advantage in presenting his point of view.

Lundy spent disheartening weeks in the winter of 1835–36 composing a series of essays in which he presented his interpretation of the origin and character of the Texas Revolution. No longer having a newspaper of his own, he submitted the work to the abolitionist editor Robert Walsh, who agreed to publish it serially in his Philadelphia *National Gazette*. Lundy insisted that the articles appear under the pseudonym "Columbus," because he imagined that the exposé would so damage the interests of certain speculators and politicians that disclosure of its origin would imperil his life.[18]

At the moment the essays appeared, southern and antislavery interests were clashing once again in Congress, this time over the reception of antislavery petitions. The American Anti-Slavery Society's campaign to engulf the House of Representatives with a flood of petitions against slavery and the slave trade was succeeding so spectacularly that the regular business of the House faced suspension as thousands of petitions demanded official attention. Southern congressmen used this fact as an excuse to refuse to receive the documents; John Quincy Adams made himself champion of the right to present the petitions over all objections by his southern colleagues. During the ensuing wrangle Adams took occasion to argue also against another sectional issue, the recognition or the annexation of Texas.[19]

---

[18] Lundy to John Quincy Adams, May 14, 1836, Adams Papers.
[19] Samuel Flagg Bemis, *John Quincy Adams and the Union* (New York, 1956), pp. 360–370.

Lundy saw in Adams a valiant and useful partner in the antislavery cause. He had watched Adams' antislavery views develop slowly over the years and had long considered him a potential ally. As early as 1831 he visited Adams in Washington to acquaint the former President with his antislavery plans, and in the eyes of proslavery advocates the two were linked. "The last we heard from Mr. Adams," maliciously wrote the editor of the *United States Telegraph* during the presidential campaign of 1828, "he was on his way to New-England to aid the editor of the Genius of Universal Emancipation in getting up a Manumission Society." [20]

In the spring of 1836 Lundy, whose circumstances in life had never before given him entrée to high places,[21] arranged an effective antislavery alliance with the former President who now represented Massachusetts' Plymouth district in Congress. He bundled up the issues of the *National Gazette* containing the first four of his anti-Texas essays and mailed them to Adams at Washington on the chance the old statesman might find in them something useful to his political maneuvers.

Lundy did not disclose his authorship, but assured Adams that on account of his own close observation of Mexican affairs he could vouch "that the remarks of the writer of these essays are strictly correct." In the letter accompanying the essays he told Adams what the former President already suspected: "There can be *no doubt* of the fact, that the grand object of the insurgents is, the re-establishment of slavery in Texas. Evidence enough can be adduced to substantiate the assertion." [22]

Adams responded to Lundy's overture with an eagerness

---

[20] *United States Telegraph* (Washington, D.C.), August 18, 1828.
[21] Lundy to John Quincy Adams, June 9, 1836, Adams Papers.
[22] Lundy to John Quincy Adams, May 9, 1836, *ibid.*

beyond his expectation. The packet of essays tantalized Adams. He had felt in his bones that the Texas Revolution must be a plot engineered by slaveholders to further southern interests, but he had found little beyond intuition to support his view. Now Lundy had supplied evidence that appeared to substantiate his darkest suspicions. Who was the author, Adams wanted to know. The facts were so important that he must be told at once. He appealed to Lundy for still more information about Texas and promised to make the facts known to the entire country.[23]

Lundy could not ignore so flattering a proposition. He had hardly dreamed of such success. After years of lonely and unrewarded struggle to acquaint the public with the menace of slavery and the slave power, a former President of the United States had offered to join his enterprise! At last he might reasonably expect to influence the nation's policy at a fateful moment in its history. He promised Adams the information he sought and pridefully confessed that it was he who had written the "Columbus" essays, though he pledged Adams to keep the fact a secret. Lundy then set himself to gathering maps, pamphlets, copies of Mexican laws — anything that might serve as ammunition in the old statesman's battle — and sent them off to Washington.[24]

Adams welcomed every item, but he still considered the essays from the *National Gazette* the most valuable. It was the "Columbus" essays, Adams assured Lundy, that had supplied "nearly all the facts" he possessed about events in Texas. "I earnestly entreat you to continue the series of your publications upon this subject," he wrote, and to forward any material "serviceable to my purpose of making known to the Nation the designs affecting them and their Liberties which

---

[23] John Quincy Adams to Lundy, May 12, 1836, *ibid.*
[24] Lundy to John Quincy Adams, May 14, 19, 23, 24, 25, 1836, *ibid.*

have long been in operation, and are now in the process of being disclosed and ripening. . . ." [25] Later he wrote, ". . . it will be a favor to me, and may promote the cause in which you take so much interest, and to which probably more than anything else, the remainder of my political life will be devoted." [26]

The Lundy-Adams combination bore its first fruit in the form of a long anti-Texas speech delivered by Adams on May 25 in the House of Representatives. Although the address began as a defense of the right of petition, it soon diverged into an account, based on the "Columbus" essays, of the dangers to be expected from the annexation of Texas.[27] Adams' charges of the sinister character of southern intentions received wide notice, especially in the North, where they helped marshal opposition against hasty governmental action either to recognize or annex the new republic. Lundy dashed off a congratulatory letter to his distinguished partner. "I perceive the 'ice is broken' in the House of Representatives," he wrote. "Perseverance, *perseverance*, my friend!" [28] Adams replied in similar vein: ". . . and I say in return to you also *persevere*." He pointed out to Lundy that for much of the substance of the speech he was indebted to Lundy's writings, a fact the enthusiastic Quaker would hardly have missed.[29]

With so much encouragement from Adams and also from his friends in Philadelphia, Lundy decided to reprint the "Columbus" essays in a thirty-two–page pamphlet, *The Origin and True Causes of the Texas Revolution Commenced in the Year 1835*. He sent Adams a dozen copies as a sample, where-

---

25 John Quincy Adams to Lundy, May 20, 1836, *ibid.*
26 John Quincy Adams to Lundy, May 30, 1836, *ibid.*
27 *Register of Debates*, 24 Cong., 1 Sess., XII, part IV, 4046–47.
28 Lundy to John Quincy Adams, May 27, 1836, Adams Papers.
29 John Quincy Adams to Lundy, June 2, 1836, *ibid.*

upon Adams ordered a hundred copies for his own use.[30]
Through Adams' speeches and the wide circulation of the
"Columbus" pamphlet, Lundy's interpretation of the Texas
Revolution became standard among abolitionists and northerners generally. William Goodell reprinted the essays in the
Friend of Man, thus making them available to still more readers. That paper claimed that fifty northern editors who did
not consider themselves abolitionists accepted the truth of
Lundy's charge that the Texas Revolution originated in a
plot to perpetuate slavery. No other man in the United States,
said Goodell, knew as much about political affairs in Mexico
and Texas as Lundy; no one else could claim to speak so
authoritatively on the subject.[31]

Lundy himself never doubted the validity of his interpretation of events in Texas. "My intercourse with many of the
actors in the great drama, has given me numerous opportunities to understand their motives and designs," he wrote. "It
is indeed impossible that I should be mistaken in the one or
the other." [32] He took much satisfaction in recording information that seemed to confirm the accuracy of his view. In
the middle of June 1836 he learned from "a member of
the present *Texas revolutionary government*," who passed
through Philadelphia on a journey to New York, that in order to acquire additional portions of the seacoast the Texans
planned to extend their aggressions southward by establishing the Texas boundary some 200 miles below the Rio
Grande.[33] He forwarded to Adams an extract from a letter
General Santa Anna had written to a correspondent in Phil-

[30] Lundy to John Quincy Adams, May 31, 1836, and Adams to Lundy,
June 6, 1836, *ibid.*
[31] *Friend of Man* (Utica, N.Y.), August 18, 25, 1836.
[32] *Genius*, XIV (October, 1836), 178.
[33] Lundy to John Quincy Adams, June 14, 1836, Adams Papers.

adelphia in which the defeated Mexican leader asserted that speculators and adventurers headed the Texas revolt.[34] When Lundy heard that the Texas Congress by unanimous vote had offered command of its army to James Hamilton, former governor of South Carolina and a leader of South Carolina's nullification movement, he maintained that the truth of his charge had been proved — collusion between southern slaveholders and the Texas rebels demonstrably did exist.[35]

Despite the personal satisfaction both Lundy and Adams derived from widespread acceptance of their views, neither man could be hopeful that the movement to annex Texas had been scotched. Adams reached solemn conclusions after studying the mountain of evidence Lundy had presented. "I see no alternative but that the whole Mexican Confederation is destined to be overrun by our landjobbers and Slavemakers, and that the dissolution of our own union must precede the final struggle between Slavery and Freedom," he wrote.[36] Lundy, equally apprehensive, predicted the imminent secession of the South; ". . . unless the Despots of the Slave States can establish their authority over the Union, safely and *permanently*, they will, *ere long*, endeavor to set up for themselves," he wrote. "Depend on it, we *are* upon the eve of an important *crisis*. The plans for a *Southern Confederacy* are maturing. Let the sentinels on the watch-tower of *our Union* look to it." [37] By the summer of 1836 he was predicting that the United States would soon become involved in war with Mexico: ". . . it will be almost impossible for our government to keep its fingers out of the pie." In New York, Boston, and Philadelphia partisans of the Texans had joined with

---

[34] Lundy to John Quincy Adams, June 9, 1836, *ibid.*
[35] *Ibid.*
[36] John Quincy Adams to Lundy, June 27, 1836, *ibid.*
[37] Lundy to John Quincy Adams, June 9, 1836, *ibid.*

southerners to support the rebels. As a result men, money, and weapons had left the United States to strengthen the Texans. "Who are they, indeed, that are *now* waging the war against Mexico?" asked Lundy. "How would the 'laws of nations' decide this question?" [38]

Such fears were not to be realized immediately, however, and despite a flood of pro-Texas memorials and John C. Calhoun's fervid demand for annexation, Congress adjourned early in July 1836 without the United States' having become officially involved in the war and with Texas' independence still unrecognized. Both Adams and Lundy could take satisfaction in having helped delay those events.

With the business of Congress suspended for the summer, Adams traveled to Philadelphia to spend several weeks with his Quaker friend Nicholas Biddle, president of the Second Bank of the United States. Lundy, looking upon the visit as an opportunity to bring Adams firmly within the abolitionist circle, arranged to spend many hours in conversation with him and persuaded the Quaker reformer Lucretia Mott to invite a company of antislavery workers to meet with Adams at her home.[39]

Early one morning, shortly after Adams arrived in the city, Lundy called at Biddle's house to urge Adams to address the local antislavery society. Adams declined. Not easily dissuaded, Lundy came back in the afternoon with his abolitionist associate Edwin Atlee in hope of changing the old man's mind.[40] But if Lundy was persistent, so was Adams. He would not speak to an antislavery society. Three days later Lundy spent two hours at Biddle's house, acquainting Adams "with his principles, projects, and purposes relating to Slavery."

[38] Lundy to John Quincy Adams, June 14, 1836, *ibid.*
[39] Lundy to John Quincy Adams, June 25, 1836, *ibid.*
[40] John Quincy Adams Diary, entry for July 8, 1836, *ibid.*

Lundy must have realized that Adams already knew these fairly well; his particular object was not to educate Adams but to try to persuade him to help reestablish Lundy's suspended antislavery newspaper. Although Adams listened patiently while Lundy presented a lengthy appeal for aid, he finally decided it would be best "not to give him any expectation of it." Later that same day Lundy escorted Adams to a tea party James and Lucretia Mott had arranged in the congressman's honor. Adams hugely enjoyed himself and appeared to be at one with the abolitionists who attended. "I had free conversation with them till between ten and 11 o'clock," he wrote in his diary, "upon Slavery — the abolition of Slavery and other topics of all which the only exceptionable part was the undue proportion of the talking assumed by me, and the indiscretion and vanity in which I indulged myself." Much encouraged that he had made a convert, Lundy walked back to the Biddle house with Adams and talked with him there for another hour.[41]

All these conversations and urgings failed to accomplish their purpose, however. Adams was too wary a politician to commit himself to the abolitionist cause, whose success and effect still remained in doubt. He would use the abolitionists when they served his purpose, just as they would use him, but firm commitment to their program he regarded as out of the question. Although Adams refrained from identifying himself with antislavery societies, as Lundy wished him to do, and declined to aid Lundy in his publication ventures, the two nonetheless became close friends. Adams visited Lundy in Philadelphia in May 1837,[42] and they maintained regular correspondence as long as Lundy lived. However much they might differ on formal adherence to abolition, they nonethe-

---

[41] Adams Diary, June 11, 1836, *ibid.*
[42] Adams Diary, May 11, 1837, *ibid.*

less remained as one in their views on the evils of slavery and the annexation of Texas.

Lundy never doubted Adams' loyalty to abolitionist principle. When early in 1839 Adams enraged some abolitionists by announcing that he opposed immediate emancipation in the District of Columbia, Lundy affirmed his faith in Adams' antislavery conviction. "We know the opinion which he entertains, *but refuses to express* until the door of free discussion shall be opened in Congress . . ." Lundy wrote. "He has contributed his full share in propelling the *Abolition Car*, within the last two or three years. And though he may yet prefer the application of horse power to that of steam, in the crowded metropolis, we opine that he would use an engine of *adequate force*, in the broad and open fields of the nation." [43]

Without any aid from Adams Lundy managed in the summer of 1836 to reestablish himself at the head of an antislavery press. On August 3, 1836, he issued the first number of the weekly *National Enquirer and Constitutional Advocate of Universal Liberty*, and announced the revival of the *Genius* as a quarterly magazine. The new journal's policy, he said, would be the same that he *"long had in view,* — to plead the cause of the oppressed; to promote the ends of justice and equality of human rights. . . ." [44] Its specific object, of course, was to prevent the annexation of Texas. Presumably Texas would be kept out of the Union by political action within the framework of the Constitution, a procedure Lundy long had advocated. In selecting the name *Constitutional Advocate* for his newspaper, he thus accomplished two ends. He defined the mode of antislavery operation he would favor, and at the same time he distinguished himself from other abolitionists whose method and argument were primarily re-

[43] *Genius*, XVI (March 8, 1839), 10.
[44] *National Enquirer*, August 3, 1836.

ligious. Lundy thereby ranged himself among the earliest exponents of the revived political trend in antislavery thought
and action. During the Texas crisis Lundy continued to be
much more than merely a political free-soil advocate, however.
As always he aimed at the abolition of slavery; mere contain-
ment of it would never satisfy him. "Slavery must be met, and
put down, by a concentration of moral and political
power . . ." he wrote; "the idea that the system of slavery
may be limited or restricted, while suffered to exist in its present form is erroneous. All experience teaches this." [45]

The most immediate antislavery issue, however, remained
the annexation of Texas. No one could be sure that the session
of Congress which convened in December 1836 would not carry out the goal of the expansionists. Lundy continued his un-
relenting agitation to persuade northerners to accept his view
of the Texas Revolution as a slave-power conspiracy. He prepared an enlarged edition of his anti-Texas pamphlet, which
in its new form he called *The War in Texas*. He sent a copy
of it, together with an issue of the *National Enquirer*, to every
member of Congress and to the Cabinet. [46] He also prepared a
resolution against recognizing Texas' independence, and under his guidance the Young Men's Anti-Slavery Society of
Philadelphia called upon similar groups in other states to
form a united front on the issue. As chairman of the society's
committee on Texas Lundy forwarded the resolution to
Adams for presentation in the House of Representatives. [47]

With the abolitionists once again besieging Washington
with antislavery petitions, Adams became somewhat impatient
with their energy and counseled them to cease. Their pleas

[45] Lundy to John Quincy Adams, June 9, 1836, Adams Papers.
[46] Lundy to John Quincy Adams, December 17, 1836, *ibid.*
[47] Lundy to John Quincy Adams, January 21, 1837, *ibid.*; *National Enquirer*, January 28, 1837.

were impractical, he advised, and their efforts useless in changing the views of congressmen.[48] Adams' advice was wasted,
for as the abolitionist Lewis Tappan reminded him, the abolitionists did "not expect so much to convert members of
Congress, as their constituents." [49] Their purpose was propaganda — to persuade northern public opinion that southern
policy endangered civil rights — and in this way they succeeded magnificently. Lundy heeded Adams' advice no more
than other abolitionists did. By August 1837 he was circulating
a new anti-Texas memorial.[50] No other issue in the sectional
contest aroused such widespread interest in the North; none
had proved so effective in obtaining support from men who
did not consider themselves abolitionists.

Lundy could take much credit for this result through the
wide circulation of his pamphlets. The first printing of his
War in Texas was soon exhausted, and late in August 1837
he prepared a second, enlarged edition of 5,000 copies.[51] In
December 1837 he printed an extra number of the *National
Enquirer* devoted to Texas and some 23,000 copies of a small
pamphlet, *Facts for the People*, which was a condensation of
The War in Texas. He sent one of each to every member of
Congress and to state officials throughout the country, some
of whom returned them folded in such a way as to require
him to pay heavy postage on them.[52]

All such literature had its effect, as its argument was read
and repeated throughout the North, but it was John Quincy
Adams who provided the drama that gave life to the issue.

---

[48] Bemis, *John Quincy Adams*, p. 351.
[49] Lewis Tappan to John Quincy Adams, May 3, 1837, Adams Papers.
[50] Lundy to John Quincy Adams, August 5, 1837, *ibid.*
[51] Lundy to John Quincy Adams, August 21, 1837, *ibid.*
[52] Lundy to John Quincy Adams, December 15, 1837, *ibid.*; *Genius*, XV
(January, 1838), 141–142.

Once again the Massachusetts representative maneuvered southern congressmen into a position of seeming to deny the basic right of petition while they favored annexing Texas. At the beginning of the regular session of the Twenty-fifth Congress in December 1837, Adams presented the House with a group of anti-Texas petitions and moved that they be referred to a select committee. Loud southern objections naturally followed. In the debate that resulted, Adams managed to make some of his sharpest comments against the South and slavery and the annexation of Texas. Southern efforts to prevent discussion of slavery in Congress had failed once again. Lundy read the speech and sent his congratulations at once. "Well! — I see thee again on the ramparts, battling for *the rights of man*, against the hosts marching under the banners of oppression." Such episodes, Lundy believed, created abolitionists who would soon make their opinion felt by political parties. "The *people* are pretty well aroused," he added, "and their representatives will be expected to do their duty." [53] The petition controversy, which was Adams' creation, and the issue of Texas, which was Lundy's, had joined to create the basis for organized antislavery political activity.

For all Lundy's satisfaction at standing with the vanguard of a new political movement, his publishing venture, which advocated the movement, languished, and subscriptions remained too few to defray expenses. Probably it soon would have succumbed had not the Young Men's Anti-Slavery Society of Philadelphia taken over sponsorship in November.[54] Hope for further support soon appeared in a movement during the fall of 1836 to form a state antislavery society. A com-

---

[53] Bemis, *John Quincy Adams*, pp. 361–363; Lundy to John Quincy Adams, December 15, 1837, Adams Papers.
[54] *National Enquirer*, October 8, November 5, 1836.

mittee of correspondence of which Lundy and his old friend
James Mott were members began a campaign to organize backing, and at a meeting in Philadelphia on October 18 Lundy
offered the resolution to call a state antislavery convention at
Harrisburg.[55]

Lundy, with twenty-six other men, met at Harrisburg on
January 31, 1837, to form a state antislavery society, a procedure followed at about the same time in other states across
the North. The convention passed a resolution singling out
Lundy for special commendation on account of "the self-deny-
ing zeal and untiring efforts . . . by which he sustained *The
Genius of Universal Emancipation* for eight years of general
apathy on the subject of slavery, when no pecuniary embar-
rassment, no privations of society, no cold neglect or indifference to his warning voice could dissuade him from his
fixed principles of duty, but finally the attention of many
was roused by it throughout the land. . . ."[56]

Lundy's worsening deafness prevented him from taking the
large part in the proceedings that might otherwise have been
expected; nonetheless, the convention appointed him to a
committee to draft a remonstrance to Congress against annexing Texas, and he delivered a forceful speech on the
necessity for political action against slavery. His most notable contribution to the proceedings, however, was an address demanding jury trial for Negroes alleged to be fugitive
slaves.[57]

Pennsylvania's location made it an inevitable hunting
ground for slaves escaped from Virginia and Maryland, a fact
that had distressed Pennsylvania Quakers for at least a gener-

[55] *Ibid.*, October 29, 1836.
[56] Armstrong, *Lundy Family*, pp. 393–394.
[57] John G. Whittier to Joshua Leavitt, January 1, 1837, in *National Enquirer*, February 18, 1837.

ation and led to the passage in 1826 of the nation's first personal liberty law.[58] Lundy now expressed the growing northern discontent with legal requirements for returning fugitives to bondage. He did not deny that federal law obliged the states to surrender fugitives when adequate evidence had been presented, but he contended that the states also had the right to prescribe jury trial to determine the sufficiency of evidence. He went so far as to claim that the states might constitutionally prohibit their judiciary from acting in the matter at all, thus placing sole responsibility on United States courts and officials.[59] In such reasoning, of course, lay the germ of the personal liberty laws, soon to be passed in many northern states, to prevent state officials from participating at all in the enforcement of the Fugitive Slave Act.

During the next months Lundy worked closely with State Senator Francis James in advocating a bill to establish trial by jury for fugitive slaves.[60] The effort failed. In the house the bill lost in the committee of the whole; in the senate it was rejected by a vote of twenty to ten. According to John G. Whittier, every Whig and Democratic legislator voted against the bill; anti-Masons voted for it.[61] The defeat contributed to abolitionist determination to use political power for antislavery ends. Lundy comforted himself with the prediction that legislative opponents of the measure would soon "find themselves a little behind *the spirit of the age* in which they live." He would not be surprised, he wrote, "if they soon get leave

[58] William R. Leslie, "The Pennsylvania Fugitive Slave Act of 1826," *Journal of Southern History*, XVIII (November, 1952), 429–444.
[59] *National Enquirer*, February 18, 1837.
[60] Lundy to Francis James, February 13, 27, 1837, H. M. Jenkins Autograph Collection (Friends Historical Library).
[61] *Liberator*, April 14, 1837.

to *stay at home*. The eyes of their *constituents* are upon them." [62]

Lundy still hoped that the state constitutional convention, which was about to meet, would provide for trial by jury. It did not do so. Thaddeus Stevens' measure to that effect was rejected by a vote of seventy-five to thirty-eight, and the convention even retrogressed by depriving Negroes in Pennsylvania of the right to vote. Lundy's intemperate reaction gauged the extent of the mounting abolitionist fury. "Proscribe them," he wrote, "— trample them — kick them out!!" [63]

Such transactions within the state coupled with events at Washington to emphasize again the utility of antislavery political action. The issue of Texas, which would finally be decided by government, and the question of Negro rights in Pennsylvania reinforced Lundy's long-standing interest in politics. During the Missouri contest he had tried to organize political pressure against the extension of slavery; during the convention struggle in Illinois in 1824 he had thrown his influence on the antislavery side of a political contest; in Baltimore he had helped to form an antislavery political party; repeatedly in the *Genius* he had insisted that slavery finally must be ended by government. Now that the extension of slavery, civil rights for Negroes, and the right of petition all had assumed great public importance, he stepped up his campaign to awaken antislavery advocates to their political responsibilities: ". . . *we must have* more POLITICAL ACTION," he wrote. "The time, indeed, is near at hand, when we must TRY THE VIRTUE OF THE BALLOT-BOX, for the maintenance of our rights — even the *privilege*, granted

---

[62] Lundy to Francis James, February 27, 1837, Jenkins Autograph Collection.

[63] *National Enquirer*, June 3, 1837; *Genius*, XV (January, 1838), 143, 145.

us by the God of Heaven, to raise our voice for the relief of suffering humanity." [64]

Through his newspapers he attempted to sway local political contests. He urged voters to reject Joseph McIlvaine as a candidate for the state legislature because he had led opposition to the bill to provide jury trial for fugitive slaves. Although McIlvaine won the election, Lundy claimed that abolitionist opposition had cut his vote to 500 below the average received by other candidates.[65] Under Lundy's urgings, the Pennsylvania abolitionists began to question candidates to learn their views on such issues as the right of petition and the annexation of Texas.[66] Lundy advised abolitionists in the third congressional district of Pennsylvania to stay home on election day unless an antislavery candidate should present himself, although he grudgingly admitted that the Whig Charles Naylor, who promised to defend the right of petition, was more worthy than Charles J. Ingersoll, his Democratic opponent. When Naylor won by the narrow margin of 5,192 to 4,941, Lundy claimed that abolitionists were "solely" responsible for his victory.[67]

Lundy accurately stated the abolitionists' new attitude toward politics. They would not, he said, "by their suffrages, elevate to stations of power and trust persons who are in favor of the ACQUISITION OF TEXAS, and its incorporation into the Union. This question will be a positive *sine qua non* with every true friend of our cause, which must be promptly and distinctly answered by all who may solicit our support at the *ballot-boxes.*" [68]

---

[64] *National Enquirer*, April 22, 1837.

[65] *Ibid.*, October 12, 1837.

[66] Lundy to John Quincy Adams, August 5, 1837, Adams Papers.

[67] Samuel Webb to John Quincy Adams, August 1, 1837, and Lundy to Adams, August 5, 1837, *ibid.*

[68] *Genius*, XV (October, 1837), 37–38.

Lundy's call for antislavery political action was heard even as far west as Michigan. From the town of Schoolcraft in Kalamazoo County, Nathan M. Thomas — who had been born in Lundy's former home, Mount Pleasant, Ohio — sent Lundy money that he had collected for fourteen subscriptions to the *National Enquirer* and two for the *Genius*. Thomas reported that since the first issues of the newspaper had arrived in the neighborhood he had obtained 423 signers for a petition against the annexation of Texas, "a greater number of signatures than were ever voters polled in those townships where it circulated." [69] The congressman to whom Thomas sent the well-signed petition reported that it was the first of its kind ever to be received from Michigan.[70] Thomas soon followed it with others. He secured 388 signatures for abolishing slavery in the District of Columbia, 387 to abolish it in the territories, 384 to abolish the domestic slave trade, and 414 not to admit another slave state.[71] Some candidates for public office in Kalamazoo County, Thomas reported, boasted in 1837 that they favored abolition and charged that their opponents did not. This had never happened before; indeed, something like a revolution toward abolition had taken place there during the year. Antislavery groups, following Lundy's advice, had begun to apply pressure to local candidates. Their purpose, Thomas explained, was to demonstrate to aspirants for office that they held the balance of power between the two parties and would refuse to vote for candidates who failed to take an antislavery position.[72]

---

[69] Nathan M. Thomas to Lundy, September 22, 1837, in *ibid*. (December, 1837), 108.
[70] Lucius Lyons to Nathan M. Thomas, September 20, 1837, Thomas Papers.
[71] Nathan M. Thomas to Lucius Lyons, December 22, 1837, *ibid*.
[72] Nathan M. Thomas to Jesse Thomas, Sr., December 29, 1837, and Thomas to Lundy, ——, 1837, *ibid*.

Public opposition of the sort manifested in Michigan appeared throughout the North in the summer of 1837 and prevented the annexation of Texas at that time. The widely circulated anti-Texas petitions and the anti-Texas resolutions adopted by abolition societies and other groups provided undeniable evidence of heightened public interest in the issue. Politicians could not be blind to that fact. Especially in New England, where Garrison's opposition to political action had its largest influence, an aroused electorate demanded exclusion of Texas. Probably the most persuasive anti-Texas tract published in New England was William Ellery Channing's *A Letter to the Hon. Henry Clay, on the Annexation of Texas to the United States*, which repeated Lundy's argument and borrowed his evidence.[73]

Lundy, through his newspapers and pamphlets, and Adams, through his speeches in Congress (based on Lundy's information), could properly claim a large share of the credit for arousing popular hostility against annexing Texas. At the same time Lundy's newspaper had helped awaken northern antislavery voters to a new awareness of their power and responsibility to influence elections and to sway candidates toward antislavery positions. Both were momentous developments in the sectional controversy. They were the last great accomplishments of Lundy's life, products of his otherwise unsuccessful Texas ventures.

---

[73] William Ellery Channing, *A Letter to the Hon. Henry Clay, on the Annexation of Texas to the United States* (Boston, 1837). See especially pp. 14–17, 19, 34–35. Channing's disclaimer (pp. 5–6) that with Lundy's "reasonings and opinions, I have nothing to do . . ." can hardly be taken seriously.

CHAPTER XIV

To the Illinois Prairies

The appearance of such specifically political issues as the "gag rule" and the annexation of Texas had inevitably led abolitionists to give increased attention to political candidates and to elections. Yet at the same time one of their chief spokesmen, William Lloyd Garrison, had begun to advocate a course based on abstract morality that would largely divorce himself and the *Liberator* from such mundane concerns. Lundy, for years committed to the necessity of using political power against slavery, opposed and condemned Garrison's views. The *Liberator*, he believed, had endorsed so many bizarre ideas that it was bound to create discord by alienating those abolitionists who could not accept novel stands on politics, religion, and women's rights. Garrison's name had become a byword for extremism on nearly all subjects to the detriment of the antislavery cause.

Lundy sided with Garrison's antagonists, who first made their opposition felt in New England itself.[1] There a formal

---

[1] *National Enquirer*, November 9, 1837.

division appeared within the movement when dissidents split the Massachusetts Anti-Slavery Society by seceding to form the anti-Garrison Massachusetts Abolition Society. Their dissatisfaction with Garrison's leadership centered about his religious views, which had become increasingly unorthodox, and his political theories, which verged on Christian anarchy. Lundy reproved his former partner for injecting religious controversy into the antislavery movement and thereby sacrificing much needed support. He deplored too the "severity of personal censure" which Garrison directed toward all who failed to meet his own standard of abolitionism. Lundy, who had himself smarted from Garrison's barbs, attached no blame to severity of censure as such, but he accused Garrison of being "sometimes too hasty in his criticisms, and too indiscriminate in his charges against both advocates and opponents" of abolitionism.[2]

When Garrison's Pennsylvania supporters read Lundy's critique, they were furious and threatened to withdraw support from the *National Enquirer*.[3] Probably the declining fortunes of the newspaper may be attributed in part to their alienation. Nonetheless, Lundy did not relent in his disapproval of Garrison's course. After it became certain that the Massachusetts movement had been split beyond repair, Lundy announced his sympathy with the division and his approval of the establishment of the new society's *Massachusetts Abolitionist* as a rival to the *Liberator*.[4] Garrison had only himself to blame for his troubles, thought Lundy, for the *Liberator* under his editorship had become "erratic and dogmatical," and its policy "whimsical and unreflecting." He al-

---

[2] *Genius*, XV (October, 1837), 61.

[3] Charles C. Burleigh to J. Miller McKim, November 13, 1837, in Garrison and Garrison, *William Lloyd Garrison*, II, 322n.–323n.

[4] *Genius*, XVI (July 12, 1839), 22.

luded also to Garrison's "arrogance" and to the "wild and absurd theories" and the "vagaries" which he had injected into the antislavery controversy. The whole movement suffered, Lundy believed, from Garrison's unwillingness to concentrate his attention on slavery alone. Blame for the schism in New England, Lundy indicated, must be charged directly to Garrison. And, he added, "were we not too well acquainted with his disposition, we would indulge the hope that he might profit by the lesson. . . ." [5]

Garrison discounted Lundy's comments by noting that the Quaker had "suffered a jealous and envious spirit . . . to take possession of his breast. . . ." [6] This may well have been true, for Lundy had come to feel that those who magnified the importance of such newer abolitionists as Garrison had lost sight of his early contributions to the antislavery movement, and Lundy's children later seem to have blamed Garrison for many of their father's troubles.[7] But Lundy's opinion of Garrison's folly in agitating extraneous issues was not eccentric. It was a view widely held, particularly by western abolitionists, not many of whom could reasonably be accused of harboring "a jealous and envious spirit" toward him.

The apparent diminution of Garrison's power within the movement after 1837 gave Lundy no satisfaction whatever, for he regretted such discord as harmful to the antislavery cause. Furthermore he himself suffered at the same moment from difficulties that allowed him little satisfaction from the discomfiture of others. In spite of the importance of his antislavery work in Philadelphia Lundy nonetheless judged his present contributions inadequate and the place he occupied inappropriate, the result of chance rather than of his free

---

[5] *Ibid.* (June 28, 1839), p. 19.
[6] Garrison and Garrison, *William Lloyd Garrison*, II, 321–322.
[7] *Genius*, XVI (March 29, 1839), 14.

choice. By early 1838 he had experienced moments bordering on despondency as he questioned his value to the antislavery cause.[8]

Lundy conducted his war against Texas during a time of widespread economic dislocation and collapse. Everywhere the Panic of 1837 hampered reformers in carrying out their enterprises, much as it hampered businessmen. Lundy's activities, dependent as they were on a steady flow of financial contributions and newspaper subscriptions, were much handicapped by the severe money shortage that developed during the summer of 1837. The *National Enquirer* escaped the spreading paralysis only when the executive committee for the eastern district of the state antislavery society assumed financial responsibility for its operations. The members themselves finally were compelled to advance most of the money that kept the newspaper alive. But even they could barely sustain it. By midsummer its debts totaled nearly 1,000 dollars. Only thirty-three dollars had been contributed to its support from outside Philadelphia.[9]

Lundy received next to nothing for his editorial labors. By late August when the executive committee of the state antislavery society sent out a desperate appeal for aid, Lundy's personal funds had become so low that he could not even pay his board. He planned to leave the city and retreat to his father's farm in New Jersey, where at least there would be enough to eat. Only a gift of fifteen dollars from Jane Howell enabled him to stay in the city and continue his antislavery work.[10]

Such extreme poverty added to, but did not originate, the

---

8 Lundy to John Quincy Adams, March 26, 1838, Adams Papers.
9 William Harned and Isaac Parrish to Paxson Vickers, August ——, 1837, Lundy-Vickers Papers.
10 Jane Howell to Thomas Chandler, October 12, 1837, Chandler Papers.

discontent Lundy had felt ever since he returned from Mexico. Not even the founding of his new weekly and the revival of the *Genius*, necessary as he believed both to be to the antislavery cause, had fully satisfied him. Lundy had always intended to issue his newspaper in the South, where he thought he might reach the ears of men who could themselves abolish slavery. Hopeless as such a prospect was, Lundy could not altogether relinquish his youthful dream of converting southerners, and he still considered the effort of antislavery journals on northern soil partly misdirected.[11]

But the most profound source of Lundy's discontent was his changed relation to the antislavery movement. He felt lost among the crowd of antislavery workers who now surrounded him. No longer was his voice preeminent among the abolitionists. Younger, more vigorous men dominated the field. Lundy, in contrast to them, had reached that season of his life when he felt his powers ebbing. He was not so much envious of fellow workers as he was simply conscious that many surpassed him in youthful capacity and talent. The efforts of which he was now capable seemed to him feeble in contrast to theirs. His newspaper which once had stood virtually alone as an exponent of abolitionist creed now vied for attention with a half-dozen ably edited journals.[12] In dealing with the great issues growing out of the Texas Revolution, Lundy still had an important job to do for which no one else was so well qualified, but in the work of general antislavery agitation he had been passed by.

He sometimes thought of settling again in the West, where

[11] *National Enquirer*, March 11, 18, 1837; Lundy to James G. Birney, March 27, 1836, in Dwight Lowell Dumond (ed.), *Letters of James Gillespie Birney, 1831–1857* (New York, 1938), I, 314–315.

[12] "Prospectus for the Genius of Universal Emancipation," in *Genius*, XV (July, 1837), 4.

antislavery newspapers still were few and the need for additional strong voices still urgent. He hinted to the antislavery editor James G. Birney that he might be willing to join him in conducting the *Philanthropist* at Cincinnati.[13] He particularly admired Birney's emphasis on constitutional issues and his reasoned, unemotional analysis of slavery. Birney, however, seems not to have responded to Lundy's overture; indeed, he apparently had the bad grace a year later to chide the Quaker veteran for so long advocating free-labor emigration experiments.[14]

Lundy relinquished whatever hopes he may have had of moving West in 1836 and 1837. He decided that duty required him to remain in Philadelphia, not only because "it would not be proper . . . to seek repose, during the heat of the great moral warfare," but also because the state antislavery society had agreed to underwrite the *National Enquirer* only on condition that he remain as editor.[15] But by the spring of 1838 he regarded his obligations in Philadelphia as fulfilled. He had thoroughly publicized the facts of the Texas Revolution as he understood them. By means of newspapers and pamphlets and through such allies as John Quincy Adams, Lundy had been instrumental in arousing the North to oppose the annexation of Texas. He concluded that he could add little to the contributions he had already made to the antislavery cause.[16]

Furthermore, he was tired and ill. He had never recovered

---

13 Lundy to James G. Birney, March 27, 1836, in Dumond (ed.), *Birney Letters*, I, 314.

14 Lundy to James G. Birney, May 27, 1837, Autograph Collection of Simon Gratz (Historical Society of Pennsylvania).

15 Lundy to William and Susan Wierman, April 6, 1837, in Armstrong, *Lundy Family*, p. 395.

16 Lundy to John Quincy Adams, March 26, 1838, Adams Papers.

from the ordeals of his travels in Mexico. Since his return the strains of incessant labor had further impaired his health. Frequent spells of sickness in 1836 and 1837 incapacitated him for weeks at a time. Late in August 1837 illness forced him temporarily to leave the city for the peace of the New Jersey countryside; during much of the next winter he was too indisposed to perform his editorial work. He thought that he suffered from a lung ailment; friends were shocked to see that the muscles in his face had become partially paralyzed.[17]

Finally in February 1838 Lundy announced the inevitable. John G. Whittier would succeed to the editorship of the *National Enquirer*, and Lundy would leave the East altogether. "I must now look somewhat to the affairs of my own household," he explained.[18] The Pennsylvania State Anti-Slavery Society's official announcement of the retirement was little more revealing. Lundy had made his decision, the executive committee said, because of "circumstances of a personal nature, which seem to require, at his present period of life, more attention to his own interests. . . ."[19]

Lundy had concluded that the time had come when he must reestablish his broken family ties. Declining health had made him long for the companionship of his children. His older daughters — Susan and her husband, William Wierman, and Elizabeth and her husband, Isaac Griffith — had moved from York Springs, Pennsylvania, to Putnam County, Illinois, in 1837, taking Lundy's three other children with them. Lundy's brother-in-law William Lewis, with his abolitionist wife, Lydia Stanton, had settled in Putnam County

---

[17] *National Enquirer*, August 31, 1837; Lundy to John Quincy Adams, August 21, 1837, Adams Papers; Jane Howell to Thomas Chandler, October 12, 1837, March 29, 1839, Chandler Papers.

[18] *National Enquirer*, February 22, March 8, 1838.

[19] *Liberator*, March 23, 1838.

the year before.[20] Lundy decided that he must join his family in Illinois.

Although he would give up editorship of the *National Enquirer*, neither he nor his fellow abolitionists expected him to relinquish antislavery work altogether. In the spring of 1838 he attended the business sessions of the American Anti-Slavery Society, where he was named one of its managers for Illinois. At the same time, perhaps with the encouragement of the national society, he developed plans to reestablish the *Genius* on the Illinois prairies.[21] His prospectus announced that the first number of the new volume would be issued in July 1838, although he could not yet say exactly where it would be published. "There has been no change of opinion on the part of the editor," Lundy declared, "no alteration in the general course pursued by him — and none is contemplated." He would continue to advocate *"Free Discussion*; the TOTAL ABOLITION OF SLAVERY: and the firm establishment of the *constitutional*, inalienable, and 'universal' rights of man." [22] But despite these announcements it was clear to most antislavery workers that the most important stages of Lundy's career lay behind him.

At Lundy's announced retirement tributes to his labors appeared from many quarters. Julius R. Ames, a New York abolitionist, sent him 100 dollars to use for his own comfort. Garrison commented in the *Liberator* that a "statue of gold, erected to him by his country, would be only the shadow of

---

[20] Lundy to William and Susan Wierman, April 6, 1837, in Armstrong, *Lundy Family*, pp. 394–395; Nathan M. Thomas to Jesse Thomas, Sr., May 13, 1836, Thomas Papers.

[21] *Liberator*, May 4, June 1, 1838; Lundy to John Quincy Adams, May 5, 1838, Adams Papers.

[22] Prospectus in Erastus Wright Papers (Illinois State Historical Library, Springfield).

a reward for his invaluable labors." The executive committee of the Pennsylvania Anti-Slavery Society praised him as
"one of the earliest and most unflinching friends of the man of
color — as one who has been largely instrumental in arousing
an anti-slavery feeling in Pennsylvania . . . in promoting
an effective organization," and in publicizing the "designs
of slaveholders in annexing Texas."[23] To Lundy perhaps
the most affecting of all tributes was that given by a group
of Philadelphia Negroes who met with him before he left
the city. With James McCrummell as chairman and James
Cornish as secretary the meeting resolved to "view Benjamin
Lundy as the father of those benevolent exertions, which have
done, and are yet doing, so much for the amelioration of the
condition of our oppressed people in this country. . . ."[24]

In preparation for the long journey to Illinois Lundy
moved out of his boardinghouse and stored his belongings in
the antislavery office located on the first floor of the newly
completed Pennsylvania Hall at Sixth and Haines streets, a
structure built by public subscription and dedicated to freedom of speech. Although the building would be open to many
kinds of public gatherings, it was most closely identified with
abolition. At the dedicatory ceremonies on May 14 David
Paul Brown, a Philadelphia lawyer, delivered an antislavery
address, and two days later the Anti-Slavery Convention of
American Women began its sessions in the hall, with many of
the best known of the abolitionists attending. Lundy and
Theodore D. Weld were there, and large audiences gathered
to hear Garrison, Maria W. Chapman, Angelina Grimké
Weld, Esther Moore, Lucretia Mott, and Abby Kelly speak.
Mobs demonstrated in the streets outside as opposition de-

[23] Williams, "Benjamin Lundy."
[24] *Liberator*, August 31, 1838.

veloped to the racially mixed assembly. When public wrath increased even more the next day, the mayor prohibited additional sessions of the convention and in the interest of peace closed the hall. But his action did not assure tranquility. That night a mob of several thousand people gathered about the building, broke down the doors, and finally set the hall afire.[25]

Lundy's boxes and trunks did not escape the mob's fury. Some of the mob members broke into the antislavery society's office and began hurling books and pamphlets into the flames. Lundy's belongings met the same fate. One of his small trunks which held the journal of his trip to Mexico was somehow saved; a few of his letters and other manuscripts passed into friendly hands and thus escaped the general destruction; but all the other accumulations of a lifetime spent in antislavery work were destroyed.[26] Lundy arrived at the scene while smoke still rolled from the building and flames colored the lowering clouds. "Methought I could read, on this mighty scroll, the woeful destiny of this nation of oppressors," he commented.[27]

Everything he owned was gone; he was left without even a change of clothing. "$5000 would have been refused a few hours earlier for what I lost," he told John Quincy Adams. Lundy decided to postpone his departure for Illinois in the hope of recovering some of his papers and securing compensation for his losses. He issued a public appeal to the citizens of Philadelphia for the return of any manuscripts that might have survived what he termed "the late *auto da fe . . .*" and

25 Lundy to Julius R. Ames, May 18, 1838, Gratz Autograph Collection; Garrison and Garrison, *William Lloyd Garrison*, II, 214–216.
26 [Earle], *Life*, pp. 302–303; *Liberator*, June 15, 1838; [Samuel Webb], *History of Pennsylvania Hall, Which Was Destroyed by a Mob on the 17th of May, 1838* (Philadelphia, 1838), p. 170.
27 Lundy to John Quincy Adams, May 18, 1838, Adams Papers.

he entered a claim with city authorities for 2000 dollars in damages. A grand jury eventually awarded him 900 dollars, but it deducted 100 dollars for expenses, and authorized payment of the rest in "county stock." [28]

Aided by friends who gave him small amounts of money, Lundy left Philadelphia on July 24, 1838, to begin his westward journey. In the middle of September he arrived at Hennepin in Putnam County, Illinois. The peace that he longed for appeared to have been attained ("I am here among my children, at last," he wrote),[29] but this was illusion, for he now found himself placed in the midst of the struggles of Illinois abolitionists to recover from the loss inflicted on their movement some ten months earlier when a mob at Alton had killed antislavery editor Elijah P. Lovejoy. Perhaps in no northern state had conflict between abolitionists and their opponents raged more bitterly than in Illinois. Lundy had written even before he left Pennsylvania that he anticipated "a sore battle" in his new home.[30] He largely succeeded in evading the battle, however, for he had the good fortune to settle in one of the few parts of the state where antislavery sentiment prevailed. In Putnam County antislavery Quakers and Presbyterians, some of them refugees from the South who had for a time lived in abolitionist communities in Ohio, had joined to create a community free from serious division over slavery. William M. Stewart, one of the most fiery abolitionists in the entire country, lived unmolested in Putnam. Stewart, a wheelwright by trade, had gained national attention three years earlier with a fervid antislavery address delivered

[28] Ibid.; Liberator, June 15, 1838; Jane Howell to Thomas Chandler, May 29, 1838, Chandler Papers; Samuel Webb to Lundy, April 4, 1839, in Williams, "Benjamin Lundy"; Genius, XVI (June 28, 1839), 19.
[29] [Earle], Life, p. 304.
[30] Lundy to John Quincy Adams, June 30, 1838, Adams Papers.

at the Presbyterian General Convention in Pittsburgh.[31] Lundy need have no fear that he was settling among enemies.

He did, however, find himself immediately engaged once more in the abolitionist cause. Only a few days after he arrived at Hennepin, an antislavery convention met in the village. Lundy attended its sessions, and as an important national figure naturally attracted much attention from the delegates. He was invited to address the gathering, "and in a very modest manner stated his object in migrating" to Illinois and "his determination to co-operate with the friends of freedom in effecting the total abolition of American slavery, and in securing the universal rights of man." The convention's chairman, the Reverend James H. Dickey, appointed him to a committee with Stewart and Hooper Warren (the former editor of the Edwardsville *Spectator* who had helped defeat the Illinois constitutional convention in 1824) to prepare a memorial to the state legislature for the repeal of "all oppressive laws growing out of slavery whether applying to slaves, free Negroes, or whites. . . ."[32]

Lundy reported to one of his friends his pleasure with the meeting. He especially liked the several "excellent resolutions" which the convention passed.[33] The reason Lundy found them so satisfying was that he was their author. With little dissent the delegates approved Lundy's resolutions (1) approving John Quincy Adams' course in advocating the right of petition and opposing the annexation of Texas, (2) praising the abolition of slavery in the British Empire and citing the experiment in Antigua as proof that immediate emancipation

---

[31] Merton L. Dillon, "Abolitionism Comes to Illinois," *Journal of the Illinois State Historical Society*, LIII (winter, 1960), 393–403; Samuel Rezneck, "Diary of a New York Doctor in Illinois, 1830–1831," *ibid.*, LIV (spring, 1961), 42–43; *Liberator*, June 27, 1835.

[32] Peoria (Ill.) *Register*, October 6, 1838.

[33] Lundy to Thomas Gregg, September 23, 1838 (Illinois State Historical Society).

was practical, (3) rejecting colonization as a means of effecting abolition, (4) endorsing petitions against the annexation of Texas — "that unhallowed scheme; which, if successful, will certainly involve our beloved country in difficulties and disasters, and probably soon prove destructive to our free institutions," (5) affirming the full and exclusive power of Congress to abolish slavery and the slave trade in the District of Columbia and the territories, and (6) stating their faith that petitions would be acceded to "in some degree at least, before we find it necessary to speak thro' the ballot box." [34]

Most gratifying of all to Lundy, however, was the convention's action in voting unanimously to recommend the location of the *Genius* at Hennepin and resolving to support it.[35] With the death of Lovejoy and the destruction of his press at Alton the Illinois abolitionists had been left without a newspaper. A journal called the Alton *Observer* had been printed at Cincinnati by Elisha W. Chester during the winter of 1837–38, but its location made it inadequate to serve the needs of the Illinois antislavery movement.[36] Leaders of the movement had failed in their efforts to make more satisfactory arrangements; Lundy's arrival in the state therefore offered hope that their problem had been solved. When Lundy attended the first anniversary meeting of the Illinois State Anti-Slavery Society at Farmington on October 1, a committee composed of George W. Gale, Edward Beecher, and William M. Stewart recommended support for the *Genius* and its adoption as the official organ of the state society.[37]

Encouraged by these several promises of patronage, Lundy

---

[34] Peoria *Register*, October 6, 1838.
[35] Lundy to Thomas Gregg, September 23, 1838 (Illinois State Historical Society).
[36] Cincinnati *Journal*, February 14, 1838.
[37] Illinois State Anti-Slavery Society Minutes (Chicago Historical Society), pp. 55–56.

hastened arrangements to establish his newspaper. Efforts to purchase the press and type used by the suspended Hennepin *Journal* failed, so, except for one number of the *Genius* issued during November, publication was delayed until the end of February 1839, when the Illinois abolitionists finally purchased printing equipment for his use. Lundy decided to publish his paper not in Hennepin but at Lowell, a newly established town nearby where the proprietors offered free lots to mechanics. It was on such terms that Lundy received five town lots on condition that he establish a printing office in the village. On one of these he built himself a small home and printing office. His twin children came to live with him. Esther kept house, and young Benjamin did chores around the office. For the first time since the death of his wife more than a decade earlier, Lundy lived with his family in a home of his own.[38]

But not all his problems had been solved. Difficulties appeared when he tried to find a printer. Although the veteran Hooper Warren would have joined him, the terms he proposed seemed too demanding for Lundy to accept. Thomas Gregg, a young printer from Ohio who now lived in Iowa Territory, refused an offer of employment. Finally in the winter John W. E. Lovejoy, the idealistic young brother of the martyred Alton editor, came to work with him, and later Zebina Eastman, an experienced printer from Vermont, joined in the enterprise. With such abundant aid Lundy enjoyed plenty of time to engage in antislavery work and to tend to his personal affairs.[39]

Through the winter he attended conventions of antislavery

---

[38] Lundy to Paxson Vickers, May 19, 1839, Lundy-Vickers Collection; [Earle], *Life*, pp. 304–305; Williams, "Benjamin Lundy." The newspaper was datelined Hennepin because Lowell had no post office.
[39] Lundy to Thomas Gregg, February 24, 1839 (New-York Historical Society); Lundy to John Quincy Adams, February 4, 1839, Adams Papers.

societies and helped organize new ones, each of them emphasizing the importance of antislavery political activity and the
need to aid free Negroes.[40] He kept his eye on Texas and on
developments in Congress, and he circulated antislavery memorials and forwarded them to John Quincy Adams for presentation to the House.[41]

All this activity seemed to improve Lundy's health and out-
look. He began to envision a new life for himself, which
would even include a new marriage. On the way from Philadelphia he had stopped in Chester County, Pennsylvania,
to visit the Paxson Vickers family, where he became well acquainted with a young spinster, Mary Vickers. In the months
afterward the two corresponded frequently. Lundy composed
romantic verse addressed to her, though he seems not to have
mailed it, and finally they agreed that they would marry as
soon as Lundy had become better established in his new location.[42]

As soon as he could arrange it, he began to buy land in
Putnam County, no doubt hoping to improve his fortunes in
anticipation of his marriage. He purchased a small tract of
timbered land some dozen miles southeast of Hennepin and
a preemption claim to a half-section that already had ten
acres of wheat growing on it. In the spring of 1839 he rode
to the land office at Galena to enter additional land for himself and also for members of the Vickers family, whom he
hoped to encourage to move to Illinois.[43]

---

40 *Genius*, XVI (February 26, 1839), 5; (March 8, 1839), p. 9; (March 29,
1839), p. 13.
41 Lundy to John Quincy Adams, October 13, 1838, February 4, 1839,
Adams Papers.
42 [Earle], *Life*, p. 304; Susan M. Wierman to Mary Vickers, May 3,
1840, Lundy-Vickers Collection.
43 Lundy to Paxson Vickers, May 19, 1839, in Armstrong, *Lundy Family*,
pp. 395–396; Lundy to Vickers, May 9, 1839, Lundy Papers.

Lundy and his sons, Charles and Benjamin, went to work building fences on the farm and breaking more land. In May he suspended the *Genius* for several weeks while he spent his time improving his farm.[44] In July he explained to his readers that "a little pressing business out of the printing office, has again prevented the editor from devoting as much of his attention to the paper as he desired. Among other matters, a small wheat harvest required his care." [45] He left the business of printing to Eastman, who by the summer was his only help, for Lovejoy had remained with him only a few months. Eastman too announced his intention to leave and return to New England. Not even Lundy's offer to divide his town lots with him and to give him a share of his preemption claim could persuade the boy to change his plans.[46] But despite such annoyances Lundy's prospects had never looked fairer. He expected his land to rise in value, he lived among his children, he would soon marry again, and once more his newspaper ably served the antislavery cause.

But none of this promise would be fulfilled. Early in August Lundy fell ill. Farm work had overtaxed his strength, and he contracted a fever that then prevailed in Illinois. At the same time his daughter Esther suffered from the ague, which, Lundy had written earlier, "still *shakes* his rod . . . bidding defiance to doctors and drugs." [47] The child could no

---

[44] Lundy to Paxson Vickers, May 19, 1839, in Armstrong, *Lundy Family*, pp. 395–396.

[45] *Genius*, XVI (July 19, 1839), 31. The newspaper had only 500 subscribers. Peoria *Register*, October 19, 1839.

[46] George A. Lawrence, *A Pioneer of Freedom; an Address . . . upon the Life and Services of Benjamin Lundy* (Galesburg, Ill., 1913), p. 44. Lundy's death led Eastman to decide to stay in Illinois as an antislavery journalist.

[47] Lundy to Thomas Gregg, February 24, 1839 (New-York Historical Society).

longer take care of the house, and Lundy became too ill to nurse her. He wrote to his daughter Susan requesting her to take Esther into her own home where she could be properly cared for, since he was himself confined to bed more than half the time.

From this illness Lundy was not to recover. He worked in his office for the last time on the morning of August 21; in the afternoon severe pains seized him; the next day he grew worse; and at eleven o'clock on the night of August 22, 1839, he died. The next day his body was taken to the house of his son-in-law Isaac Griffith near Magnolia, and on August 24 he was buried in the Friends' burying ground near McNabb in Putnam County.[48]

When news of Lundy's death reached the East, tributes poured forth extolling his services to the antislavery movement, none of them more generous than Garrison's, whose biographical account of Lundy occupied three-and-a-half columns in the *Liberator*.[49] The Massachusetts Anti-Slavery Society passed Garrison's resolution stating that "to no man is the country so deeply indebted for the mighty impulse it has received on the subject of abolition, as the first cause of all protracted effort for the overthrow of slavery. . . ."[50] The Uwchlan Anti-Slavery Society in Pennsylvania praised him as "the principal promoter of the exertions now making on behalf of the deeply injured and cruelly oppressed descendants of Africa. . . ."[51] John Quincy Adams remarked to John G.

---

[48] [Earle], *Life*, p. 305; Lundy to William and Susan Wierman, August 21, 1839, in Armstrong, *Lundy Family*, p. 396; *Genius*, XVI (July 26, 1839), 35; (August 16, 1839), p. 39.

[49] *Liberator*, September 20, 1839.

[50] *Ibid.*, January 31, 1840.

[51] *Ibid.*, December 13, 1839.

Whittier that he mourned Lundy "as a Brother." [52] Free Negroes in Philadelphia, Boston, and elsewhere held services commemorating him as one of their principal benefactors.[53] At a meeting in the First Colored Presbyterian Church in Philadelphia, Robert Purvis, James Cornish, T. C. White, and Frederick A. Hinton delivered speeches testifying to Lundy's importance to the antislavery cause and acknowledging their race as chief "recipients of benefits from his early, devoted, and uncompromising efforts in behalf of human rights. . . ." Afterward the assembled representatives of the city's Negro population passed a memorial expressing their gratitude to the Quaker saddler whose entire life had been devoted to the cause of universal emancipation.[54]

Lundy died in the midst of the battle against slavery and oppression, when the prospect for victory in the struggle for human rights still seemed impossibly far off. Although his unceasing labor moved the antislavery crusade nearer its goals, the glory of his life did not lie in success, for he never achieved that. Final, unchallenged success in the cause to which he dedicated his life always eluded him as it eludes all men. But success postponed is neither failure nor tragedy. The record of his triumph remains vivid for all to read — a life lived selflessly in devotion to the cause of human equality and freedom.

---

[52] John Quincy Adams to John G. Whittier, November 11, 1839, Adams Papers.
[53] *Liberator*, December 27, 1839.
[54] *Ibid.*, October 18, 1839.

BIBLIOGRAPHY

Most of Lundy's personal collection of papers was destroyed in the burning of Pennsylvania Hall, and no vast store of his letters to contemporaries has yet come to light. However, the Benjamin Lundy Papers at the Ohio Historical Society in Columbus and the Benjamin Lundy and Paxson Vickers Collection in the Library of Congress include revealing letters and documents from all periods of his life. The Pennsylvania Abolition Society Manuscript Collection in the Historical Society of Pennsylvania in Philadelphia contains some of his correspondence from the 1820's; the extensive series of letters by and about him in the Elizabeth M. Chandler Papers in the Michigan Historical Collections at the University of Michigan, Ann Arbor, concern especially the years after 1830; the same depository also holds the Nathan M. Thomas Papers, which contain accounts of Lundy and his associates and indicate his influence in Michigan after 1830; Lundy's relations with John Quincy Adams from 1836 to 1839 may be followed in their lengthy correspondence in the Adams Family Papers at the Massachusetts Historical Society. The Lyman Spalding Collection in the Regional History Collection at Cornell University, Ithaca, New York, includes correspondence about his Texas projects; several letters are in the Gerrit Smith Papers at Syracuse University. The Friends Historical Library at Swarthmore, Pennsylvania, the

New-York Historical Society, the Boston Public Library, the Illinois State Historical Society Library at Springfield, and the Oberlin College Library also have Lundy correspondence. The Papers of Elihu Embree at the Historical Society of Pennsylvania are rich in information about one of Lundy's contemporaries.

Lundy's newspapers, the *Genius of Universal Emancipation* and the *National Enquirer,* are invaluable sources for a study of his life and opinions, as well as for the antislavery movement in general. Lundy's other published writings include *The Origin and True Causes of the Texas Revolution Commenced in the Year 1835* (Philadelphia, 1836) and *The War in Texas: A Review of Facts and Circumstances, Showing That This Contest Is the Result of a Long Premeditated Crusade Against the Government, Set on Foot by Slaveholders, Land Speculators, &c. with the View of Re-establishing, Extending, and Perpetuating the System of Slavery and the Slave Trade in the Republic of Mexico* (Philadelphia, 1836).

Two genealogies preserve the account of Lundy's ancestry as well as provide documentary material which has otherwise disappeared: William Clinton Armstrong, *The Lundy Family and Their Descendants of Whatsoever Surname with a Biographical Sketch of Benjamin Lundy* (New Brunswick, N.J., 1902), and Ambrose M. Shotwell, *Annals of Our Ancestors; or Our Quaker Forefathers and their Posterity* . . . (Lansing, Mich., 1897).

The only published book-length work on Lundy is Thomas Earle's compilation of documentary material, *The Life, Travels and Opinions of Benjamin Lundy, Including His Journeys to Texas and Mexico; with a Sketch of Contemporary Events, and a Notice of the Revolution in Hayti* (Philadelphia, 1847). Approximately half the book consists of Lundy's valuable Mexican diary; only twenty-six pages are devoted to the important years of his life before 1830, and much of that account is inaccurate. The remainder chiefly consists of extracts from his newspapers. Garrison had proposed to write Lundy's biography, but unfortunately abandoned the project when Joseph Lundy and other relatives objected.

Glimpses of Lundy's early years in Ohio are provided in Nathan Macy Thomas, *Nathan M. Thomas, Birthright Member of the Society of Friends, Pioneer Physician, Early and Earnest Advocate of the Abolition of Slavery, Friend and Helper of the Fugitive Slave; an Account of His Life Written by Himself* (Cassopolis, Mich., 1925). Two works by Ruth Anna (Ketring) Nuermberger, *Charles Osborn in the Anti-Slavery Movement* (Columbus, Ohio, 1937), and *The Free Produce Movement, a Quaker Protest Against Slavery* (Durham, N.C., 1942), illumine important facets of Lundy's life and concern. Rinaldo R. Williams, "Benjamin Lundy, Pioneer, Hero, and Martyr," in Chicago *Inter-Ocean*, March 7 and 14, 1897, is useful for preserving documentary material and for portraying Lundy's last months in Illinois.

Frank Sanborn attempted an early biographical appraisal in "Benjamin Lundy," *Friends' Intelligencer and Journal*, XLVI (May 18, 1889), 308–310, 325–327; a later brief sketch is George A. Lawrence, *A Pioneer of Freedom; an Address . . . upon the Life and Services of Benjamin Lundy* (Galesburg, Ill., 1913). Fred Landon more recently published a series of well-written accounts based chiefly on the Earle compilation. The most important among these are "Benjamin Lundy, Abolitionist," *Dalhousie Review*, VII (1927), 189–197; "Benjamin Lundy in Illinois," *Journal of the Illinois State Historical Society*, XXXIII (March, 1940), 57–67; and "Benjamin Lundy, Abolitionist, 1789–1839," in John Swaney School Alumni and Society of Friends, *A Memorial to Benjamin Lundy, Pioneer Quaker Abolitionist, 1789–1839* (n.p., 1939).

Lundy's career may be seen in its Quaker context in Thomas E. Drake, *Quakers and Slavery in America* (New Haven, Conn., 1950), and, by implication, as the product of new humanitarian emphases within the sect in Sydney V. James, *A People Among Peoples; Quaker Benevolence in Eighteenth-Century America* (Cambridge, Mass., 1963). Edward Needles, *An Historical Memoir of the Pennsylvania Society for Promoting the Abolition of Slavery* (Philadelphia, 1848), is an early account of the society which supported many of Lundy's activities. Lundy's place in the larger antislavery movement is assessed in Dwight Lowell Dumond's monumental *Antislavery: The Crusade for Freedom in America* (Ann Arbor, Mich., 1961), by far the most comprehensive and morally vigorous work on its subject, and in Louis Filler's *The Crusade Against Slavery, 1830–1860* (New York, 1960), which relates antislavery to other reforms.

The New England Garrisonian abolitionists long enjoyed prestige so great as to cause them to overshadow both their predecessors and their western contemporaries in nearly all historical accounts, popular and professional alike. Important exceptions to this distortion were Alice Dana Adams, *The Neglected Period of Anti-Slavery in America, 1808–1831* (Boston, 1908), a demonstration of the vigor of pre-Garrisonian protests, and William Birney, *James G. Birney and His Times* (New York, 1890), which placed Lundy in accurate perspective. An early article by E. A. Snodgrass, "Benjamin Lundy, a Sketch of His Life and of His Relations with His Disciple and Associate, William Lloyd Garrison," *Northern Monthly*, II (March, 1868), 501–520, correctly portrayed the relationship between Lundy and Garrison. Wendell Phillips Garrison and Francis Jackson Garrison, *William Lloyd Garrison, 1805–1879* (Boston, 1885–89), a vast source collection, includes much vital material on the Lundy-Garrison association. Two recent biographies, Walter M. Merrill, *Against Wind and Tide, a Biography of William Lloyd Garrison* (Cambridge, Mass., 1963), and John L. Thomas, *The Liberator, William Lloyd Garrison, a Biography* (Boston, 1963), recount in traditional terms Lundy's influence on Garrison.

Works on slavery which portray that institution much as Lundy saw it are Frederic Bancroft, *Slave-Trading in the Old South* (Baltimore, 1931), Kenneth Stampp, *The Peculiar Institution; Slavery in the Ante-Bellum South* (New York, 1956), and Richard Wade, *Slavery in the Cities: The South, 1820–1860* (New York, 1964). Robert McColley, *Slavery and Jeffersonian Virginia* (Urbana, Ill., 1964), documents the power of slavery to withstand liberal ideology. Two works by Clement Eaton, *Freedom of Thought in the Old South* (Durham, N.C., 1940), and *The Growth of Southern Civilization, 1790–1860* (New York, 1961), trace the growing rigidity and influence of the slaveholding culture. William Sumner Jenkins, *Pro-Slavery Thought in the Old South* (Chapel Hill, N.C., 1935), amply documents the retreat of the southern intellectuals from their earlier Jeffersonian position; Glover Moore, *The Missouri Controversy, 1819–1821* (Lexington, Ky., 1953), gives the background and consequence of that important event; the colonization movement is analyzed in P. J. Staudenraus, *The African Colonization Movement, 1816–1865* (New York, 1961); Charles S. Sydnor, *The Development of Southern*

Sectionalism, 1819–1848 (Baton Rouge, La., 1948), shows the weakness and inefficacy of the southern antislavery movement.

Samuel Joseph May, *Some Recollections of Our Anti-Slavery Conflict* (Boston, 1869), helps explain the transition in antislavery thought from gradualism to immediatism, as does William Goodell, *Slavery and Anti-Slavery; a History of the Great Struggle in Both Hemispheres; with a View of the Slavery Question in the United States* (New York, 1852). The most successful modern effort to interpret this aspect of abolitionist history is David Brion Davis, "The Emergence of Immediatism in British and American Anti-slavery Thought," *Mississippi Valley Historical Review*, XLIX (September, 1962), 209–230; Stanley M. Elkins, *Slavery, a Problem in American Institutional and Intellectual Life* (Chicago, 1959), explains abolitionist espousal of immediatism in terms of the atomization of American society and the abstraction of American thought.

Samuel Flagg Bemis, *John Quincy Adams and the Union* (New York, 1956), discusses the relation between Adams and Lundy during the Texas controversy. All modern accounts of the Texas Revolution dismiss Lundy's interpretation of its origin as wrong or at best as naive. The magisterial work of Eugene C. Barker, Texas-born and Texas-trained historian at the University of Texas, was largely responsible for establishing the prevailing view. This may be seen most clearly in his article, "The Influence of Slavery in the Colonization of Texas," *Mississippi Valley Historical Review*, XI (June, 1924), 3–36, and in his major work, *The Life of Stephen F. Austin; a Chapter in the Westward Movement of the Anglo-American People* (Nashville, Tenn., 1925), the subtitle of which succinctly states his explanation of the Texas Revolution. Barker's interpretation had been anticipated in some respects by Lester G. Bugbee, also of the University of Texas, in "Slavery in Early Texas," *Political Science Quarterly*, XIII (1898), 389–412, 648–668; and by Chauncey S. Boucher in *"In Re* That Aggressive Slavocracy," *Mississippi Valley Historical Review*, VIII (September, 1921), 13–79.

INDEX

Abolition Intelligencer and Missionary Journal, 50

Abolitionists: ideas of early, 26, 60–68, 77–78; and Negro emigration, 88, 123; J. Barbour condemns, 114; and evangelicalism, 151–153; as revolutionists, 153–154; as a menace to southern interests, 155; attitude toward Lundy's Texas project, 184–185; hostility toward, 214; and political action, 242

Adams, John Quincy: and presidential campaign of 1828, 116; and right of petition, 227; and annexation of Texas, 227–233 *passim*; relations with Lundy, 228–238 *passim*, 250, 254; predicts secession, 232; visits Philadelphia, 233; opposes immediate emancipation, 234–235; commended by Illinois abolitionists, 256; mourns Lundy's death, 261–262; mentioned, 150, 222, 259, 244

Adams-Onís Treaty, 221

Adrian (Michigan) Library Company, 173

Alabama: Lundy's proposal to settle slaves in, 96

Albany, New York: First African Baptist Church of, 137

Almonte, Juan N., 200, 201, 202, 216

Alton (Illinois) *Observer,* 257

Amalgamation, 150

American Anti-Slavery Society, 208, 218, 227, 252

American Colonization Society: founded, 23; program of, 23–24; and race, 25; opposition to, 26–27, 31–32, 145, 147, 149–150, 161, 168; Lundy's view of, 27–28, 31, 130, 163; educative work of, 28; weakness of, 87; and Negro settlement in Haiti, 94; loss of southern support, 109; in Baltimore, 112, 123–124; contribution to antislavery thought, 127; in Boston, 136; G. Smith supports, 170; mentioned, 67. *See also* Colonization

American Convention for Promoting the Abolition of Slavery: T. H. Genin's address to, 31; and gradual emancipation, 67; organized, 79; meeting of 1823, 79–83; and the *Genius,* 83; and colonization, 88; supports antislavery petitions, 124; endorses *Journal of the Times,* 138; meeting of 1829, 151; studies free produce, 178; lends Lundy money, 188; mentioned, 13

American Convention of the Free People of Color, 190

American Economist and Weekly Political Recorder, 70

Enlightenment, 12, 61–62, 151–152

Evangelicalism: and abolition, 151–153

Evans, Ruth, 213

Facts for the People, 237

Federalists, 37

Filibusterers, 221

Flower, George, 93

Foley, Thomas, 51

Forbes, G. V. H., 207

Fox, George, 7

Francis, 157

Free labor: Lundy advocates, 76–77, 96, 113, 187–188; superior productivity of, 97; colony proposed, 98–99; and British antislavery movement, 211. *See also* Free produce

Free Negroes. *See* Negroes, free

Free produce: store founded, 99; organized movement for, 128, 178–179; in Texas and Mexico, 180; advocated by Lydia Child, 217. *See also* Free labor

Free Produce Society of Philadelphia, 188

Friend of Man, 231

Friends of Humanity, 16, 37, 60, 75

Fugitive Slave Act, 240

Fugitive slaves: jury trial advocated for, 239, 240, 241

Gabriel conspiracy, 10

"Gag rule," 245

Gale, George W., 257

Galveston Bay and Texas Land Company, 225

Garrison, William Lloyd: and G. Bourne, 15; edits *National Philanthropist*, 131; early admiration for Lundy, 132–133, 138–139; reaction to criticism, 136–137; edits *Journal of the Times*, 138, 144; Lundy's influence on, 138; as associate editor of *Genius*, 144, 145–149, 156; association with W. Goodell, 144–145; espouses immediate emancipation, 145; in Baltimore, 145–161 *passim*; contrasted with Lundy, 146–147; position on colonization, 147, 148; and Woolfolk family, 156–157; libel trial, 157, 161; supports H. Clay's American System, 158; partnership with Lundy dissolved, 158–159; religious views, 159; lectures against colonization, 161; efforts to re-establish *Genius*, 160–161; campaign to found *Liberator*, 161, 162, 163; relations with Lundy, 162, 189–190, 209–212, 247; supports Negro settlement in Canada, 167; at free Negro convention, 168; G. Smith opposes, 171; supplies *Liberator* to Elizabeth Chandler, 173; and free-produce movement, 179; and Texas colonization, 184, 209–210; and Chandler memoir, 214; opposes purchase of Texas, 222–223; opposes po-

163; Lundy's opinion of, 163, 245, 246; received by Elizabeth Chandler, 173; mentioned, 167, 176
Liberia, 165, 167
Liberty party, 8, 42
Livermore, Arthur, 14
Lockport, New York, 137, 171, 186
London Anti-Slavery Society, 84
London Yearly Meeting, 22
Lovejoy, Elijah P., 255, 257
Lovejoy, John W. E., 258
Lowell, Illinois, 258
Lundy, Benjamin: childhood and youth, 1–3; religious views, 2, 5; as a saddler, 4, 9, 10, 36, 47, 193; and antislavery commitment, 5; and Stanton family, 8, 47; marriage, 9; antislavery views of, 9, 38–39, 59, 61–64 passim, 123; antislavery influences on, 16–17; and Union Humane Society, 18, 21, 35; and Philanthropist, 22; views of colonization, 24, 27–28, 90–91; opinion of slavery, 27–29; views of race, 28–29, 91, 177; view of abolition, 29–30; early opposition to, 51; supports American Colonization Society, 31, 163; decision to become journalist, 32; trips to Missouri, 32–33, 35–40; and political action, 38, 42, 74, 75, 110, 235, 236, 241–242; effects of Missouri controversy on, 41–42; contrasted with other abolitionists, 42;

and Elihu Embree's death, 45; founds Genius, 45–46; limited resources of, 46, 199; moves to Tennessee, 48; use of rhetoric, 53–54; emancipation plans, 56–58, 67–68, 96–97; and immediate emancipation, 58, 107–108, 148, 163; republican views of, 63; and necessity for compulsion, 66; and gradual emancipation, 67–68, 148; financial affairs, 69–70, 127–128, 212–213; and Humane Protecting Society, 70–71; founds American Economist, 70; and Tennessee farm problem, 71; and Illinois constitutional convention, 72–73, 74; and conspiracy theory, 73, 222, 223, 224; and election of 1824, 74–75; and anti-institutionalism, 74–75; and churches, 75; and free labor, 76–77; and economic argument against slavery, 76–78; at American Convention of 1823, 79–83; and British antislavery pamphlets, 84, 106–107; moves to Baltimore, 85; travels in North Carolina and Virginia, 85; and Haitian colonization, 88–89, 90–92, 94, 98; Negro associates of, 89; fears slave rebellion, 91; and racial equality, 91, 177; visits Haiti, 99–102, 142–143; wife's death, 102; and Maryland Anti-Slavery Society, 110; and Baltimore slave trade, 118; as-

Lundy, Susan, 36, 251
Lynn, Massachusetts, 135

McCrummell, James, 253
McDuffie, George, 124
McIlvaine, Joseph, 242
McManus, Jane, 225–226
McNabb, Illinois, 261
Magnolia, Illinois, 261
Maine, 126
Malcom, Howard, 135, 136
Manumission Intelligencer, 33, 44
Manumission Society of Tennessee. *See* Tennessee Manumission Society
Maryland: political antislavery movement in, 110–117; slave trade in, 117–118; House of Delegates of, 151
Maryland Anti-Slavery Society, 99, 110, 115–116
Massachusetts: legislature endorses antislavery resolution, 104
Massachusetts Abolitionist, 246
Massachusetts Abolition Society, 246
Massachusetts Anti-Slavery Society, 246, 261
Matamoras, Mexico, 202–204 *passim*
May, Samuel J., 127
Methodists, 49, 134, 135
Mexico: antislavery policy of, 169, 180, 224; and free produce, 180; prohibits American settlers, 180; free Negroes and, 176, 203, 204; absence of racial prejudice in, 204; re-

jects American offer to buy Texas, 223
Michigan Territory, 170, 174
Milam, Benjamin R., 200
Miner, Charles, 125, 137–138
Minge, David, 95
Mississippi: Lundy's proposal to settle slaves in, 96
Missouri: Friends of Humanity in, 16; Lundy's travels in, 32, 34, 36–40, 179; slaveholders in, 34; admission opposed, 35; antislavery movement in, 37–40, 222; effect of admission controversy, 40–41, 42, 44; Compromise, 105, 241
Monclova, Mexico, 193, 195
Moore, Esther, 253
Mott, James, 234, 239
Mott, Lucretia, 233, 234, 253
Mott, Robert F., 82
Mount Pleasant, Ohio: Lundy moves to, 7; Quakers in, 7–8; and abolitionism, 7–9, 20; visited by C. Osborn, 17; and Union Humane Society, 18; as Quaker center, 21; *Genius* founded in, 45; Lundy visits, 185; mentioned, 5, 243

Nacogdoches, Texas: Lundy in, 181–182, 200
Nashoba, society of, 97
Nashville, Tennessee: Lundy in, 181, 198, 206–207
National Anti-Slavery Tract Society, 127, 141
National Enquirer: founded, 235; distributed to public officials, 236; extra printed,

237; financial problems, 238,
248; Michigan subscribers to,
243; W. L. Garrison's friends
withdraw aid from, 246; supported by Pennsylvania State
Anti-Slavery Society, 248,
250; Lundy resigns from, 251;
J. G. Whittier edits, 251;
mentioned, 252
National Gazette, 227, 228
National Philanthropist, 144
Natural rights philosophy, 61–
62
Naylor, Charles, 242
Negro convention movement,
145, 168
Negroes: economic importance
of, 25; and colonization, 25;
Lundy on, 29; T. H. Genin's
view of cultural accomplishment of, 31; Sunday school
for, 49; necessity for colonization of, 87–88; Haitian government offers aid to, 90; in
Haiti, 94; southern need for,
97–98; Quakers send to Haiti,
100; education of, 134; Lundy
escorts to Haiti, 142; and
Mexican settlement, 207; disfranchised in Pennsylvania,
241; mentioned, 149
Negroes, free: in Mount Pleasant, Ohio, 21; oppose colonization in Africa, 27, 89; in
North, 81; support emigration, 88, 92, 165; in Baltimore, 92, 99, 145; in Illinois,
93; persecution of, 93, 165–
166; sent to Haiti, 93; feared
as competitors, 111; support
immediate emancipation,

155; laws against, 166; support Canadian settlement,
167; conventions of, 167, 168;
conditions in Upper Canada,
172; interest in Texas colony,
176, 185, 198; support for
Lundy, 197; in Mexico, 203,
204; Texas as refuge for, 222;
tributes to Lundy, 253, 262
Newburyport, Massachusetts,
157
New England: and antislavery
movement, 13–14, 126, 149;
Lundy's plan to found antislavery societies in, 127; racial
prejudice in, 177; opposes annexation of Texas, 244
New Haven, Connecticut, 134,
166
New Jersey, 3, 104
New York, 126, 128, 137, 161,
170
New York Manumission Society, 80
Niles, Hezekiah, 158
Niles Register, 158
North Carolina: antislavery
movement in, 17, 22, 108, 109;
advocates of immediate emancipation in, 66–67; legislature
of, 109
North Carolina Manumission
Society, 66–67, 93, 149–150
Northwest Ordinance of 1787,
73
Nullification movement, 232

Ohio, 4, 104, 166, 174–175
Ohio University: Philomathian
Society of, 72
Osborn, Charles: antislavery